*"A Vision for the Aging Church* offers both scientific learning and spiritual wisdom on the increasingly important issue of aging in our society today. A groundbreaking work in the field, we have here a valuable resource for professionals, pastors and laypersons everywhere."

**Timothy George,** founding dean of Beeson Divinity School of Samford University and the general editor of the Reformation Commentary on Scripture

"With the explosion of the older adult population, this insightful and powerful book encourages and motivates church leaders to take seriously the ministry to their seniors. It provides the needed resource to accomplish that goal. If you want to catch a vision for the aging church, and you want to learn how to respond to that vision, read this book!"

**Dave Gallagher,** author of *Senior Adult Ministry in the 21st Century* and *Healing Takes Time*

*"A Vision for the Aging Church* offers much-needed insight into the future of our aging congregations. Houston and Parker offer sage advice to both the elderly and their pastors and congregations for best practices of serving—and being served by—the seniors in our churches."

**Harold G. Koenig, M.D.,** director of the Center for Spirituality, Theology and Health, Duke University Medical Center

"I am distinctly honored to call James Houston and Michael Parker friends and colleagues in mission. These two cultural 'evangelists' advocate for a paradigm shift in both church and society—one in which our elders are proudly embraced and engrafted into vibrant leadership and ministry. . . . Read this book and be inspired!"

**Daniel C. Potts, M.D.,** associate clinical professor, College of Community Health Sciences, The University of Alabama School of Medicine

"James Houston and Michael Parker provide a wake-up call to the church. Despite biblical commands to honor and care for older adults, the church has failed to value the lives of the rapidly increasing numbers of older members by excluding them from ministry and failing to provide help for them and their caregivers when it is needed. This book challenges older adults to embrace their important God-given roles as leaders and elders in the modern church. Every church leader and seminary student needs to read this book and heed the call to let the elders enlighten them."

**Richard M. Allman, M.D.,** professor of medicine and director of the Center for Aging and Division of Gerontology, Geriatrics, and Palliative Care at The University of Alabama at Birmingham

"This is a must-read for sociologists, social/behavior scientists, gerontologists, priests, pastors and ministers of our modern churches."
**Daniel K. Winstead, M.D.,** Robert G. Heath Professor and Chairman, Department of Psychiatry and Behavioral Sciences, Tulane University School of Medicine

"This impressive book by Houston and Parker offers a thoughtful exploration of the important role and place of an increasing number of older persons in our faith communities. *A Vision for the Aging Church* provides an invaluable resource for both the church as well as the social work profession."
**Rick Chamiec-Case,** executive director, North American Association of Christians in Social Work

"Houston and Parker have written a critical book for our day. They detail well how the prejudicial practice of 'ageism' by Western culture and the church has far-reaching and devastating results for our time. As one with an interest in spiritual formation, I'm grateful that we finally have someone providing a vision for the church regarding how the elderly are a potential powerhouse of spiritual depth and vitality as well as examples in life and sacrificial caring for others. Without elderly persons' profound leadership, involvement and interaction, the church, family and society are destined to become a truncated community bent on self-referential consumerism and impersonal overproductivity. God help us in opening to this timely message."
**John H. Coe,** director, Institute for Spiritual Formation, Biola University

"Railing against a culture that is often dismissive of the aged or that socializes the retired primarily toward ease and sometimes toward despair, Houston and Parker not only articulate a countercultural vision of aging, they demonstrate its potential vitality. Fresh insights emerge throughout as these authors set commonly referenced scriptural texts in the context of aging, offer insightful gerontological research to faith communities, and guide congregations and organizations in ministry both to and from older adults. Reading these pages one feels the acquired excellencies of soul that can emerge in the later stages of life when a person does not lose heart. How grateful we can be to James Houston and Michael Parker for giving us in this book a much-needed, contemporary, theological anthropology for eldership."
**Chris Kiesling,** Asbury Theological Seminary

"What a wealth of wisdom and insights on the future church! So many people speak of the 'future church' as being young, unchurched and skeptical. In reality, the future church will be old, spiritually inclined and receptive. This book is a great resource for leaders of the real future church!"
**Charles Arn,** professor of outreach, Wesley Seminary

# A VISION FOR THE AGING CHURCH

## Renewing Ministry for and by Seniors

### JAMES M. HOUSTON
### & MICHAEL PARKER

IVP Academic

An imprint of InterVarsity Press
Downers Grove, Illinois

*InterVarsity Press*
*P.O. Box 1400, Downers Grove, IL 60515-1426*
*World Wide Web: www.ivpress.com*
*E-mail: email@ivpress.com*

*InterVarsity Press® is the book-publishing division of InterVarsity Christian Fellowship/USA®, a movement of students and faculty active on campus at hundreds of universities, colleges and schools of nursing in the United States of America, and a member movement of the International Fellowship of Evangelical Students. For information about local and regional activities, write Public Relations Dept., InterVarsity Christian Fellowship/USA, 6400 Schroeder Rd., P.O. Box 7895, Madison, WI 53707-7895, or visit the IVCF website at <www.intervarsity.org>.*

*Design: Cindy Kiple*

*Images: senior woman portrait: © Martina Ebel/iStockphoto*
    *elderly African man: © MShep2/iStockphoto*
    *senior woman with glasses: © Özgür Donmaz/iStockphoto*
    *male Japanese senior: © Roberto A Sanchez/iStockphoto*

*ISBN 978-0-8308-3948-3*

*Printed in the United States of America* ∞

**Library of Congress Cataloging-in-Publication Data**

*Houston, J. M. (James Macintosh), 1922-*
  *A vision for the aging church: renewing ministry for and by seniors*
*/ James M. Houston and Michael W. Parker.*
    *p. cm.*
  *Includes bibliographical references and index.*
  *ISBN 978-0-8308-3948-3 (pbk.: alk. paper)*
  *1. Church work with older people. 2. Older Christians—Religious*
*life. I. Parker, Michael W., 1947- II. Title.*
  *BV4435.H68 2011*
  *259'.3—dc23*

2011023156

| **P** | 19 | 18 | 17 | 16 | 15 | 14 | 13 | 12 | 11 | 10 | 9 | 8 | 7 | 6 | 5 | 4 | 3 | 2 |
|---|---|---|---|---|---|---|---|---|---|---|---|---|---|---|---|---|---|---|
| **Y** | 27 | 26 | 25 | 24 | 23 | 22 | 21 | 20 | 19 | 18 | 17 | 16 | 15 | 14 | 13 | 12 | | |

# CONTENTS

# PREFACE

*Ask . . . your elders, and they will explain to you.*

DEUTERONOMY 32:7

• • •

As far back as I (Dr. Parker) can remember, older people have played a crucial and unique role in my life. Until she died, I adored and appreciated my maternal grandmother who showered me with unconditional love, wise counsel and faithful availability. As I grew older, I continued to exhibit an affinity for those much older than I, which resulted in a strong sense of appreciation for the unique contributions that elders offer to the rest of the world. When I became a Christian, I observed the traditionally assigned roles (or lack thereof) of seniors in the church. Basically, they were put out to pasture, so to speak, relegated to elderly Sunday school classes and occasional recreational trips. Personally, I have benefited immensely from the love and acceptance of several older and wiser Christian mentors. These experiences and the unconditional love of my own father directly influenced my decision to focus my professional career on advancing the status of seniors.

My association with Dr. James Houston and our subsequent collaboration on this book are, perhaps, good examples of a younger generation Christian benefiting from the faith and experience of an older Christian. Now still writing more books at age eighty-eight, Dr. Houston has a contagious, boundless energy and joy that engages you quickly in friendship. Later in our association, Dr. Houston and I presented together at a Southeast Regional Alzheimer's Dementias' Conference,

Hope: Prevention, Care and Cure.[1] At the conference, I was able to introduce him to some other members of an interdisciplinary team of Christian professionals in history, geriatric medicine, elder law, psychology, neuropathology, neurology, kinesiology, geriatric pharmacy, social work and psychiatry. We welcomed him on board as a much-needed resident theologian to our band of brothers and sisters. He discussed, among other wide-ranging topics, the dangers of professionalism, while he unknowingly served as a loving example of how to age successfully. Just as my colleagues and I became better connected to an elder like Dr. Houston, none of us should be surprised when God hooks us more intimately into the life of a new elder-mentor-friend or reminds us to appreciate members of our own aging social convoy of friends and family.[2]

At about the ten-year mark in my military career, I had to face my father's progressive frailness. He was dying. I had an opportunity to spend two weeks with him in the hospital before departing for an overseas assignment during Desert Storm. I remember my departure like yesterday. My wife, three children and I were to board a plane within the hour, a plane that would take my family and me to another country, where I would be given huge responsibilities in the European Theater of Operations during Desert Storm. Somehow I managed to recognize the significance of the moment: *I might not see my father alive again.* As always, God was present at the point of need. Little did I know that his providential hand would lead me through a series of remarkable changes and opportunities that would result in some mid-career changes and a new set of assignments.

In the movie *Dad*, Jack Lemmon has a deathbed scene with his son,

---

[1]M. W. Parker and J. Houston, "A Theology of Dementia and Life Review," paper presented at the Southeast Regional Alzheimer's Dementias' Conference, Hope: Prevention, Care and Cure, University of Alabama, Tuscaloosa, Ala., August 25, 2010.

[2]The term *convoy* is used to evoke the image of a protective layer, in this case, of family and friends, who surround the individual and help in the successful negotiation of life's challenges. Each person can be thought of as moving through life surrounded by a group of people to whom s(he) is related through the exchange of social support. Convoys are thought to be dynamic and lifelong in nature, that is, changing in some ways but remaining stable in others across time and situations. See T. C. Antonucci and H. Akiyama, "Social Networks in Adult Life and a Preliminary Examination of the Convoy Model," *Journal of Gerontology* 42 (1987): 519-27.

played by Ted Danson. When I watched the movie for the first time, I was struck by its similarity to what happened with my own father. At one point, the father says to his son, "There is a lot of good and bad in this world, but when I look at you, I know I did something right." The son responds by climbing into the hospital bed with his dad and places his head on his shoulder. As my family said their separate farewells, I remained alone with my father. As I stood next to his bed, I was taken back to a vivid childhood memory. It was bedtime, and I had just slipped into my bed. I must have been about eight years old. My dad quietly entered my room. I knew that he thought I was asleep, and I was careful to promote that misperception. He leaned over the bed and gently kissed me on my forehead. Like many members of the stoical World War II generation, my father was rarely demonstrative. I presume that is, in part, why that moment is so meaningful to me after so many years. How I wanted at that instant to return to a childhood time of innocence and safety. Like so many adult children who experience a reversal of roles with their aging parents, I found myself as a father to my own dad. So, I turned to him and said: "Dad, I'm going to do something now that you did for me many years ago when I was a child." I leaned over and kissed him on his forehead. After his death and funeral, I returned to my overseas position with 7th Medical Command. My brothers and sisters in uniform held a memorial service for my father, and I learned after the ceremony that many of them faced aging parent issues as well. These Spirit-led experiences prompted me to pursue post-doctoral study in aging, a direction that required additional divine assistance.

The University of Michigan offered a National Institute of Aging (NIA) Post Doctoral Fellowship Program, but in order to attend, I would have to secure permission from the Army Medical Department for long-term civilian training, a program offered to only a few officers each year. Once the Army and the University of Michigan selected me, I was told by my colleagues in psychiatry that we are a "young Army," meaning there was no need for an NIA fellowship at Michigan. Instead, they planned to recommend that I complete a child and family fellowship at Walter Reed. I declined and was promptly told my career was in jeopardy. Someone suggested I talk with my boss, a two-star general who was at the time in charge of all medical care for Desert Storm. He had the weight of the world on him, but sensing God's direction, I scheduled an appointment. During the first few minutes, he mirrored the words of my colleagues. Then he asked what I planned to do at Michigan in terms of research. I told him that I wanted to help military families with aging parent issues. His entire countenance changed. He shared how he had just received a call from his family priest. "I just came from your mother's home," the priest said, "and she didn't know the gas on the stove was on. What do you want me to do?" The general looked at me and said, "I didn't have a clue what to tell him, but you tell those people that are opposing your assignment to the University of Michigan after the war that I support you." I never told anyone anything, but the next day my colleagues congratulated me for "sticking to my guns." So after the war, I was reassigned to the University of Michigan and my professional life changed dramatically.

After completing the NIA Post Doctoral Fellowship and later, after completing other duties with the military, I felt God's prompting to transition from a military to an academic research career in the field of aging. I joined the faculties of two major universities, and, after a few years, the Gerontological Society of America selected me as a Hartford Foundation Geriatric Scholar.[3] Through these marvelous programs and opportunities, I became personally linked to leading scholars across the world in the field of aging. After these mid-career professional experiences, I felt more qualified to address the complex challenges and opportunities facing older persons, the church, our communities and the nations of the world. I especially took note of the disparity I had observed in the expectations the church has of its seniors. Spurred on by my association with Dr. Houston, one of the most successful Christian agers I have encountered, I began a collaboration with him that resulted in this book. Together in these pages, Dr. Houston and I have probed one of the most pressing and vital dilemmas faced by today's church: benefiting from an ever-increasing elderly population. We have

---

[3]The Hartford Foundation and The Gerontological Society of America selects academic leaders in gerontology for advanced training and research support; I received this award in 2002.

approached this undertaking as theological and scientific partners and as members of powerful but different generations.

Though most of my research and interdisciplinary work with older persons and the church has been in the fields of psychology, geriatrics and gerontology (and is, therefore, buried in scientific journals) we hope to share more thoroughly some of our findings in this book and in our next collaborative effort with other scholars, *A Church Handbook on Aging*. In this second text, we will bring to light even more of what we and our interdisciplinary team of colleagues know about aging successfully God's way, in a practical manner that can be taught in seminaries and implemented by local churches and communities of all sizes. In this book, Dr. Houston and I will draw on the latest research, scholars of the past and present and, most importantly, the Scriptures to discern how the church has arrived at the current stage of her development with regard to older persons.

The statistics on America's rapidly aging population underscore the value and urgency of encouraging elderly men and women to embrace late-life missions that mirror those of seniors like Dr. Houston. The modern church must avail itself of information about seniors—both biblical and scientific—that can be used by church leaders to challenge seniors to greater ministry and health.

Even scholars previously contemptuous of organized religion, like two-time Pulitzer Prize winner and Harvard biologist Edward Wilson, are calling for partnerships between the church and science in the hope of saving the earth.[4] Yet in this era of collaboration, many orthodox believers are troubled by the proliferation of academic efforts that appear to secularize faith and force a false, conventional religious consensus. Others are concerned about pejorative characterizations of their religion, and some are offended by unholy unions between church and state, particularly when such associations result in a loss of religious identity, community and purpose.

This book represents an effort to join science and religion in ways that most positively impact the partnership between today's churches

---

[4]Edward O. Wilson, *The Creation: An Appeal to Save Life on Earth* (New York: Norton, 2006).

and seniors. This is not easily accomplished. In many cases, our world-view informs and shapes our lives. It influences our values, ethics and capacities, and it directs our life trajectories. Despite the scientific claim of objectivity, historians of science, like Thomas Kuhn, have argued that scientists' worldview affects what they choose to investigate and how they discuss the implications of their research findings.[5] Let me openly state: I share Dr. Houston's worldview that faith is of divine origin. My research and public service interests have been influenced by my faith in Christ; however, I am, nonetheless, open to what science aims to do: to describe truth truthfully. I do not claim that Christ can be proven, but I do believe that the effects of faith can be analyzed and described. Relatively recently, science has been more open to the meas-urement of religion and spirituality on health, but this endeavor has its consequences and temptations.

After my military career and during my early academic years, I real-ized that any attempt to join the two worlds of academia and spiritual-ity would usually be met with skepticism or outright rejection by most fellow academics and by leaders in the church. As is probably the case with many Christians teaching in large, public universities, I found myself falling into a tenure-track mode involving the solicitation of public and private sources of funding for "my" state of science research agenda, the publication of "my" outcomes in tier-one journals and the presentation of "my" findings at national and international professional conferences. After some success with this trajectory, I realized that I could easily isolate myself from Christian community with sugar-plum notions of "expert" dancing in my head. How could I reconcile my call-ing to service from Christ with my self-centered proclivities and newly acquired standards of academic excellence to address the all-important areas of faith, health and aging that affect every area of our lives? Dr. Houston has helped me and some Christian colleagues to reevaluate our research and professional careers by emphasizing the importance of being more relational with our own families, students, colleagues and patients.

---

[5]Armand M. Nicholi, *The Question of God: C. S. Lewis and Sigmund Freud Debate God, Love, Sex and the Meaning of Life* (New York: Free Press, 2002), p. 7.

Providentially, I became connected to elderly mentors in the African American and white churches of the South, underserved elderly men and women who helped me face the collective challenges associated with developing religious-academic partnerships: hierarchical religious sources of community power that blocked ecumenical work, pejorative thinking among academics about organized religion, resistance to partnerships between universities and their surrounding communities ("town and gown" collaborations), myopic-minded researchers and institutional racism and ageism. As I experienced the love and mentorship of many senior saints, I came to see through their resilient eyes the staggering needs as well as the exciting potential of today's elders. I was literally put in touch with elders whose added years were foundations for hope, not despair.

Repeatedly throughout this book we will return to generational themes, drawing on differences and common needs in young adults, mid-lifers and older persons while addressing the cultural tensions between science, history and the Bible. Openly, we promote the idea that our elders minister to us. We provide evidence from our history of research and from organizing conferences and programs that it is possible to outline vibrant, sustainable initiatives for every community that every church can put into practice. Seniors of faith, our true spiritual elders, can reflect what happens to people when they have experienced the love of Christ across a lifetime. May this book help all senior saints rediscover the adventurous spirit that can define their final season of life. May these seniors and those who value the place of older persons in the church "rise up and help us build" together, as in the days of Nehemiah (Neh 2:18).

*Michael Parker*

*Teach us to number our days aright,*
*that we may gain a heart of wisdom.*

**PSALM 90:12**


*Do not cast me away when I am old;*
*do not forsake me when my strength is gone.*

**PSALM 71:9**

# PROLOGUE

## Distressed Communities

...

*They said to me, "Those who survived the exile and are back in the
province are in great trouble and disgrace. The wall of Jerusalem
is broken down, and its gates have been burned with fire."*

NEHEMIAH 1:3

In the book of Nehemiah, Jerusalem was initially pictured as a vulnerable community, not unlike those without a social support system today. With exhortations to stand on the strength of their faith, all the people of Jerusalem joined together to rebuild the wall of their city and thus refortify it. As we know, Nehemiah and his people rebuilt far more than the wall; they renewed their religious traditions, the symbols of their dependency upon God. Nehemiah's aim was pure: anticipating opposition, he began with a prayer of repentance, knowing that his fight was against the spiritual wickedness of his day (Eph 6:12). The wall was important, but it was the joint effort to rebuild that wall that best pictures what can be accomplished in our own communities when all ages join together, under the banner of Christ, for the common good. Today there are pastors, doctors, lay leaders, senior saints and researchers who believe that older, successfully aging elders can be leaders in rebuilding the walls of communities across America and the other nations of the world, one at a time, from the restoration of communities affected by Hurricane Katrina and the massive earthquakes affecting Haiti and Japan, to the revival in the inner cities, to one-on-one mentoring between the younger and older generations through effective parenting, grandparenting and small group involvement. The church needs to be in a position of leadership in these matters, but, unfortunately, tends to be silent and unprepared on issues related to aging.

In seeking solutions for the ills of society, liberal extremists have rejected all the conventional forms of religion, particularly the Christian church. They substitute into the void their own vision of a perfect and just society, often ironically adopting a rigid adherence that brooks no opposition. As a result, the church can often be left out of the organizing purview of scholars, researchers and scientists seeking modern day solutions. The church shares fault because of its failure to live up to its scriptural moorings in developing programs that communicate God's grace and love in practical ways. Instead, the church has tended to be suspicious of efforts to evaluate its programs or tell its story in an evidence-based manner so that effective programs can be duplicated. This is an egregious mistake when we consider what is possible with our aging populations throughout the world, particularly in America, where churches exist in practically every community.

As an example, when secular, community-based, community and national "aging in place" initiatives (like those that would allow older persons to walk rather than drive to the grocery store or to live in their homes rather than in long term care facilities like nursing homes) are implemented, the church as an organizing entity is rarely represented in the planning process. According to a recent report by the National Association of Area Agencies on Aging America's communities are not prepared for an aging population.[1] Many communities fail to provide older adults with a proper range of needed preventive health care services, emergency services, workforce development, opportunities for civic engagement and volunteer opportunities, aging/human services,

---

[1]"The Maturing of America—Getting Communities on Track for an Aging Population," National Association of Area Agencies on Aging, accessed June 13, 2011, www.n4a.org/pdf/MOAFinalReport.pdf.

tax and finance assistance, adequate public transportation and housing options. A review of their "best practices" by communities does not include one faith-based initiative.[2]

The Robert Woods Johnson Foundation (RWJ) developed another national community based program, the Faith in Action Initiative.[3] Dr. Parker served as a reviewer on this multi-million project. Relatively small grants were awarded competitively based upon specific criteria including the ability to sustain ecumenical partnerships across different religions in order to fill gaps in services provided to older persons. Though an extremely worthy endeavor, many of these programs had difficulty sustaining local financial support after RWJ funding ceased. In some communities, this may have been related to the requirement to work across organized religions. We describe some excellent, sustainable, church-based programs in part three. Fortunately, our growing body of interdisciplinary research suggests that many church leaders are not defensive about discussing or addressing shortfalls in their program offerings to elders. Instead, they are open to the possibilities of ecumenical partnerships across denominational lines within organized religious boundaries. They respond well to sharing responsibilities for programs that benefit elders in their community and to pedagogical input from creative leaders in the fields of aging who acknowledge and recognize the importance of the organized church.

Dr. Parker led an interdisciplinary research team in partnership with a local senior ministry association.[4] Their goal was to foster collaborations among 350 congregations to address gaps in services to senior

---

[2]"Best Practices," MetLife Foundation, accessed June 13, 2011, http://aipi.nonprofitsoapbox .com/index.php?option=com_content&task=view&id=21&Itemid=50

[3]"What Is Faith in Action" Faith in Action National Network, accessed June 13, 2011, www .fianationalnetwork.org/what-is-faith-in-action.cfm.

[4]His interdisciplinary team was awarded the Premiere Award, Outstanding Faculty-Initiated Community Engagement Effort by the Office of Community Affairs (2009) from the University of Alabama, presented May 1, 2009; two of our Ph.D. students involved in the project were awarded the 2010 Group for Advancement of Doctoral Education's (GADE) National Leadership and Service Award. L. Dunn et al., "Building Sustainable Community Partnerships to Promote Successful Aging: A Preliminary Study of Local Congregations and Agencies," *Journal of Community Engagement and Scholarship* (forthcoming); M. W. Parker et al., "Helping to Unite an Aging Southern Community: An Internet Directory Project and Telephone Survey of Local Congregations," *Journal of Community Engagement and Scholarship* (forthcoming).

adults and to promote greater use of existing local, state and national resources for older people.[5] Over thirty-five graduate students worked with the group, interviewing local service agencies and local pastors and lay leaders; they developed local, state and national resource directories for all participating organizations to better connect the community as a whole. Phone surveys were completed on approximately half of the 600 congregations in one community, which identified a number of service gaps. The continuing plans for this initiative include the development of caregiver support programs, life review initiatives, improved home visitation and transportation programs, catastrophic planning projects and local successful aging conferences targeting congregations.[6] Other outcomes from our research suggest that churches must partner to provide services and systematic challenges for senior ministry. The vast majority of congregations in the community surveyed consisted of congregations of two hundred or fewer members, and even large, well-resourced churches were strapped and overwhelmed with meeting the growing needs of seniors and their caregivers. Many church leaders in the study expressed particular concerns about staff capacities to properly conduct home and long term care facility visitation, and others were frustrated with managing travel and tour programs for retirees while continuing the essentials of church like Sunday school, preaching, baptisms, marriages and funerals.

In this five-part book, we present a biblical approach to the aging

[5]X. Li, N.S. Park, L. Dunn, S. MacCall, C. Spencer, R. Harrell, H. Lee, M. Parker and S. Martin, "A Preliminary study of community-based services and resources provided by faith-based organizations to older persons in one southern community," poster presentation at the 12th Annual Graduate School Association Research and Thesis Conference, Tuscaloosa, Ala., March 2009; M. Parker, L. Dunn, X. Li et al. "Advocacy for Older Adults," invited presentation at the Alabama Public Health Association Annual Meeting, Mobile, Ala., March 2009; M. W. Parker (Principal Investigator) and N. Park, H. Lee, L. Dunn, S. Martin, A. Li and S. MacCall (Co-Investigators), "A qualitative and quantitative study of faith based organizations and agencies providing services to older persons," UA Community Affairs Office (2009); M. W. Parker (Principal Investigator) and N. Park, H. Lee, L. Dunn, S. Martin, A. Li and S. MacCall (Co-Investigators), "A qualitative and quantitative study of faith based organizations and agencies providing services to older persons," UA Community Affairs Office (2008).
[6]M. W. Parker, J. Bellis, M. Harper, P. Bishop, C. Moore, P. Thompson and R. A. Allman, "Multidisciplinary Model of Health Promotion Incorporating Spirituality into a Successful Aging Intervention with African American and White Elderly," *The Gerontologist* 42, no. 3 (2002): 405-15.

imperative faced by the church and our communities. This prologue provides an introductory overview of the book, and in part one, we describe the ageist spirit that exists in our culture. We discuss why the church is not more involved in addressing the challenges posed by an increasingly aged society and why we must confront the common thinking that older persons are more of a burden to the church than a gift. In part two, we investigate the historical, cultural and biblical roots behind the loss of status for elders and discuss the consequences of these themes. In part three, we put forward samples of tested solutions for congregations and communities, and part four lays out our thoughts on achieving significance in late life. Finally, we address the theme of finishing well in part five.

The church has a number of scriptural admonitions to fulfill regarding late life. How do we as Christians respond to late life issues associated with caregiving, poverty, disability, chronic disease, immobility, isolation, depression, dementia and death? Are we acting as a salt in preserving the value of all older persons irrespective of their health status? Are we preparing people for longer lives of significance and for the great tests of character that come with caregiving? Some might argue that these are more properly the concerns of our government and our medical professions, but the readiness and availability of professionals to solve these problems without the help of the church is limited. More and more, our society is looking to faith-based organizations during economic down times to help with instrumental and emotional support of elders, and federal agencies and secular nonprofits recognize that religious involvement is the most common choice among seniors for organizational participation among all other options. Simply stated, churches have access to older persons that other organizations cannot reach—churches have access to older persons who otherwise might not be reached by community agencies. We provide some answers and share some solutions by offering some tested, church-based programs that target predicable, developmental tasks associated with late life, and we identify ways younger people can benefit from vibrant, reciprocal relationships with older persons. All professions critically need gerontological pedagogy, and the pastorate should lead this movement, being as it is on the frontline of these issues every day! After all, the church is represented in practically every community in the modern world, and no one should ignore the value of this infrastructure.

Despite the possibilities afforded by increased longevity, our research and that of others indicate that today's church seems largely out-of-touch with its aging membership. Our research confirms that "senior ministry," when present at all, is almost universally considered to be a ministry *to* rather than *from* elders.[7] The reciprocity of exchange, in the vein of the great exchange we have from Christ, is absent. A leading authority from one of the largest protestant churches in America shared recently that her particular community church, located near a major university, had the *only* adult-senior ministry to college-aged youth in her entire denomination. The implication is that older persons have nothing to offer younger generations! Some large denominations are actually downsizing their work with seniors. We challenge the church to examine and evaluate the place of elders in its congregations, to consider the sample state-of-science recommendations made in this book concerning seniors, and to advance the status, purpose and health of all senior members. These gains can be made in the midst of fostering relationships that connect older persons to younger people. The ever-growing, aging church is no burden; instead, this burgeoning reservoir of accumulated experience and talent can provide a lasting legacy of God's love to the younger generations. Because of our society's tendency to relegate seniors to lives relatively disengaged from the lives of younger generations, most of us under the age of sixty-five have little knowledge of what we are missing with our senior saints.

The following simple story illustrates what can happen when the young lose contact with the old.

> It is said that once upon a time the people of a remote mountain village used to sacrifice and eat their old men. A day came when there was not a single old man left, and the traditions were lost. They wanted to build a great house for the meetings of the assembly, but when they came to look at the tree-trunks that had been cut for that purpose, no

---

[7]Dunn et al., "Building Sustainable Community Partnerships to Promote Successful Aging" (forthcoming).

one could tell the top from the bottom: if the timber were placed the wrong way up, it would set off a series of disasters. A young man said that if they promised never to eat the old men any more, he would be able to find a solution. They promised. He brought his grandfather, whom he had hidden; and the old man taught the community to tell top from bottom.[8]

This tale highlights the irreplaceable value of our elderly and the danger of forgetting that value. Though our society would have us believe we must cling to our youth at all costs and avoid growing old as much as possible, our culture has not yet descended to the idea that older people simply need to be eliminated (though we now have a growing number of states and nations with laws make active euthanasia[9] and assisted suicide[10] more possible).[11] Already, older patients with end-stage kidney disease are being asked to rethink the "free dialysis" care available to them. Physicians are being taught to suggest medical management without dialysis.[12] While, at the other end of the continuum, homes are being designed so that older people might age in place, and cars are being designed specifically for older drivers. Despite these efforts, our youth-dominated tendencies are contributing to a situation that may ultimately have the same outcome as the tale you just read—a society that cannot tell its top from its bottom!

The church is in a unique position to positively affect how seniors are viewed and treated and is, therefore, able to tap into a wiser reservoir of knowledge, faith and love found in the late life generations. Churches who foster the rich, intergenerational connection available only through our elders will ensure that their unique legacy of faith and

---

[8]Simone de Beauvoir, *The Coming of Age* (New York: C. P. Putnam's Sons, 1972), p. 77.

[9]Deliberate steps taken to bring about someone else's death by administering a lethal injection or by some other means, with and without the consent of the dying person. The Netherlands has an involuntary program that can be implemented without the consent of the dying person.

[10]Physician-assisted suicide occurs when the physician prescribes medication, usually barbiturates, knowing that the individual intends to use it to commit suicide.

[11]Currently, the state of Oregon has legalized physician-assisted suicide as a choice for patients who are diagnosed by two doctors as having less than six months to live; several other states are reviewing similar legislation: Maine, California, Alaska and Hawaii.

[12]Gina Kolata, "When Ailments Pile Up: Asking Patients to Rethink Free Dialysis," *New York Times*, March 31, 2011, www.nytimes.com/2011/04/01/health/01dialysis.html?_r=1.

love is made available systematically and intentionally to younger generations. The lives of the younger set are enriched, and seniors who become more actively engaged with life also benefit by aging more successfully.

We believe that aging, rather than being an inevitable stage of life worthy only of despair, provides a reason for hope. God planned the splendor and potency of the young adult years to be predominately corporeal and the magnificence and vigor of old age to be first and foremost, lovingly spiritual. Sadly, while society grapples with what to do with its ever-increasing aged population, the church seems unaware of how long its own people are now living. Yet the church, more than any other institution, needs to be prepared to answer the demands and challenges of prolonged life for its seniors. This overriding theme of the church assuming a primary role in supporting its aging members is affirmed in the Scriptures and by history.

In this book we address the part today's church must play in meeting the demands and embracing the opportunities of senior living. Not since biblical times, when it was not unusual to live past one hundred years, has the church been faced with such a tremendous opportunity. While many within the church look upon older persons as a burden, it is critical to recognize a larger, divine purpose behind the aging of America and other nations' populations. We suggest the possibilities of what could happen to our nation and the world if an army of spiritually inspired, successfully aging elders entered the fray, grounded in the gospel. On a practical level, we hope our words serve as a manual of hope for those who envision the possibilities available to and through our elders. People of all ages today are desperate for love, and our elders may hold the keys to the blessings of intergenerational Christian fellowship so needed today. In loving others, we must remain committed to the gospel, preaching it first to ourselves daily and then to others. Our elders, who have lived the longest with the ever-present power of the Holy Spirit, may be most able to share the Father's love in a Christlike manner.

"I am not ashamed of the gospel, because it is the power of God for the salvation of everyone who believes: first for the Jew, then for the Gentile, for in the gospel a righteousness from God is revealed, a righteousness that is by faith from first to last, just as it is written: 'The righteous will live by faith'" (Rom 1:16-17). As in staying committed to the gospel, we must remain sensitive to contemporary challenges to its authenticity. Martin Luther said, "If you preach the gospel in all aspects with the exception of the issues which deal specifically with your time, you are not preaching the gospel at all."[13] To preach the gospel in these days, we must address the opportunities and challenges of God's aging church.

This book is not so much about what is wrong with the methods utilized by today's churches in dealing (or failing to deal) with the burgeoning senior population, but about celebrating the wonderful news that our parents, grandparents and great grandparents are living longer—on average, almost two decades longer than those at the beginning of the twentieth century. Beyond providing state of science information on preparing for our final seasons of life, we propose the idea that longer lives can be more fulfilled lives. This contemporary gift of added years affords mature people the opportunity to reframe the second half of their lives. Age-restrictive traditions about vocation, ministerial calling and love no longer apply as a new and growing wave of elders are empowered to dedicate themselves more completely to God-given, recreated visions and purposes. Though the church has floundered in this area, we want to help by presenting practical guides that will attract and engage our seniors on a local level. They must be assured that their wisdom, testimony and courage are needed in the church, and that their personal aging needs will be addressed as practically as possible. The evidence is clear: older, community-engaged elders age more successfully and are, therefore, better equipped than uninvolved and unconnected seniors to serve to God, the church and the world.[14] The majority of older Christians, by virtue of living so long, have experienced the hopelessness of soul that comes from self-reliance, when everything seems to be perishing and life has rubbed them "red raw." They are, therefore, more likely to have learned to surrender God-

---

[13]C.R. Swindoll, *The Finishing Touch* (Dallas: Word Publishing, 1994), p. 146.
[14]M. W. Parker and G. Fuller, "Successful Aging," in *Finishing Strong* (Dallas: LifeWay Publishers, 2002), pp. 63-70.

ward than toward self-reliance when the storms of life come.

Hold us in quiet through the age-long minute
While Thou art silent and the wind is shrill:
Can the boat sink while Thou, dear Lord, art in it?
Can the heart faint that waiteth on Thy will?[15]

[15]Quoted in Elisabeth Elliot, *The Life and Legacy of Amy Carmichael* (Grand Rapids: Fleming H. Revell, 1975), p. 278.

# PART ONE

...

# AN AGEIST ZEITGEIST

# 1

# THE AGING CHURCH

## A Future Katrina?

*Storms like Hurricane Katrina wash away the surface of society,
the settled way things have been done. They expose the underlying
power structures, the injustices, the patterns of corruption
and the unacknowledged inequalities.*

DAVID BROOKS, *THE NEW YORK TIMES*

• • •

Major catastrophes like 9/11, Hurricane Katrina and the 2008 Haitian earthquake can serve as a wakeup call to individuals, families, communities and nations about the necessity of being prepared. These events also reveal clearly that seniors suffer disproportionately during natural disasters.[1] From the now-forgotten tragedy of the flooded nursing home in New Orleans to the abandoned nursing home in Haiti, the higher mortality rates among seniors found in China and Japan serve as tragic reminders that our old people are vulnerable during disasters. Dr. Parker led an interdisciplinary team in New Orleans that helped con-

---

[1]M. W. Parker, Richard Powers, L. Roff, B. Ford and M. Hollingsworth, "Evacuation of the Frail Elderly During Katrina: Lessons and Solutions," paper presented at the Forensic Psychiatry Post-Katrina: Lessons Learned Post Disaster Conference, Tulane University, New Orleans, La., April 13-15, 2007; James Appleby, quoted in "Growing Field of Literature Outlines Necessary Steps for Elder Disaster Preparedness in Emergency," News-Medical, March 19, 2011, www.news-medical.net/news/20110319/Growing-field-of-literature-outlines-necessary-steps-for-elder-disaster-preparedness-in-emergency.aspx.

gregations to use geographic information systems able to map patterns of vulnerability in advance, allowing first responders to intervene more effectively. Congregations can provide help to their older members through proactive planning, using "go kits," multitiered evacuation plans, contact information with families, lists of relevant health care providers, a week's supply of prescriptions and over-the-counter medications, etc. Unfortunately, his most recent research confirms that congregations do not think about helping their elderly members prepare in a systematic, proactive way for high probability disasters in their geographic locations (e.g., fires, power outages, tornadoes).

Elderly disabled people with mobility limitations are particularly vulnerable in disasters. During 9/11, before the Twin Towers collapsed, people in wheelchairs were were systematically evacuated to a midlevel staging area, essentially condemning them to death. Only one seriously disabled person was successfully evacuated before the towers collapsed. She later shared what the fireman who was carrying her down the stairs said after he looked at the faces of people sitting in their wheel chairs: "Lady, I ain't leaving you here!"[2] We need that kind of honest assessment and commitment to do the necessary work in the church today, and elders should be a vibrant, essential part of this effort.

Hurricane Katrina was different from 9/11 and the Haitian and Chinese earthquakes and the more-recent tsunami that hit Japan because of advance warning. Yet despite the opportunity to prevent some of the hurricane's devastation, vulnerable members of the community were lost. When the water rose to the rooftops in New Orleans, many citizens drowned, including, as is well-publicized, the entire resident population of one nursing home. Although many able-bodied people had evacuated safely prior to Hurricane Katrina's landfall, thousands remained in their homes, either refusing or unable to evacuate. Many others died as a consequence of the way they were evacuated. This was particularly true of those over sixty-five. Roughly one half of New Orleans' poor households did not own a vehicle, and among New Orleans'

---

[2]D. Brooks, "Katrina's Silver Lining," *New York Times*, September 8, 2005, quoted in M. W. Parker et al., "Evacuation of the Frail Elderly During Katrina: Lessons and Solutions."

elderly population, 65 percent were without vehicles.

When the levees (walls) protecting the city fractured, large parts of New Orleans and nearby Louisiana parishes were destroyed. Approximately ninety thousand square miles of the Gulf Coast, an area roughly the size of Great Britain, was declared a federal disaster area. Katrina exposed the stench of societal neglect, injustice and inequality in one of our nation's poorest cities. After the hurricane made landfall, contaminated floodwaters covered much of New Orleans for almost two months. Health concerns were elevated for residents and cleanup workers because the polluted waters contained a mix of raw sewage, dead bodies, bacteria, millions of gallons of oil, heavy metals, pesticides and toxic chemicals.[3]

Over a thousand people in the New Orleans area would die as a result of Hurricane Katrina. Seventy four percent were over sixty years old; 50 percent were over age seventy-five. These proportions are shockingly high, considering the fact that the elderly constituted only 11.7 percent of New Orleans' population.

The disproportionate number of elderly deaths during Hurricane Katrina may seem unrelated to the church at large. But consider, however, that in most communities, more than 95 percent of the elderly do not live in nursing homes, yet approximately 80 percent are members of religious congregations. In subsequent chapters, we present a more thorough examination of the problem of connecting elderly church members with the younger members in a church. Yet the example of Katrina begs the question, why were frail elderly and disabled people without the capacity to evacuate themselves during Hurricane Katrina not helped by more able-bodied members of their congregations? If the fastest-growing age group is eighty-five and older, and almost half in this age group suffer from dementia, why didn't the congregations of the elderly who needlessly perished during Katrina play a more proactive role in rescuing their own and others in the city of New Orleans?

---

[3]M. W. Parker et al., "Evacuation of the Frail Elderly During Katrina: Lessons and Solutions"; James Appleby, quoted in "Growing Field of Literature Outlines Necessary Steps for Elder Disaster Preparedness in Emergency"; Brooks, "Katrina's Silver Lining," *New York Times,* September 8, 2005, in M. W. Parker et al., "Evacuation of the Frail Elderly During Katrina."

Perhaps it is because the effects of aging on a person, a family, a congregation, a community and a nation are typically experienced more subtly and insidiously. Perhaps, like other institutions (political, medical, marketing and entrepreneurial), the church is both actively and clandestinely ageist. Like other "isms" (such as racism), *ageism* is a self-defeating societal ill that has many forms of expression. Simply stated, it is the presence of negative stereotypes, incorrect assumptions and distorted characterizations about older people and their capacities. Chapter twelve debunks some myths about aging by examining the latest research, but here we explore what researchers have found in some instances: the presence of ageist attitudes and practices actually shortens the quality and length of the lives of older persons and their contributions to society. Hurricane Katrina presents a severe case, in which many improperly evacuated older and disabled persons died.

### Examples of Ageism

Do some churches—or, at least, people in positions of power or influence within them—view older people as selfish, dependent, helpless and unable to contribute? In truth, the vast majority of seniors are active consumers who have more assets than younger people and possess a great deal of available talent, training and (perhaps) time. Most important, many older persons have years of experience in living out their faith. This gives them a unique capacity to represent the love of Christ to others. Our research indicates clearly that though ageism exists in the modern church, many church leaders want to do something about it.[4] Ageism is not just another issue churches need to be conscious of but a neglectful sin that has resulted in the loss of life of older members.

One specific example of ageism is a widespread tendency to design ministries and Sunday school classes around age-graded thinking.

---

[4]L. Dunn et al., "Building Sustainable Community Partnerships to Promote Successful Aging: A Preliminary Study of Local Congregations and Agencies," *Journal of Community Engagement and Scholarship* (forthcoming); M. W. Parker, J. Bellis, M. Harper, P. Bishop, C. Moore, P. Thompson and R. A. Allman, "Multidisciplinary Model of Health Promotion Incorporating Spirituality into a Successful Aging Intervention with African American and White Elderly," *The Gerontologist* 42, no. 3 (2002): 405-15.

While eighty-five-year-olds can be "younger" (more vivacious) than some eighteen-year-olds both psychologically and spiritually, separating believers by their ages deprives everyone of the chance to learn from and care for each other across ages. Like the decision to place disabled people on a midlevel floor after the 9/11 attack, such a decision has a profoundly negative effect on older saints and makes fostering intergenerational connections almost impossible during the Sunday school hour. Given the high divorce rate within the modern church, for example, newly married young couples might benefit from association with older couples, some of whom have been married for over fifty years.

In another example of ageism, recent research suggests that pastors stop visiting elderly members of their congregations who reside in long term care facilities once they detect or have confirmed that a resident is suffering from dementia.[5] Because almost half of those who reach eighty-five or older will suffer from a form of dementia, believers must encourage the church to view these senior members as people with tremendous value. Anyone who is rendered helpless and dependent still has worth in the eyes of Christ. Learning to love under these circumstances can carry a price for those extending the love, and the church must be there to help caregivers and care recipients in ways that make a real difference. Platitudes or promises of prayer cannot replace the necessity of practical forms of assistance and state of science care. The biblical truth that receiving often follows giving holds true in such circumstances. Those who lovingly serve older people incapable of returning their love will be blessed through their efforts many times over because they learn how to love unconditionally. Though corporate sins of neglect are largely sins of omission, only the church can preach the God-given value of those who are losing their intellectual capacities and foster the spiritual growth available to their caregivers.

One senior pastor of a large Presbyterian church characterized his seniors in categories "no go, slow go and fast go: If someone is a *no go*, she tends to be frail and demented, dependent upon others, while the

---

[5]M. W. Parker and R. Powers, "The Parent Care Readiness Program," paper presented at the Alabama Medical Directors Association's Fifteenth Annual Conference, Aging in America, Destin, Fla., July 25, 2009.

*fast go* is strong and independent; a *slow go* is somewhere in between." The church should ask the hard question, what value to society is a "no go"? And we should answer confidently, "An incontinent, dependent, person suffering from late stage Alzheimer's disease provides the person's family and her church with one of life's most important lessons, an opportunity to learn how to love a person unconditionally, without any expectation of something in return." Because dementia care is complicated and challenging, we discuss how the church can help develop caregiver support groups and maintain directories of community-based and national resources in a later chapter.

### Senior Ministry: Both To and From

Although the health status of aging members does affect the type of ministry extended to them or expected from them, the church must confront the reality that almost all members must be included in some type of ministry. In the coming years, it will become more and more crucial to create connections with aging members; in fact, it is a biblical responsibility to maintain cutting edge ministries "to" and "from" elders.

Like the failed faith-based system in New Orleans, if the church ignores and mishandles its aging members, the effects can have a devastating outcome. As we will learn in subsequent chapters, our society in general is unprepared for its aging population as disasters have revealed. If our society fails to train our religious, medical, legal, financial and entrepreneurial leaders about these matters, systems of support will be like a broken levee, unable to deal with the multiplying needs in elder care. The church of all institutions needs to take a stand. Sadly it may be the least prepared.

We need older persons of faith to help us address the problems we face today individually, as families, as members of our communities and as citizens of great nations. We cannot afford to deny and minimize the facts concerning the elderly, perpetuate our rationalizations about them, and project our personal and religious responsibilities toward them onto other people and institutions. Christ warned us about the consequences of losing that which places and preserves faith in him in the Sermon on the Mount. "You are the salt of the earth. But if the salt loses its saltiness, how can it be made salty again? It is no longer good for anything, except to be thrown out and trampled by men. You are the light of the world. A city on a hill cannot be hidden. Neither do people light a lamp and put it under a bowl. Instead they put it on its stand, and it gives light to everyone in the house. In the same way, let your light shine before men, that they may see your good deeds and praise your father in heaven" (Mt 5:13-16). If the church continues to relegate its responsibilities toward its senior members to other institutions in society and fails to recognize the gifts that lay within those members, it will become like salt that has lost its taste, its purpose and its capacity to preserve that which is good, and it will have lost its capacity to light the way. The aging church is not an accident. It is God himself who has granted longer life for his purposes, and we believe that elders hold the keys to solving many, if not most, of society's problems.

# 2

# Is Society Prepared for
# Its Aging Population?

*They will still bear fruit in old age,*
*they will stay fresh and green.*

PSALM 92:14

• • •

How did an increase in the population of elderly in our society come about, and why? Who or what is responsible for our increasingly aging population? Is it due to the skills of physicians, advances made by scientists or is it part of God's providential plan? For America's largest generation, some 70 million plus born approximately between 1946 and 1964, increases in life do not necessarily mean the dreamed-for retirement. But could longer life open up divine opportunities for the intervention of a wise God? Is society prepared? Is the modern church ready for the aging tidal wave that is hitting the beaches of America's communities?

These issues are underscored by the 2009-2010 health care debate in the United States. As an example of misinformation, physicians on the till by large pharmaceutical companies have presented false information before Congress, and the media is quick to present anecdotal cures for Alzheimer's disease. So misled, many in Congress, thinking we will have a cure for the dreaded disease in the next three to five years, have failed to address the needs of millions of family caregivers whose work is largely unrecognized and unappreciated but absolutely essential to the nation's welfare.[1]

According to the Institute of Medicine, starting in 2011, a baby boomer will turn sixty-five every twenty seconds.[2] The United States Social Security Administration expects to receive ten thousand applications per day for the next twenty years just for members of the baby boomer generation who are reaching ages of entitlement. Because of increasing longevity, most Western cultures have moved from a three-generational family structure to a four-generational one. Older people live longer and nuclear families have fewer children, meaning that kinship relationships are less among siblings and more across generations. Social scientists describe this new societal structure as the *beanpole family*, in which both parents work full time, divorce is more prevalent, and fewer daughters and sons are available to honor and care for parents as they age.[3] This is a major concern for the United States; for the first time, those over age sixty-five now outnumber those age eighteen and younger. And most modern nations are in the same boat.

## Challenges Associated with an Aging Population

As our senior population increases, we face a variety of challenges associated with this unprecedented growth. Centenarians represent the fastest growing age group in our country. In this century, some people are expected to reach 120 years, generally considered by scientists to be the maximum age for human beings. Surveys and experts indicate that most people, when asked, underestimate their longevity and therefore fail to plan adequately for it.[4] As an example, many older Americans are

---

[1]M. W. Parker and R. Powers, "The Parent Care Readiness Program," paper presented at the Alabama Medical Directors Association's Fifteenth Annual Conference, Aging in America, Destin, Fla., July 25, 2009.

[2]Gerontological Society of America, "Forecast Underscores Need for Aging Careers," *Gerontology News*, January 2009, p. 1.

[3]V. C. Bengtson, "Beyond the Nuclear Family: The Increasing Importance of Multigenerational Bonds," *Journal of Marriage and the Family* 63 (2001): 1-16. See also V. C. Bengtson and N. M. Putney, "Future 'Conflicts' Across Generations and Cohorts," in *The Futures of Old Age*, ed. J. Vincent, C. Phillipson and M. Downs (London: Sage, 2006).

[4]L. Roff, S. S. Martin, L. K. Jennings, M. W. Parker and D. K. Harmon, "Long Distance Parental Caregivers' Experiences with Siblings: A Qualitative Study," *Qualitative Social Work Research and Practice* 6, no. 3 (2007): 315-34; D. Myers, L. L. Roff, H. W. Harris, D. L. Klemmack and M. W. Parker, "A Feasibility Study of a Parent Care Planning Model with Two Faith-Based Communities," *Journal of Religion, Spirituality and Aging* 17, no. 1/2 (2004): 41-57;

uncomfortable talking about their own death, even though death is an undeniable reality. The church should be addressing the fears of death more completely, so that people might prepare for it emotionally, spiritually and financially. When asked what people fear the most about death, they register concerns about extended pain and suffering, loss of control and the afterlife.[5] Most older people die from chronic diseases like congestive heart failure or cancer. Many suffer unnecessarily at the end of life from symptoms like nausea or pain, because their physician, family and pastor fail to recommend in a timely way hospice[6] and palliative care programs.[7] Both these initiatives, aimed at alleviating these fears, remain largely underutilized.[8]

In America, the old-age poverty rate is about the same as that among non-elderly. However, the experiences of older women differ significantly from men economically, often because of life course issues related to household duties, career interruptions, limited pensions, lower wages and social security benefits, caregiving duties, higher rates of widowhood and other factors. Women represent the majority of our fastest growing age group, the oldest old, and they form one of the poorest groups in our society.[9] Almost 40 percent of African American and Latina women age eighty-five and older are living below the federal poverty level.[10] Marriage often protects women against experiencing poverty in old age. Given these factors, let us consider the biblical

---

M. W. Parker, V. R. Call, R. Toseland, M. Vaitkus and L. Roff, "Employed Women and Their Aging Family Convoys: A Life Course Model of Parent Care Assessment and Intervention," *Journal of Gerontological Social Work* 40, no. 1 (2003): 101-22.

[5]M. J. Christopher, "The New Place of End of Life Issues on the Policy Agenda," *Public Policy and Aging Report* 13 (2003): 23-26; V. G. Cicirelli, *Older Adults' Views on Death* (New York: Springer, 2002); V. G. Cicirelli, "Fear of Death in Mid-Old Age," *Journal of Gerontology: Psychological Sciences* 61B (2006): 75-81.

[6]A comprehensive program of care for dying persons aimed at emphasizing the dignity of the dying person.

[7]Palliative care is a program and philosophy of relief from pain and suffering for people of all ages facing a terminal illness.

[8]Robert Woods Johnson, "Study to Understand Prognoses and Preferences for Outcomes and Risks in Treatment," in Nancy Hooyman and H. Asuman Kiyak, *Social Gerontology: A Multidisciplinary Perspective*, 9th ed. (Boston: Pearson Education, 2011), pp. 559-60.

[9]Administration on Aging, "Profile of Older Americans: 2008," www.aoa.gov/AoAroot/Aging_Statistics/Profile/2008/index.aspx.

[10]Federal Interagency Forum on Aging-Related Statistics, *Older Americans 2008: Key Indicators of Well-Being* (Hyattsville, Md.: U.S. Independent Agencies and Commissions, 2008).

mandates to care for widows beside the fact that non-married women account for 56 percent of those aged eighty or above, and most of these are widows as defined by Paul in 1 Timothy 5. Many widows are in poverty because of gender inequities in social security, divorce or a husband's failure to provide a pension.[11] In Mark 12 and Matthew 23, the teachings of Christ to religious leaders are clear regarding widows.

These tremendous gains in life expectancy are not being greeted with optimism by many within our society, but are instead being received with tales of impending doom, grounded in depressing realities like the rising cost of medical care for the elderly. At present, elder caregiving is largely a woman's challenge and issue. The typical caregiver is a forty-seven-year old woman who works outside the home and spends more that twenty hours per week providing unpaid care to her mother. Now that American mothers and daughters, the traditional caregivers for older persons, are more involved in the full-time labor force than in any other nation in the world (68 percent of mothers work full time), they are less available to care for the growing number of older loved ones.[12] When working women are required to provide such care, they are often burdened by juggling outside work and combinations of child care and eldercare.

In the United States alone there are approximately 34 million family caregivers at any point in time, and the estimated economic cost to American families (e.g., lost revenue, direct costs associated with transportation, shopping, bathing, feeding, contacting agencies) has been estimated at $350 billion dollars, equivalent to the entire gross sales from Wal-Mart. Or spent by Medicare ($342 billion) and Medicaid ($300 billion) in 2005.[13] The cost to the workplace and working caregivers is tremendous. Thirty-seven percent of caregivers report quitting their job or reducing work hours. Unfortunately, our work with congregations suggests that the church is doing little to support the needs of caregivers in their congregations.[14]

---

[11]Administration on Aging, "Profile of Older Americans: 2008," www.aoa.gov/AoAroot/Aging_Statistics/Profile/2008/index.aspx.
[12]M. W. Parker et al., "Employed Women and Their Aging Family Convoys, " pp. 101-22.
[13]Hooyman and Kiyak, *Social Gerontology,* pp. 394-95.
[14]D. Myers et al., "A Feasibility Study of a Parent Care Planning Model with Two Faith-Based

Western culture, communities, families and congregations face incredible financial challenges related to our aging populations. Who will pay for national and state entitlement programs to support this pool of seniors? Spending on Medicare and Medicaid represents almost 25 percent of the federal budget,[15] and these costs are growing at a rate that far exceeds the economic growth rate of the United States. Sadly, older people and their caregivers pay a larger portion of the incomes on health care services than they did before Medicare and Medicaid were created in 1965, and those below the poverty line pay almost 30 percent of their total income on health care.[16] The vulnerabilities of Medicare Trust Fund are estimated to be greater than those to Social Security.[17] Current debates about health care in the United States have not properly addressed these issues. According to recent estimates from the MetLife Mature Market Institute and other research groups, the current costs of long-term care (for example, aging-in-place facilities, nursing homes, assisted living and dementia care units) will test the savings plans of even the very rich.[18] Though some congregations have gotten involved in developing affordable aging-in-place facilities that allow a person to move from independent housing to assisted living to nursing home status to cognitive-care units, this is much more the exception for most communities. Most older Americans prefer to avoid nursing homes altogether, but new resident-centered paradigms of care are emerging, and congregations and denominations need to be more involved.[19]

Communities," pp. 41-57; M. W. Parker et al., "Parent Care and Religion: A Faith-Based Intervention Model for Caregiving Readiness of Congregational Members," *Journal of Family Ministry* 17, no. 4 (2004): 51-69; L. Dunn et al., "Building Sustainable Community Partnerships to Promote Successful Aging: A Preliminary Study of Local Congregations and Agencies," *Journal of Community Engagement and Scholarship* (forthcoming).

[15]*The Budget and Economic Outlook: Fiscal Years 2008 to 2017* (Washington, D.C.: Congressional Budget Office, 2007), <www.cbo.gov/ftpdocs/77xx/doc7731/01-24-BudgetOutlook.pdf>.

[16]Federal Interagency Forum on Aging and Related Statistics, *Older Americans 2008: Key Indicators of Well-Being* (Washington, D.C.: Government Printing Office, 2008).

[17]M. Crutsinger, "Social Security, Medicare Facing Unhealthy Future: Benefit Programs Will Be Depleted Before Projections," *The Boston Globe News* (national), May 13, 2009, p. 7.

[18]"MetLife Market Survey of Nursing Home and Home Health Costs" (Westport, Conn.: MetLife Mature Market Institute, 2006), www.nyc.gov/html/olr/downloads/pdf/ltc/2006_ltc_survey.pdf.

[19]See, for example, the Eden Alternative in W. H. Thomas, *The Eden Alternative Handbook*

How are families (the primary caregivers of older Americans), governmental agencies and other societal systems in the United States going to meet the current and expanding need for services to seniors without the help of congregations? Given the shortages of geriatric professionals in the majority of communities, how can congregations help? What role, if any, does the church play—and what role should it play—in these challenges?

## The Church's Response

The church must be a visible, key shareholder in the aging of America, yet many of its structures and programs are outdated. Most programs of senior ministry, much like the United States' Social Security and Medicare Programs, were developed during the nineteenth and twentieth centuries and were based on the foundational premise of a relatively short life span and health care system designed for acute and not chronic medical care. Now that life expectancy is much longer, the vast majority of church programs are grossly obsolete like many of the United States' national programs and policies. Churches are generally thought of as institutions that neglect the training of their leaders, particularly in gerontology, and professional organizations therefore discount the church as a positive change agent in society. But churches stand to benefit—both in effectiveness and in impact—by becoming more involved on a local level with professional organizations that focus on aging well; learning to partner with other congregations to share in the financial costs of innovative, effective programs that promote lifestyle changes associated with successful aging; and offering countercultural programs that value the role of older people.

We think caregiving will be the great test of character this century, and yet the modern church is virtually mute on the topic. Almost half of those eighty-five and older, one of our fastest growing age groups, face the probability of dementia (about two-thirds will be diagnosed with the dreaded Alzheimer's disease). Recipients of such a diagnosis are virtually guaranteed years of dependency on others. Traditionally,

(Sherburne, N.Y.: Eden Alterantive Foundation, 1999); or see the Green House Concept and the Pioneer Network.

families have provided most late-life care. According to our research, very few churches provide systematic help to familial caregivers, and when such a program is offered, those who manage it often feel overwhelmed, unprepared and underresourced.[20] Community-based, ecumenical partnerships will become a necessity. Employed adult children or elderly spouses are often unable to provide the all the help needed. If elder care is the number one human resource problem in most organizations, why wouldn't it be the case for the church? Some churches are literally aging to death; actually, they already have for the most part in Western Europe.

The church provides little if any planning for late life. At present, if a woman in the United States lives to sixty-five years of age, she can expect to live, on average, another nineteen years, five of which will be years of dependency. Many widows suffer financially without the church's knowledge or intervention. For men, life expectancy after sixty-five is approximately fifteen years, with three anticipated years of dependency. The church has an obligation to become part of the solution for these new aging challenges.

Profound shortages exist in the geriatric care work force. Take for example the number of geriatric certified (trained) physicians in the United States: there are approximately eight thousand, but only about one thousand practice exclusively with older persons. United States medical schools combined have only five specifically geriatric medicine departments; the balance is absorbed in other divisions of medicine (internal medicine, family practice). In contrast, Japan, Great Britain and Canada have separate departments of geriatric medicine in most of their medical schools. In the United States, the number of medical students selecting primary-care vocations (family practice, internal medicine) is decreasing. As noted earlier, our systems of care remain focused on acute, not chronic, care, and many primary care doctors are not choosing geriatrics because they will make more money in other specialties. As professional groups address this problem, the church also should be helping church members locate trained professionals; em-

[20]L. Dunn et al., "Building Sustainable Community Partnerships."

ploying geriatric care managers (geriatric-trained nurses and social workers) to help congregates navigate the long-term care system; and insisting that seminaries provide geriatric and gerontological training to its future pastors.

Without adequate resources for mobility, many seniors face isolation, depression and poor health, and society faces increased costs of care and a loss of the vital contributions of older generations. The first step toward improving this situation comes through gaining insight into the issues and creating a vision for change in which the church is a clear stakeholder. The church can help identify and target at-risk groups and provide interventions and training. For example, spinal and hip fractures resulting from falls are epidemic among the elderly, and the church easily could offer a variety of fall prevention programs.[21]

Medical and legal professionals in the United States are ill equipped to address the coming age wave associated with the baby boomer generation. The first boomers have already qualified for social security. In past years, one worker in five contributed to social security; now, one in two workers contributes to the funding of entitlement programs like Medicare and Social Security. Law schools across the United States affiliate with only a paucity of elder law clinics. Notably, the Hartford Foundation has attempted to support the gerontological training of physicians, social workers and nurses, but its efforts are not sufficient to meet the growing need.

Preliminary research suggests that similarly only a few seminaries offer an elective course on aging and ministry, though all pastors will have older persons in their congregations. Those clergy inclined to blame or ignore the elderly may know little about them. Only a very small number of seminaries offer solid accredited courses on the implications of a graying church for ministry. As early as 1988, Hutchinson estimated that only twenty seminaries offered pastoral courses on an age-related topic.[22] He also reported that in 1985 fifty seminary profes-

---

[21]A fall prevention evaluation should ideally include a physical examination performed by a doctor, a progressive exercise regime implemented by a physical therapist and an environmental precautions analysis, especially of home hazards.
[22]"Coming to Grips with an Aging Church," *Christian Century* (February 22, 1988): 206.

sors and deans gathered to consider what courses should be taught and how they could encourage and stimulate the seminaries to teach gerontological insights in theology. Hutchinson further reported that the Institute on Religious Life and the AARP office published a substantial document, "Aging Society—A Challenge to Theological Education." Twenty-four scholars in eight disciplines prepared stimulating material suggesting a theological basis for seminaries to consider (and simultaneously provide) courses in the church and aging field. Though these leaders hoped that gerontological insights would someday pervade the entire seminary curriculum, Watkins provided a more recent but similarly bleak view of seminaries and the availability of such courses.[23] J. L. Knapp and J. Elder also confirmed these patterns of neglect by seminaries in their research, which indicates that some seminaries have added a course focusing on the needs and concerns of older adults, but gerontological content remains a minor consideration among the vast majority of seminaries.[24]

Only a few seminaries consider these courses basic to the theological education of prospective ministers and therefore require them for graduation. Occasionally they are incorporated in courses on pastoral theology. In our research, we could not locate one American seminary that has conducted a comprehensive review of its curricula to insure that it is "geriatrically enriched" and truly reflective of our aging congregations and population. Education in pastoral ministry lacks what the John A. Hartford Foundation and the Gerontological Society of America does for schools of medicine, social work and nursing. These organizations have provided substantial funding and research to examine the overall curricula offered in the colleges of these three professions. When we have approached seminaries, they have shown little inclination to apply for grants that might provide for such an intense review and overhaul of their curricula. For the church to lag behind such secular programs removes the church from its proper position of leadership

---

[23]*Religion and Aging: An Anthology of the Poppele Papers* (New York: Haworth Pastoral Press, 2001), pp. 1-5.

[24]J. L. Knapp and J. Elder, "Ministry with Elderly: Training Needs of Clergy," *Educational Gerontology* 28, no. 3 (March 2002): 207-17.

in addressing the pressing agendas regarding older persons. Such issues—many even moral in nature—are not completely addressed without a Christian perspective.

We believe that the church is obligated to act as a countercultural, biblically based advocate on critical matters with regard to aging. Churches can and should promote the care and employment of seniors, healthy caregiving practices, caregiving support, late-life planning, aging-in-place initiatives and strategies for successful aging, and they should uphold the inherent value of dependent, disabled people. Many churches are "aging to death" because they are unable to attract younger members, and rather than taking an intergenerational perspective that would connect the younger members with more elderly members, some national denominations have dramatically cut their programs for seniors in favor of youth ministries.

A growing number of pastors are asking for help. Some have simply aged out of youth ministry. Some feel overwhelmed and burdened by their aging congregations and lack a clear sense of direction in solving the mounting challenges with their senior members. During one presentation I (Dr. Parker) gave to a large gathering of ministers to seniors, a majority of the audience reported feeling frustrated at not having received specific training in how to minister to seniors; indeed, many of them felt more like modern day travel agents than ministers-to-seniors. Encouragingly, many had received personal callings to minister to their older members and were hungry for new and effective strategies that would assist them in that ministry.[25]

Boomers with frail, dependent parents are also frantically seeking advice for understanding and coping with America's long-term care system. The needs of their parents can erupt in periodic crises or stretch on for several years. Such crises can thrust a church member into a bureaucratic maze of trying to make successive care arrangements in a

---

[25]Dunn et al., "Building Sustainable Community Partnerships to Promote Successful Aging"; Parker et al., "Multidisciplinary Model of Health Promotion," pp. 405-15. See also M. W. Parker, L. Dunn, J. Goetz, S. Ousley, M. Rogers, M. Piper, R. Harrell, H. Lee, N. S. Park, S. MacCall, J. Williams, C. Spencer and X. Li, "Helping to Unite an Aging Southern Community: An Internet Directory Project and Telephone Survey of Local Congregations," *Journal of Community-Based Partnerships* (forthcoming).

badly fragmented long-term care system. The nation's patchwork of nursing homes, foster homes, adult day centers and home health care agencies offer a dizzying array of often unsatisfactory options for the church and society. It is imperative that the church step up and offer guidance and assistance to its caregiving and senior members.

People in the church are beginning to see their need with regard to elder care issues, and we think there are reasons to be hopeful that the church is on the precipice of an exciting impact on our culture. Facing up to the ways society's admiration of youth diminishes our churches is a first step in reenvisioning the role of seniors in the church today.

# 3

# THE CONFUSED CULTURAL ROLE
# OF SENIORS IN SECULAR SOCIETY
# AND THE CHURCH

...

We are convinced that elders have an irreplaceable role in churches and communities, and church history of the last two millennia provides a proper perspective about elders as vital players in reviving today's church. Despite the existence of ageism within the church, the individual lives of all older Christians continue to contribute to our congregational life, particularly when the church recognizes the eternal significance of their unique, spiritual narratives, etched and shaped by historical events. Tom Brokaw's depiction of the World War II Generation as the "greatest generation" underscored for many the importance of a particular generation.[1] But his book did little to change the youth-oriented systems of power within the church and our culture.

## The Context: American Self-Reliance

Certainly de Tocqueville, at the beginning of the nineteenth century, recognized a new social experiment was taking place in the colonization of North America. Its immigrants were cut off (or had voluntarily cut themselves off) from their traditional roots to explore and occupy a new continent. He called it "the rise of the individual." This observation now goes without question, but it continues to have striking effects on our society. For one thing, it does make the individual

---

[1]Tom Brokaw, *The Greatest Generation* (New York: Random House, 2004).

more vulnerable, if "everyone is for himself." As former Secretary of Labor Robert B. Reich notes in his book *The Future of Success*, Americans now work over 2,000 hours a year—approximately 350 hours more than workers in Western Europe.[2]

The myth of the superiority of American higher productivity is evaporating as undesirable social trends persist. Social insecurity is high, family costs continue to rise, job satisfaction is low, loyalty to employees is disappearing, and trust of institutions and corporate entities has diminished. Yet these and related factors, together with widening inequality, actually generate even more self-interest, now more broadly interpreted as self-survival. Cultures of survival tend naturally to have "attention deficit disorders" when living "each one for one's self" becomes the norm.

"Elite culture" of aristocratic rule and of philosopher kings, giving way in turn to mass cultures of ideologies like socialism and fascism. Now in the postwar development of the professionalized "boomer generation," we have much more individualistic cultures, accelerated by the recent electronic technologies. Thus in an increasingly competitive society, innovation, individual enterprise, escalating workloads and the like will perpetuate this self-focused tendency. In fact, self-help, social independence and emphasis on personal likes and dislikes is creating a "preferential culture" (in contrast to the mass culture of the twentieth century). Today, we can choose rapidly growing, diverse ways of living. Change, instability, discontinuities, family breakup, global mobility, commuting distances, diverse family activities and interests are all leading to loss of cultural cohesion.

Seniors are being adversely affected by these changes because, in addition to the older years being a time to foster and enjoy human connection, most of them will likely be unable to be completely self-sufficient until they die. Basing one's sense of pride and personhood on autonomous success—and moreover, judging others on that basis—flys directly in the face of sufficiently learning from and caring for our elders.

---

[2]Robert B. Reich, quoted in M. W. Parker, V. R. Call, R. Toseland, M. Vaitkus and L. Roff, "Employed Women and Their Aging Family Convoys: A Life Course Model of Parent Care Assessment and Intervention," *Journal of Gerontological Social Work* 40, no. 1 (2003): 101-22.

Keeping these broad cultural perspectives in mind, we can reflect on and be challenged by the declining role of seniors within our churches. For when we see seniors treated no differently in our churches than in our society, perhaps we have an indicator of how secularized our church life is becoming and of how unaware of this connection we have been.

## Is the Church Different?

The next time you take your seat in your church congregation, take a good look around you. You may notice that a growing number of those worshiping with you have entered the "senior" category in life. In our middle-sized community of Tuscaloosa, Alabama, two of three churches in one major denomination alone are in danger of closing because their congregations consist almost exclusively of older members. The senior wisdom alone that is in jeopardy of being lost with those closings is reason enough for taking a careful look at the role those ages fifty-five and older are currently assigned in most churches today and at the manner in which today's church ministers to one of the most valuable assets in its membership.

My (Dr. Parker) wife, Lane, has shared inspiring stories of her Norwegian grandmother, Mor. Mor and her Norwegian sea-captain husband immigrated to America and settled in Mobile, Alabama. After several years of volunteerism and service, she was decorated by the King of Norway for establishing Norwegian Seamen's Missions along the Gulf Coast of the United States. Though Lane remembers the crowning event, she was influenced most of all by her regular, personal encounters with Mor. Mor's daily disciplines were consistently loving and honoring of those around her. For example, each day, coffee was served promptly at 4:00 p.m. for anyone choosing to visit. Mor provided her total attention to the needs of her guests. Few older people today have time for teaching those who are younger how to love in this manner.

When I was growing up in the 1950s, many of my Sunday school teachers (whom I still consider strong spiritual influences on my early faith) were in the senior age group. However, today's church seems to be embracing a youth-oriented recruitment system that leaves little room for our elders to serve in key leadership positions. To compound this problem, many churches promote age-graded Sunday school classes and programs that essentially isolate seniors from the younger generations.[3] Our research identified one large church that has three large Sunday school classes for seniors labeled as the "young old" (55-74), the "old old" (75-84) and the "oldest old" (85 and older). No one belonging to the first category wanted to ever be part of the second or third, and all three groups were completely isolated from the classes for younger age groups.

Today's church fails to recognize sufficiently the unique resource available in its senior members. Rather than being viewed as the age group that only needs to be cared and provided for, our elders should be heartily engaged in the inner workings of the church, lending their seasoned areas of expertise, particularly in the area of faith, to those still trying to figure out this thing called *life*. The biblical example of the old leading the young has somehow been reversed in our current society and churches; it is time to correct this fatal misdirection. As older persons continue to live healthier and longer lives, they are uniquely positioned to assume leadership roles in rebuilding our families, churches and communities. The Bible is filled with examples of God-appointed ministries in which the elderly advised and led the younger in successfully completing the work of the Lord.

Research confirms that the eighty-five-plus segment of our population is growing faster than any other group. As far as our work has determined, however, adult children faced with caring for aging parents are not finding the type of assistance they need in the church. In fact, many churches are not aware of local programs offering a variety of services to the elderly. Though there are wonderful exceptions, most pastors we have interviewed or assisted are overwhelmed with the basics of ministry. A major drawback in the current programs offered by today's church to its seniors is that they are sorely outdated. The church at large does not know how to access state of science information about critical topics that could reduce periods of dependency in its senior

---

[3]L. Dunn et al., "Building Sustainable Community Partnerships to Promote Successful Aging: A Preliminary Study of Local Congregations and Agencies," *Journal of Community Engagement and Scholarship* (forthcoming).

members, like the following: how to age successfully, how to engage and challenge elders in late life ministerial calling, how to age in place at home, how to drive safely and for longer periods using brain health programs, how to plan for caregiving and how to live with chronic conditions.

Our growing body of research indicates that churches of all sizes are not only unaware of most state of science aids to successful aging, but that they are also unprepared themselves for the aging of their congregations. Rather than placing a premium on their older members and what their years of life experience add to the overall faith and growth of their congregation, many of today's churches consider the elderly somewhat of a burden. Such unfortunate thinking results in lost opportunities for volunteerism for older persons, despite the facts that most are healthy, have retirement incomes, are readily available with their time and have the necessary faith and experience to lead. Some of the most rewarding lessons and programs in churches are those taught and overseen by senior members.

### Recapturing a Sense of Transcendence

In *War and Peace*, Leo Tolstoy uses the vast canvas of Russia to narrate the greatest war in the history of his time, Napoleon's invasion of 1812. Yet he does not depict Titans, but the love story of one man and woman, Pierre and Natasha, caught up—like many millions—in the struggle between life and death. The moral is that where there is love, there is life. Love and life are both from God. When love is awakened (or reawakened) then individual life too, is awakened and renewed. Is this not the greatest need of our time?

With prophetic insight Tolstoy, as Dostoyevsky and Turgenev before him, all realized that socialist ideology would destroy their beloved country even more than military conquest. As Tolstoy put it: "If we allow that human life can be governed by reason, the possibility of life is annihilated."[4]

When she was a child, Dr. Houston's youngest daughter was wel-

---

[4]Leo Tolstoy, *War and Peace*, trans. Richard Pevear and Larissa Volokhonsky (New York: Alfred A. Knopf, 2007), p. 1131.

comed by a childless couple living across from their house in Oxford. The husband was a famous professor of philosophy in the University. One day the conversation between Penelope and the professor went like this: "Professor Robinson, what do you do for a living?" "Well, Penny, I think, I teach about thinking, and I write about thinking." Penny's response was very disappointed: "Is that all you do?" When we speak about postmodernism today, we are culturally responding to the child's common sense: reason by itself is not comprehensive enough for human life. We are no longer enchanted by rationalism, and yet so much of our Christian faith still remains doctrinaire, or in activism, too programmatic. For the grammar of faith is not just cognitive: it is also emotional, cognitive and spiritual intelligence.

Paul expresses that his Christian education of the Thessalonians was like the nurture given by a nursing mother (1 Thess 2:7) He was equally concerned about their emotions, their will and desires, and their spiritual connectivity with each other and the Lord. We have too frequently gotten stuck in our faith by the adage "Your mind matters"; yet our soul matters most. The apostle calls his readers (including us) to live far more comprehensively as followers of Christ.

Otherwise, our personal lives are distorted and wounded by living in an impersonal universe, which we call our "scientific worldview." As C. S. Lewis has argued, we moderns disenchant our universe by making it "all fact and no meaning," seeing space as a cold, black, mostly empty vastness, with stars and planets propelled by gravitational and other forces. But the medieval universe, argues Lewis, "was tingling with anthropomorphic life, dancing, ceremonial, a festival, not a machine." As Dante reminds us, "He who moves the sun and the other stars is love." The Copernicun revolution of science—for good and ill— is irreversible, but our sense of wonder at life must not be dimmed in its wake. We need to have broader horizons than what a Blackberry can provide, more aptitude than mere technical skills that seem to put everything within our reach. What ideologies did in the twentieth century, technology is now further doing in the twenty-first, reducing a sense of transcendence.

Dr. Houston witnessed this difference quite vividly when he visited the Museum of Man directly after going to the Louvre. What a con-trast! In lieu of the religious splendor of the Louvre's medieval art, the Museum exhibits the skull of René Descartes, who revolutionized the world with his dictum, "I think, therefore I am." Another exhibit cal-culates the daily volume of global women's milk supply; it has other demographics galore, but the soul of man has vanished. Love does not exist in any of the museum's displays.

As a correspondent of the *New York Times* recently wrote, the Middle Ages can be appreciated now as "The Great Escape." Indeed for John Ruskin, Charles Williams, C. S. Lewis and Dorothy Sayers, among others, medieval culture with its vivid exercise of the imagination, of life played out in dreams, of ideals and a strong sense of symbolism, was a counter to the grubbiness of industrialism, mass manufacture, secu-larization and urbanization.[5] As Johan Huizinga wrote in *The Autumn of the Middle Ages*, "The most revealing map of Europe in these centu-ries would be a map, not of political or commercial capitals, but of the constellation of sanctuaries, the points of material contact with the un-seen world."[6] Cultural movements like climate change and the "green revolution" response find us connecting to the global effects of our choices. It is not such a stretch to reinterpret how personal yet how cosmic our Christian faith should become. Like Tolstoy, we must view the human drama in both its magnitude and yet in its personal inti-macy. Senior saints have the capacity to recognize the importance of the loving of others in the present tense. Many of their traditions make this possible. As Dr. Charles Davis,[7] one of my (Dr. Parker's) elder-mentors, writes, "Paul listed 'love' first in his description of the fruits of the Spirit because it finds expression in all of the other fruits: Joy is love's strength; peace is love's security; patience is love's endurance; kindness is love's conduct; goodness is love's character; faithfulness is love's confidence; gentleness is love's humility; and self-control is love's victory."[8] "Against such things there is no law" (Gal 5:23).

---

[5]David Brooks, "The Great Escape," *New York Times*, May 29, 2008.
[6]Ibid.
[7]Charles Davis, *New Testament Church Life: A Model for Today* (Columbus, Ga.: Brentwood Press, 2006), p. 118.
[8]Ibid.

If we need to renew our culture, as this work contends, then the book of Deuteronomy is an apposite manifesto. Deuteronomy was originally written to renew the covenant God had made with Israel. This was done on the plains of Moab, in the transition when Moses anticipates his death and prepares for Joshua to succeed him in leadership. As a covenant book par excellence, Deuteronomy is a historical text of the deeds of God as the Lord of history. It is a treaty document, recounting the past, but not like secular history, which merely traces cause and effects in human affairs. Instead, biblical history reveals what God has done in the past and is still doing today, even though we may not see and know it. Deuteronomy has also been identified with the book of the law, which king Josiah rediscovered in his reformation in the seventh century B.C. (2 Kings 22–23; 2 Chron 34–35). It is no coincidence, then, that we have chosen to focus on Deuteronomy 32:7 as the guiding theme of this book: "Remember the days of old; consider the generations long past. Ask your father and he will tell you, your elders, and they will explain to you."

Our elders are like both map-readers and map-makers of the ways of God with humans. We can now buy a map very cheaply or access one online in seconds, but the original explorers literally gave their lives to explore unknown territory. And one by one, their mapped territory has been coordinated into vaster horizons of the known. Today, we inherit all their achievements. How foolish then is contemporary culture to reject the past, to forget our map-makers and to ignore the wisdom of our seniors, all so dearly bought!

PART TWO

...

# BIBLICAL AND HISTORICAL
# THEMES OF AGING

# 4

# AGING IN A BIBLICAL CONTEXT

. . .

$A$s we will examine later in our chapters on dementia and disability, contemporary culture emphasizes the physicality of human development rather than the spirituality of aging. The Bible's emphasis, however, is upon the moral and spiritual growth of those seeking to become mature in wisdom. The Midrash Rabbah states, "How welcome is old age! The aged are beloved of God."[1] Such a culture does not see the aged as having outlived their usefulness. Rather it celebrates their age, so whatever was the measurement of life, records of years lived are carefully kept of biblical characters at their death: Isaac, 180; Abraham, 175; Jacob, 147; Ishmael, 137; Sarah, 127; Joseph and Joshua, 110. Abraham Herschel has remarked: "Old age was not a defeat but a victory, not a punishment but a privilege."[2]

## The Wisdom of the Aged

Rabbinic literature stressed the importance of older people as the source of wisdom. One quote compares them to vintage wine, in contrast to the counsel of youth as like freshly crushed grapes: "He who learns from the young is like one who eats unripe grapes and drinks wine from the winepress. But he who learns from the old is like one who eats ripe grapes and drinks old wine" (Abot 4:20[3]). To be old is to have reached the age of veneration, when the young can begin to appreciate all the

---

[1]Quoted in Marvin R. Wilson, *Our Father Abraham: Jewish Roots of the Christian Faith* (Grand Rapids: Eerdmans, 1985), p. 227.
[2]Abraham J. Heschel, *The Insecurity of Freedom* (New York: Schocken Books, 1972), pp. 71-72.
[3]Quoted in Wilson, *Our Father Abraham*, p. 230.

benefits of their parents' teachings.

The book of Proverbs begins within this setting: "Listen, my son, to your father's instruction and do not forsake your mother's teaching" (Prov 1:8). The introduction of the next six chapters begins with the summons, "my son . . . accept my words," "do not forget my teaching," "Listen, my sons, to a father's instruction," "pay attention to my wisdom," "do this, my son," "my son, keep my words and store up my commands within you." With elders the source of such a rich moral life, Leviticus 19:32 gives the injunction, "Rise in the presence of the aged, show respect for the elderly and revere your God. I am the LORD."

There are some 175 references to elders in the Bible. Today, we might call them "leading elders" who were marked by moral rather than by official authority, not elected but recognized within the community, never alone but representative of a group that reflected the well-being of the whole community. The elders were the heads of leading families, so their authority was familial and not political. Yet there were checks and balances within such a hereditary "aristocracy" (which was therefore not a "gerontocracy"). The old did not rule because of years only, but for their value and relational role within the village communities. Thus there is an allusive quality about the Jewish role of eldership that connotes age, wisdom and honor, all as they relate to community well-being. This was implicit in its Old Testament practice of covenant, which distinguished Israelite society from all its pagan neighbors. It promoted personhood, not just sociality.[4]

### The Biblical Basis of Honoring Parents

*Deuteronomy and the covenant life.* The Old Testament book of Deuteronomy lies at the heart of the covenant life. The Septuagint names it *Deuteronomion*, meaning "the Second Law" or "the repetition of the Law." Moses introduces it with two farewell addresses given in his old age, both of which renew the covenant life of the Israelite community. Now that Israel has established its own territory, the people are reminded by Moses, as only an old leader can do from his own long ex-

---

[4]Ray S. Anderson and Dennis B. Guernsey, *On Being Family* (Grand Rapids: Eerdmans, 1985), pp. 33-36.

perience, that the uniqueness of their identity lies in relating to the uniqueness of God as the "I AM." To love God with all one's heart is the central message. In turn, the fathers sustain the memory of the I AM in the on-going life of Israel. This is done in the preaching about the covenant, as Moses' two addresses communicate (Deut 1:6–4:40; 5:1–28:68).[5]

Deuteronomy is not static legal material handed down, but text set within unique historical events such as the call of Moses, the exodus from Egypt, the deliverance over the Red Sea, the ascent of Moses to Mount Sinai, the giving of the Law and its renewal on the plains of Moab. All this in turn, goes back to Yahweh's call of Abraham and of the other Patriarchs. All these events reveal God's own relational character, not that of an isolated divine monad, but of Emmanuel, "God with us."

The Ten Commandments or "the Ten Words," as the account in the book of Deuteronomy describes them, are the specific stipulations of a covenant life, within a specific historical consciousness of a God-who-is-with-us. Yet basic as the Sinai revelation is in the history of God's people, it is far more than one of many historical events. Significantly, there is almost no reference to the event on Sinai in Israel's later confessions of faith and hymnody. Sinai transcends history. Yet it is a unique expression of God's self-disclosure towards humanity, incomparable with all other human covenant treaties, whose "events could be told, but the mystery behind them could not be explained," observes Marcus Barth.[6] God is the source of it all: the summons to worship; his divine self-revelation; arousing his people to accept the stipulations of his covenant. So there is certainly a historical context, but the initiative God takes is unique in all human history.

At Sinai, God brings the community of Israel into its intended relationship with him and prescribes the means for Israel to maintain that relationship. Likewise, the Ten Commandments imply that right relations with one's fellows require righteousness with God. But without

---

[5]Bruce K. Waltke, *An Old Testament Theology* (Grand Rapids: Zondervans, 1995), pp. 417-511.
[6]Christoph Barth, *God with Us*, arranged by Geoffrey W. Bromiley (Grand Rapids: Eerdmans, 1991), p. 119.

God's advent, there would be no proclamation of God's Word. This was part of the same divine action. Both presence and words are united, which explains why unbelievers who do not experience God's presence cannot accept to do his will nor become part of the community for God's fulfillment of that will. Then, however much they may love and care for their seniors, they cannot experience right relationships with them outside of the covenant community.

Without covenant relationships with God and others, the Law is still viewed as an exacting burden, instead of as the gift of grace that gives life and blesses society. Inscribed on two tablets of stone, the Ten Commandments convey two central messages: let God be God (commandments one through four) and let humans become human persons (commandments five through ten). There is no rivalry, contrary to how Nietzsche and his followers have interpreted the God-man relationship, for we can know and act freely in relation to the uniqueness of God as our Creator-Redeemer, one God as "wholly other," as we can relate to no other. God can never be confused with idols—as "things" to be seen—for a relationship to him is unique, to be loved and nurtured.

So it is pivotal to recognize the central importance of the fourth and fifth commandments. They are like two hinges uniting the two tablets. Even if the two tablets were identical copies, one for God and one for Israel, the pivotal importance of the two commandments remains. Primarily, we are "to keep the Sabbath day holy," and then "to honor your father and mother." Together, they act as the link between the character of God and the character of our humanity. All the divine commandments are, of course, founded upon the uniqueness of God in the first commandment, as the I AM. The second commandment emphasizes God is relational, not a *what* but *Who*, personal, not a thing. Thus obedience, as "listening to him" (*ob audire* means "listen to"), is basic.

Why then "Remember the Sabbath day to keep it holy"? Human activity is limited, argues Karl Barth, so that it does not occupy center-stage in human consciousness, but rather celebrates *opus Dei*, truly "the work of God."[7] The temporal uniqueness of the Sabbath day reflects

---

[7]Karl Barth, *Church Dogmatics* 3/4, ed. G. W. Bromiley and T. F. Torrance (Edinburgh: T & T Clark, 1951), p. 55.

upon this unique priority given to the I AM, over all other actions. Thus God's unique creation is separate and over all human creativity, and God's unique redemption over all our compensatory emotions in our attempts to be self-redemptive. As Barth puts it, keeping the Sabbath "demands that he[she] knows oneself only in [personal] faith in God, and that one wills and works and expresses oneself only in this imposed and not selected renunciation, and that on the basis of this renunciation one actually dares to become a new creature, as a new human being. This is the astonishing requirement of the Sabbath commandment."[8]

We are invited into this "Sabbath rest" in order to exercise absolute trust in God alone. Rather it is our workaday world which tempts us and diverts us to indulge in self-sufficiency. Instead, our true identity is a "Sabbatical identity." Karl Barth thus affirms that being truly "human" is being "caught up in responsibility before God" to keep the Sabbath.[9]

The fourth commandment, to keep "the Holy Day" of the Sabbath, then becomes pivotal in explaining the unity of the first four commandments, which all concern God's character. For it limits and contextualizes all that human beings "do" in the context of what God has already accomplished in creation and indeed in redemption. Thus it interrupts our workaday world to challenge us when we assume we are too busy to even think about God or to give him priority in our way of living. For the Sabbath symbolizes renouncing our independence from our Creator, who has done all things well. Even our creaturely nature demonstrates the therapeutic benefits of this sabbatical rest physically, emotionally and spiritually. For it serves many humanitarian purposes. Like the bodily mark of circumcision, Sabbath identifies socially a true "Israelite" or a true Christian, from all other peoples and their cultures. What mark then, do Christians bear today, to identify our "sabbatical identity," from the secularist? For like the Israelite, the Christian is not identified by the work he does, but by the sabbatical relationship he is given to enjoy God's rest. We can extend this principle today, in showing that the Christian senior is not to be discriminated against—least of all in the church—by

[8]Ibid.
[9]Ibid.

the diminishing work he or she can now perform because of age, but by the sabbatical identity that should mark the life and person of every Christian, as resting in Christ. That is to say, Christians have a more transcendent identity than a profession could ever give. It is profoundly a sabbatical identity, grounded in God and in relationship to him. While to despise another human being is to forget each of us is given to one's self, by God, to bear his image and likeness. Perhaps this is the most profound challenge of our culture today, not to live and act in defiance of this truth, that in Christ, we are a new creation.

Then the second tablet, which comprises the last six commandments, affirms the nature and proper relations of human beings, in positively honoring our parents. Then there follows a series of negatives: not being death-giving to others; not committing adultery; not stealing others' property; not lying before others; and in not being envious of the other. They all assert that to be a human person, one must acknowledge the unique reality of God, in the context of which we can legitimize the rights of each other human being. Our humanity is defined by all these social obligations, before the one God.

But of all these six realms of human relations, it is significant that the only positive command is to honor our parents. Parents reflect, as does also the biblical meaning of *father*, the source of life and then also the "issues" of life. Again they remind us of our creaturely status, of mutuality of relationships, of the self-communication and the responsiveness of the "knower" and the "known." In the role of parenting in Chinese culture, there is shame in the disclosure of intimacy from a senior to a son or daughter, even when all are adults; such self-disclosure is inconceivable. But the self-disclosure of God manifests itself intimately also in Christian family life, so all the family may share intimacy with each other as before God. Thus the authority of parents is iconic, expressive of their being a source of life, of guidance, of faith. This come not from themselves, but as they kneel "before the Father, from whom his whole family in heaven and on earth derives its name" (Eph 3:14-15).

Ultimately, we honor our parents for the sake of God as the source of all life and love, regardless of how good or bad they may be. We do so in giving them their due importance in our nurture, education and source of well-being, as all coming from God. But the parents in turn are to know the commands and will of God and by teaching them to their children, all will "live long in the land the LORD your God is giving you" (Ex 20:12). So the children will ask certain vital things: the meaning of the Passover (Ex 12:26); the dedication of the firstborn (Ex 13:14); the whole body of laws and ordinances (Deut 6:20); or how it was in former days (Deut 32:7).

*Wisdom in Proverbs.* The wisdom of the book of Proverbs is all about learning to live well from one's elders: "Listen, my son, to your father's instruction and do not forsake your mother's teaching" (Prov 1:8). Allowing ourselves to be instructed in the experiences of wisdom is truly to be "honoring" of our parents and of our seniors. Indeed, the book of Proverbs is a wide-ranging commentary on the fifth commandment. The focus of attention is on "my son," and the charge is clear: "Listen, my son, to your father's instruction and do not forsake your mother's teaching" (Prov 1:8). "If you accept my words and store up my commands within you, turning your ear to wisdom and applying your heart to understanding . . . then you will understand the fear of the LORD, and find the knowledge of God" (Prov 2:1-5). Anchored in parental teaching, the son is then to remain consistent in the instruction given, as a way of life, indeed for "length of days." It is an exhaustive commitment in an exclusive relationship. Thus the book of Proverbs details how honoring one's parents is really honoring the wisdom they communicate from the word of the Lord, the source and ground for all honor.

*Jesus' example.* Even the parents of Jesus are illustrated as shortsighted about how to properly honor God in the incident narrated in Luke 2:48-50. In returning from the visit to the temple, when Jesus was a child of twelve, his mother confronted him: "Son, why have you treated us like this? Your father and I have been anxiously searching for you [i.e., causing us such anxiety from your disappearance from us for three days]" (Lk 2:48). Had Mary already disclosed to her son her immaculate conception? Did he already know of his transcendent fatherhood by his unique conception? Jesus' response reminds her, "Didn't you know I had to be in my Father's house?" (Lk 2:49). To Mary and

Joseph's astonishment, they find Jesus is more faithfully fulfilling the fifth commandment than they!

Thus it is more than a figure of speech for the apostle Paul to claim of the Corinthian Christians, "I became your father through the gospel. Therefore I urge you to imitate me" (1 Cor 4:15-16). So he can call "Timothy my true son in the faith" (1 Tim 1:2) and Titus, "my true son in our common faith" (Tit 1:4). Yet as an upward relationship, parents as well as all teachers of faith, admit only God is our Father, as Jesus the perfect Son reminds us all: "Do not call anyone on earth 'father,' for you have only one Father, and he is in heaven" (Mt 23:9). Thus the more we acknowledge God as the source of all being, the more we show wholehearted dependence upon God by keeping the Sabbath and by honoring our parents and indeed all seniors!

Jesus, the "true Son" of the Father, draws out this same idea to confront the religious leaders in their legislation about Corban (Mk 7:6-13). Jesus castigates all legalistic sophistry as nonrelational, mere "cunning," and the Pharisees—not unlike the stereotypical lawyer in our own society—as technicians of the law rather than custodians of true justice. The magic of the Corban was its exclusivity: once a thing was declared "for God," it belonged to no one else. But when children avoided giving support to their parents by declaring their resources were Corban, it was like tax evasion or worse; it was a clever way to avoid fulfilling the fifth commandment.[10] And if God himself was being cheated in this absurd manner—not to mention parents—in what other ways were these amoral sophists further shirking their God-given responsibilities? The practice gives tangible illustration to Isaiah's lament, "These people . . . honor me with their lips, but their hearts are far from me" (Is 29:13). Jesus exposes hypocrisy in the same way as the prophet Isaiah. The practice of Corban was professedly for God's glory (Mk 7:11-12), but in fact it violates the greatest of all the commandments. Such flagrant dishonoring of parents dishonors God himself. Using such sophistry in God's name was blasphemy indeed.

More than that, Mark uses this crisis of confrontation with the au-

---

[10]J. W. D. H., "Corban," in *The International Standard Bible Encyclopedia*, ed. Geoffrey G. Bromiley et al. (Grand Rapids: Eerdmans, 1979), 1:788.

thorities of Jerusalem in the context of Sabbath-keeping to discredit the whole religious *apparat* of Jerusalem. That was why they became determined to kill Jesus and to repudiate his claim to be God's only Son. Their religious claims were all about the administration of purity laws, not about upholding the holiness of God in the first commandment. Their sophistry in "keeping the Sabbath" was likewise unaware of its true meaning and intent. It was not taboos of purity that defined their identity as God's people, it was their unique relationship with the holy God, the God and Father of our Lord Jesus Christ. Conclusively, their abuse of the two key commandments, concerning the Sabbath and concerning the honoring of parents (Corban) exposed their blindness to the divine Sonship of Jesus Christ, as "the Son of Man."

Just as I AM is the unique title given to God in the Old Testament, so the designation "the Son of Man" is given to the God-man in the New Testament and found only on the lips of Jesus.[11] Jesus tells the religious authorities, "the Sabbath was made for man, not man for the Sabbath. So the Son of Man is Lord even of the Sabbath" (Mk 2:27-28). Truly human, he is also truly God, bestowing freedom upon us to use the Sabbath in its own meaningful context.

Although espoused to Joseph, like any young Palestinian girl, Mary was purposed for an arranged marriage. Nevertheless Jesus was born of a virgin, having therefore a unique human relationship with his mother Mary, unlike any other human relationship in human history. After his public incident in the temple as a child, we hear no more of his adopted father Joseph. Was Mary widowed throughout the public ministry of Jesus? It appears probable. She appears alone with Jesus at the wedding of Cana in Galilee. Jesus presents her at his crucifixion to be taken into the household of John when Jesus said: "'Dear woman, here is your son,' and to the disciple, 'Here is your mother.' From that time on, this disciple took her into his home" (Jn 19:26-27). The Son of Man and Son of God himself displayed the seamless unity of the Ten Commandments, honoring his own mother with the natural response of a heart submitted to God's will.

---

[11]Pope Benedict XVI, *Jesus of Nazareth*, trans. Adrian J. Walker (New York: Doubleday, 2007), pp. 321-35.

# 5

## BIBLICAL ROLES FOR
## SENIORS-ELDERS

...

The term *senior* has become associated with our contemporary social apartheid of ageism. Within Christian parlance, *elder* is actually preferable, having its roots in ancient Israel, later Judaism and early Christianity.[1] *Senior* connotes advanced age while *elder* is a comparative term suggesting prior rank because of age or (later in history) of rank within a profession.[2] Having a beard may be a sign of seniority, but it may not necessarily be a sign of wisdom or conscience. *Elder* is a much richer term with more subtleties of moral evaluation, all of which apply to our contemporary social needs. The Bible points to various patterns for older members of society and religious community, and churches will miss out on a vital aspect of church health when seniors are not empowered and encouraged in such roles.

### What Roles Does the Bible Give to Elders?

*Custodians of families.* In the Semitic life of the Old Testament, the basic feature of being human is ʿam, having kinship. It may be the kinship of a family, a city, a tribe or indeed of a nation; regardless, human-

---

[1] At the same time, we agree with L. W. Countryman's warning: "There is no clear value in transposing one or another fragment of early Christian teaching directly into our world without taking account of the original social context in which that teaching came to life." L. W. Countryman, "Christian Equality and the Early Catholic Episcopate," *Anglican Theological Review* 63 (1981): 138.

[2] "Senior," in *Shorter Oxford English Dictionary* (Oxford: Clarendon, 1947), 2:1840. This indicates that the word "senior" originated in the late Middle Ages, applied later in the seventeenth century to a college officer, and in the nineteenth century to "senior partner" in a business company.

ity is a relational category. To be "a people" expresses the unity of such a grouping. For community forms "wholes" instead of isolated individuals. So the primary role of elders should be forming communities by their spiritual gifts of expressing love, loyalty, wisdom, memory, authority and example.

The Old Testament featured, in large part, the role of "the father's house" to summarize such custodianship of relational life. Thus in the various relational laws of Israel listed in Leviticus 19, those who belong to community call each other by such terms as *brother* (*'ah*) or *kinsman* (*amith*) or *neighbor/fellow* (*rea*). "Do not go about spreading slander among your people [or kinsmen]. Do not do anything that endangers your neighbor's life. I am the LORD. Do not hate your brother in your heart" (Lev 19:16-17). These terms are used comprehensively to express the serious nature of various disruptions to community well-being. A related concept was the family solidarity of *go'el*, meaning "to protect," even to redeem and repay what was needed to preserve the family inheritance. Holiness is not just a divine attribute or power but a trait reflected by God's people as they express as integrity, honesty, faithfulness and love toward one another.[3] Elders in our churches still bear a vital role in maintaining local harmony and fostering fellowship.

As the heads of households, elders were thus associated in both Jewish and early Christian house-churches with the symbols of family life—the children of God, God as our Father, being brothers and sisters in Christ, etc. All elders still bear a vital role in maintaining local harmony and fostering fellowship. Yet Christ's heavy demand of our discipleship in Matthew 10:37 and Luke 14:26 suggests that the Christian personal life and its community does transcend the analogy of family life. "If any one comes to me and does not hate his father and mother, his wife and children, his brothers and sisters— yes, even his own life—he cannot be my disciple" (Lk 14:26). This appears even more shocking than the statement of Matthew 10:37, "Anyone who loves his father or mother more than me is not worthy

[3]Frank H. Gorman Jr., *Leviticus: Divine Presence and Community* (Grand Rapids: Eerdmans, 1997), pp. 111-12.

of me; anyone who loves his son or daughter more than me is not worthy of me." The context of Luke implies that conventional morality is no substitute for being personally committed to Jesus Christ. And in Mathew, Jesus calls people to a unique and therefore transcendental relationship to Jesus Christ as Lord and Savior. (Recall that Matthew also records the double commandment that unites love of God and love of neighbor as one reality.) Luke challenges readers with the centrality of Jesus, also allowing for no personal spirituality without social spirituality and no personal devotion without social justice. Likewise the role of a Christian elder, whether within the institutional church or within the society has a much stronger character.[4] In many intimate as well as practical ways today, Christian elders bear a solemn and great responsibility to foster community, most of all when they have had a life-long experience of the love of Jesus Christ.

In Scripture, fathers receive serious moral condemnation when, instead of fostering relational life, they are the source of discord and bitterness. Thus the prophets cite a well-known saying: "The fathers have eaten sour grapes, and the children's teeth are set on edge" (Jer 31:29). But Ezekiel demands further: "You will no longer quote this proverb in Israel. For every living soul belongs to [the Lord]" (Ezek 18:3-4). A contemporary corollary is a therapist's explanation of the heritage of family systems theory from Bowen and other experts. While this may appear fatalistic—our family narrative is "the mess we live in"—instead we see family as the sphere in which "where sin increased, grace increased all the more" (Rom 5:20).

In this regard, seniors can play a significant role in providing hope, in light of their own narratives of grace. They can also facilitate relational rebonding where wounds within family life have been so damaging, not by anything they do, but simply in acting in kindly and caring ways. Twice over the apostle admonishes seniors: "Fathers, do not exasperate your children; instead, bring them up in the training and instruction of the Lord" (Eph 6:4); and again, "Fathers, do not embitter

---

[4]A. E. Harvey, "Elders," *Journal of Theological Studies* 25 (1974): 318-31.

your children, or they will become discouraged" (Col 3:21). As we well know, aging people can allow their own disabilities to make them increasingly depressed and bitter, which they then pass on in full measure to their own family members. It is not to be so among the extended family of God.

*Fully human, seasoned servants of God.* In 2 Corinthians, the apostle Paul catalogs the horrendous sufferings he endured in the school of hard knocks, (in 2 Cor 4:8-12; 11:23-29; 12:7-10). His words admonish seniors to see the advantages of the difficulties that accompany aging: "Though outwardly we are wasting away, yet inwardly we are being renewed day by day" (2 Cor 4:16). Thus older people "do not lose heart," but rather review their lives as receiving positive gain, countering the world's love for outer appearances. A senior's role in the worldliness of church life, too, prophetically counters the obsession with outward things, whatever they may happen to be in our immediate context—the building program, the financial budget, the innumerable activities of the church's programs, even the clothes we wear or don't wear! From their vantage point of long life, experiences like the repeated rehearsal of letting go rather than accumulating or the vintage of sufferings experienced redemptively should benefit the spiritual resources of a church community.

The biblical understanding of elders within the community is that they are not heroes but instead are ordinary folk. Focus upon the cult of leadership—as, for example, unquestioning reverence for particular "founding fathers"—is cultural, not biblical. Talk to Australians about leadership and they will tell you their founding fathers were convicts! In the pagan world, heroes were demi-gods with blurred distinctions between human and divine. The Bible teaches, however, that God alone is holy and wholly other. And human beings are creatures, chosen, but mortal and creaturely. Thus biblical ordination of kingship exemplifies this view: kings were those entrusted to be stewards of God's Word, humble and obedient servants of Yahweh.

The people of Israel were warned not to appoint a king over them like the other nations around them: "be sure to appoint over you the king the Lord your God chooses. . . . [The law] is to be with him, and he is to read it all the days of his life so that he may learn to revere the Lord his God and follow carefully all the words of this law and these decrees and not consider himself better than his brothers and turn from the law to the right or to the left" (see Deut 17:15, 19-20). While elders are not "perfect," they are described in Psalm 1:1-3 as being in constant meditation on God's Word and, therefore, living wholly dependent on his daily presence. All the relational fruitfulness they may bestow on others has its source in God himself.

### Seniors Must Not Present an Ambiguous Message

Seniors can be committed to lifelong learning and continual spiritual growth, or they can remain frozen by their past and condemned to regression in their old age. They inspire others when they live as exemplars of the growing stewardship entrusted to them by God, or else they become a warning to those who would also neglect of their talent, leaving it lying buried (Mt 25:14-30). Sadly, churches contain those whose reversal to a "second childhood" is worse than the first. The besetting weakness of so many churchgoers lies in false assumption that they have a "club membership" and therefore deserve to enjoy its privileges of association without much commitment and the evidence of any growth in Christ.

Elders then must maintain the imagery of the Christian life as a lifelong journey. For as the Spanish philosopher Unamuno reminds us, we have a choice of "seeing life from the balcony," looking at life as spectators, or else we choose to live "on the road," as pilgrims making progress. Like Bunyan's *Pilgrim's Progress* or the mystic pilgrims of the late Middle Ages, Christian growth moves forward from "the good," to "the better," to "the best."[5] This is an ethical and therefore inward journey of the soul, regardless of whether it is lived in prison, as the apostle Paul often was, or actually traveling as he was in his missionary pursuits. Hence the Christian elder has no vocabulary for retirement. The

---

[5]In his fourteenth century classic, William Langland depicts Piers Plowman, in this context of "do good" and of "do better" to "do best." James M. Houston, *The Heart's Desire* (Vancouver, B.C.: Regent College Publishing, 1996), p. 224.

journey is never completed this side of eternity.

The Puritans developed the theme of "living well to die well." Since we all face our mortality, from the beginning of life, how vital it is to accept and then to prepare for our demise. The best prepared are the most zestful, and can become an abundant source of spiritual blessing to others. It is as Carl Becker vividly reminds us in his book; a society living out *The Denial of Death* becomes shallow and impoverished.[6] Since seniors are living close to the edge of their lifespan, they should be infecting others with a joyous way of life. For indeed, joy expresses spiritual maturity, an emotional summation that God is doing well with our soul. The presence of such in our community is like a fragrant garden, refreshing and uplifting. As one saintly elder used to reflect, daily she could present a nosegay of a sweet spirit to refresh others. This is evidence of a true, ongoing growth of spirit, vitally alive.

### Seniors' Well-Being in Our Churches Reflects the Spiritual Quality of Our Mission

North American culture today is drifting towards increasing individualism. Christian organizations (including churches) respond by promoting more business management to centralize control and professionalize service more than before. The consequence is the decline of voluntarism. Churchgoers increasingly rely on a bureaucracy for church governance so that things can be done efficiently. This trend views everything in terms of business models of success and overlooks previous qualities of voluntary service such as loyalty, faithfulness and indeed selflessness. In such a model, seniors can seem redundant, since they served more effectively under the previous paradigm of volunteers. As the budget is given greater priority, finances become the primary concern and an impersonal forced within the community. In this respect, it may be difficult to measure differences in motivation for secular and Christian volunteers—both may be seeking some reciprocity for their efforts.

---

[6]Ernest Becker, *The Denial of Death* (New York: Free Press, 1973), pp. 188-89.

In one study, I (Dr. Parker) helped supervise, secular volunteers were motivated primarily by what they might receive (e.g., a job, some financial compensation), and in another study, I and my team found considerable evidence that church leaders think only about ministry *to* seniors and not ministry *from* elders.[7] One of my Ph.D. students from Korea recently defended her dissertation research on the topic of senior volunteerism. Though she was encouraged to include members of local congregations in her recruitment of her Korean participants, she elected to use secular, organizational forms of civic engagement and volunteerism—like senior centers—to recruit her participants because she considered the voluntary role of most religious congregations in Korea to be too small to justify the effort. American churches must compete for senior volunteers with secular organizations like the Gerontological Society of America, the American Society on Aging, the Service Corp of Retired Executives and the National Council on Aging, which operate huge volunteer engagement programs. Still, we believe that Christian elders will have an opportunity to recapture their significant role in volunteerism, because of budgetary cuts in social programs. However, this must be preceded by an attitude of change within the church about the capacities of our elders to provide ministry and by a willingness of elders to volunteer gratuitously.

Actually, the more attention is directed to fundraising, the more alienation creeps into the church and the more the church looks like the culture. Promoting relationships for the sake of funds makes members more cynical about the meaning and purpose of friendship. If the senior pastor is now operating like the CEO, can he then maintain a shepherd's heart for his flock? Or has he become more of a business executive? Yet if true relationships are not exemplified in

---

[7]L. Dunn, M. W. Parker, X. Li, M. Piper, R. Harrell, H. Lee, N. S. Park, S. MacCall, S. Martin, J. Williams and C. Spencer, "Building Sustainable Community Partnerships to Promote Successful Aging: A Preliminary Study of Local Congregations and Agencies," *Journal of Community-Based Partnerships* (forthcoming); M. W. Parker, L. Dunn, J. Goetz, S. Ousley, M. Rogers, M. Piper, R. Harrell, H. Lee, N. S. Park, S. MacCall, J. Williams, C. Spencer and X. Li, "Helping to Unite an Aging Southern Community: An Internet Directory Project and Telephone Survey of Local Congregations," *Journal of Community-Based Partnerships* (forthcoming).

church life, then where else can lonely Christians look for deep and genuine relationships? Is it the growing sense of personal alienation, which is causing more unease with church life generally? This is where seniors can play a crucial significance for younger members, in taking notice of them, showing concern, and acting as mentors for those seeking help, counsel and encouragement. So our biblical message is once more:

> Remember the days of old;
>     consider the generations long past.
> Ask your father and he will tell you,
> your elders, and they will explain to you. (Deut 32:7)

# 6

# THE PORTRAIT OF A MATURE
# CHRISTIAN SENIOR-ELDER

· · ·

While there are as many ways to be a mature Christian senior as there are such people, I (Dr. Houston) believe certain characteristics sketch the portrait of a Christian senior with much to offer the community of faith. Mature Christianity integrates the human and the divine, which is what being "godly" means. It blends living with the human spirit while being indwelt by the Holy Spirit. It has a transcendent assurance of eternal life in the face of a threatening sense of mortality.

### Constancy in Worship

Perhaps exemplary character traits mature from the growing awareness that the adoration of God is primary in the consciousness of the committed Christian. Orthodoxy is not just right belief, an assurance that we are doctrinally correct. True orthodoxy includes truth derived from right worship. Such worship, all-encompassing adoration of God as the I AM, recognizes the uniqueness of God, incomparable with other gods, for only he is "the Great I AM." As Von Hugel would highlights, "The Christian life begins, proceeds, and ends with *the Givenness of God*, in his *Otherness*, and in the *Prevenience of God*. . . . these constitute the deepest measure and touchstone of all religion."[1] By his "givenness," God is esteemed incomparable, ineffable, non-contingent, so he is not viewed as an anthropomorphic deity. God *is*. The Jews were right to recognize the inexpressible tretragrammeton of "THE I AM that I AM."

---

[1]Friedrich von Hugel, *The Mystical Element of Religion* (London: Dent & Sons, 1930), 1:xvi.

Likewise the mature Christian finds all thought and all actions, as indeed all relations, subsumed to the uniqueness of God. The apostle Paul speaks of taking "captive every thought" to Christ (2 Cor 10:5) This growing reality never ceases, so that at the end of their lives, believers esteem God with increasing adoration. Familiarity may breed contempt with earthlings, but the reverse occurs in knowing God.

God is holy, wholly other and therefore not made in our image and likeness. Too often, we tend to worship "the god of our fathers," which means we see God interpreted by the wounded emotions of our own parenting. No, reform begins within our own lives when we begin to experience the transcendence of God and the littleness of human affairs. We reject the subjectivism of liberal religion's psychologism, which can only have an anthropomorphic view of God. As J. B. Phillips expressed it, "our God is too small." As von Hugel once wrote to a directee, the reality of God is "a gift from above downwards, not a groping from below upwards . . . it is more like a glorious shower from above." As a student friend of mine, Donald Wiseman, gave as his daily greeting, "keep looking up"! We find Daniel doing so three times a day, with his window open to the heavens. Too often, if we don't "feel good" about God or his ways, we are in danger of eclipsing the majesty of God, even dismissing him from the world of his own creation.

Christian seniors can also demonstrate the providence of God from their many experiences. Not only is God mighty, but he also does mighty works. God reveals himself; he enters into our lives in many ways, loving us before we could ever love him. God initiates and inclines our hearts towards him. He renders possible any and all responses we might or can make toward him. Mature Christians hold in tension both his immanence and his transcendence within the broad canvas of all our life's experiences. Sometimes is he closer than breathing, closer than our own pulse beat. At other times, he seems so far off and we feel dry or empty. The longer we live, the more varied the dialectic becomes between his seeming aloofness and his sensed presence.

God's givenness, otherness and providence elicit from us one supreme response: adoration. Much of the prayer life and songs of Israel, encompassed in the Psalms, expresses such adoration. In his homilies on the Psalms, Augustine likewise interpreted two central aspects of prayer, adoration and petition. Without gratitude we can have little to praise God for, and gratitude flows from needy hearts of petition. As Jesus told the Pharisees, "to whom much has been forgiven, the same loves much" (see Lk 7:42-43). Alas the converse is also true: the self-righteous cannot worship, for there is no gratitude by which to adore him. As von Hugel wrote in a letter to his niece, Gwendolyn, "We are like sponges trying to mop up the ocean. We can never know God exhaustively. . . . you cannot have religion without adoration."[2] Seniors' longer experiences of God's mercy lead them to profoundly adore him. This mature response to God's ways with us is greatly needed in our church worship, where so often we applaud the musicians for their entertainment, instead of focusing with adoration on God's presence among us.

## Individual Connection

While adoration may lead us to express, like the hymn-writer, that we are "lost in wonder, love and praise," spiritual maturity also leads to a strong individuation of personal life. This we may call having a strong *attrait*, for the Good Shepherd calls us all by name. There is an extraordinary variety of human experiences and of responses to God, in which he delights to encourage our uniqueness to grow and become increasingly diversified. For human souls have the potential to be extraordinary in variety, so that the more we grow in Christ, the more varied we become. Each of us has his or her own story to narrate, and these enrich by their variation. I (Dr. Houston) found this in editing letters of God's people throughout the ages.[3] As it has been said, "souls are never mere dittos." Human experiences seem more varied than ever, and so the weakness of large churches is that the diversity of members can never been fully explored nor known. Spending time with individuals seems to diminish as the social community enlarges, and yet our Lord always had special times with individuals. The more

[2]Gwendolene Greene, *Letters from Friendrich von Hugel to a Niece* (London: Dent & Son, 1926), p. xvii.
[3]James M. Houston, *Letters of Faith and Devotion*, 2 vols. (Colorado Springs: Cook Communications, 2007–2008).

leisurely pace of living as one gets older gives one the privilege of time for individuals, paying attention (for example) to the needs and issues of younger people. As I experienced in just one day, one can listen to such an extraordinary range of human conditions that fact truly does become stranger than fiction. Giving space for each person to be what he or she is expresses kindness and facilitates personal growth in manifest ways.

Letter-writing is becoming a lost art, yet the early church itself grew in an epistolary culture; twenty-one of the twenty-nine books of the New Testament are letters, while the book of Revelation is a letter containing seven others within it. Indeed, Søren Kierkegaard interpreted the Bible as God's love letter to us. Many thousands of letters have been preserved throughout the centuries, from church fathers, monks and spiritual directors, from those more consciously into the *belles-lettres* as well as from humble, unknown folk. As John Donne put it, "letters are our selves," sharing our lives to confidants, little knowing that later generations could eavesdrop on their confidences of the heart. Some Christian fathers have been renown for their specific ministry of letter writing, such as Father Kronstadt, who after six years as bishop of St. Petersburg put aside his prestigious office simply to spend the rest of his life writing to high and low across the vastness of Russia. Perhaps there will be a revival of God's people, to take up this ministry, even if they are housebound by infirmity. Emailing today crosses so many barriers of space and culture. If a ministry of letter writing can help younger Christians to grow and mature in their individuation "in Christ," what a noble service is being done for God! I (Dr. Parker) found some evidence of hope in the lost art of letter writing by requiring my graduate students to compose letters of appreciation to guest speakers throughout the semester. Though initially resistant, the students learned to appreciate the exercise, and the speakers were grateful for the feedback they received.

## Strength in Suffering

Seniors have a long record of suffering, since our bodies begin to bear the scars of natural aging and perhaps many illnesses. A previous generation certainly bore the scars of war wounds and handicaps. While the availability of painkillers is in many senses a blessing, their mere presence can obscure the fact that suffering can be a great teacher. How can we come close to a suffering Savior and not suffer? For Christ did not avoid suffering: he met it, accepted it, endured it and transformed it. So Paul addresses the Corinthians to affirm, "In all our troubles my joy knows no bounds" (2 Cor 7:4). "Godly sorrow" he adds, "brings repentance," "but worldly sorrow brings death" (2 Cor 7:10). Few could suffer more than Paul, he insists in his catalog of sufferings at the end of 2 Corinthians. But he learned that in suffering, we can be brought very near to God. We are not to become masochists but to let the pain be well mixed with prayer. Then we may dwell with both great suffering and a strong sense of the suffering Christ in our lives. Suffering can be endured by his presence and even producing redemptive purposes for us not available through any other means. To be drawn into the healing presence of Christ through our suffering brings us into great joy. As the hymn-writer George Matheson puts it: "O joy that reaches me through pain." Suffering and joy are wondrously mixed within Christian experience, as the centrality of the cross suggests.

Suffering in Christ grows both humility and meekness. We face our creatureliness in the light of God's transcendence, to submit in obedience and trust, to acknowledge "thy will be done." From time to time, earnestly committed Christians can go through a blizzard of troubles along the lines of Job himself. There may appear no apparent reason why they should so unjustly suffer, but they do. Asking the question why becomes a sharp spear in the silence and mystery of it all. Paul himself cried out three times that "the thorn of the flesh" be removed, but it was not. Yet Paul did learn the great sufficiency of God's grace to continue to bear it. The key then is not *what* we suffer but *how* we suffer. Often I (Dr. Houston) have been tempted to ask when meeting a remarkable Christian, "Tell me how you have accepted suffering?" It is essentially a vital question for mature Christians, testing their growth perhaps more than anything else.

## Steadfast and Sacrificial in Spirit

But gentleness also is a fruit of the Spirit. Life is not just bursts of intensity or even of pain. Passion requires moderation lest we overbalance in multiple ways. The true beauty of mature Christian character lies in having a symmetry of character that is not impulse-driven, angry, ruled by an intense timetable, constantly distracted, fickle, disloyal, always seeking new fads and more. Living with an expansive, leisurely, fulfilling life provides harmony of action and an atmosphere of peace within which to shelter and nurture others. Seniors who have discovered this will listen more than talk, for they give more space for the other than for their own self-preoccupations. A gentle steadiness of purpose to live for others and to share the warmth of well-being attracts the lonely and the discouraged. Zeal for God balances out the lack of impulsive excitement for things or for always seeking new relationships. Like Badger in the children's book *The Wind in the Willows*, seniors who are spiritually mature can be dependable, even-tempered and loyal friends.

Well-rounded elders, as spiritually wise companions on the journey of faith, live in the wisdom of the book of Proverbs, seeking neither poverty nor riches. "Godliness with contentment is great gain" (1 Tim 6:6). They do not panic, but with sobriety and a genial spirit they share wide interests with those who take shelter in their kindness. They enjoy hobbies or sports, play games, read widely, entertain hospitably. Yet they dwell in a deep interior world of frequent prayer, devotional reading of Scripture and the great writings of the saints. Serenity fills their countenance as those blessed by the vision of God.

Finally, we know more as we live that the mature Christian life is sacrificial. According to the desert father Dorotheus, the egoistic will constantly gets in the way of our growth. Dorotheus observes that we cannot make big sacrifices if we have not started and practiced making small ones first.[4] In other words, get used to cutting back on minor pleasures if you want to be prepared to make big sacrifices. Doing so

---

[4]Quoted by Pierre Hadot, *What Is Ancient Philosophy?* (Cambridge, Mass.: Belknap Press, 2002), p. 245.

reveals how often being willful gets in the way of being maturely willing to do God's will. Actually, when we do what we want, we are actually will-less, falling prey of our sensate bodies instead of being self-
controlled for broader goals for our lives. How can we sell our birthright
as the children of God, like Esau did, for a mess of potage?

Likewise, expedience is a bad master to serve. Any power that threat-
ens to dominate our life must be fought by a greater power or a more
worthy objective. The sense of moral proportion must always be with
us, distinguishing lesser things from greater values. The life experiences of faithful seniors will include both success and failure in this
regard, giving them a clearer perspective about which sacrifices are
worth the cost.

Ah, you may respond, this is all too idealistic! So too is the Christian
life, its potential being far richer, if we really desired it more. In the present state of the institutional church, we greatly need a "relational reformation." How will it ever come about? By the growing awakening of
seniors to contribute by demonstrating the characteristics we have just
described. The saints have always demonstrated where and how revival
or renewal or reform needed to occur. As we fill our minds with their
writings, we begin to see the possibility of imitating them in the communion of saints. Seniors have witnessed many rapid changes in society
and therefore can warn the youth of the church some of the adverse
consequences their length of life has equipped them to anticipate.

# 7

## ELDERS AS EXEMPLARS AND
## MENTORS FOR
## CHRISTIAN RENEWAL

...

No secular appeal for the proper place for and proper treatment of seniors speaks from a sufficient basis. A church especially must consider the biblical foundations for the roles of its senior members and spiritual elders. The texts of Scripture and early Christian writing provide a window into the how elders' many years of faith can encourage renewal in the spiritual community.

### Elders Foster Community

In the ancient Near East, as with the Bedouin today, "elders" were always in the plural, perhaps expressing primitive democracy. They were recognized communally "from below" and not officially appointed "from above." So it was not like the cultural American appreciation of leaders, individualized and exalted. Hence their authority was not one of power, but of legitimacy. As is well known in political science, high legitimacy requires little real power, but more power is needed as legitimacy diminishes. An authoritarian government or individual rules where the authority of legitimacy no longer exists. Thus in principle, elders are never authoritarian in their influence. They are neither professionals nor politically appointed members of society. Their legitimacy is personal, not one of power. Priests, Levites, kings and princes are therefore distinguished from elders in the Old Testament, while in the New Testament they are distinguished from the deacons who are appointed or from the apostles who were uniquely selected. As Alastair Campbell explores the history of elders, he notes that *elders* is consistently "an imprecise and flexible term of honor."[1]

The biblical climax on the role of elders is witnessed in the book of Revelation, where "twenty-four elders" hold eternal court (Rev 4:4), perhaps to suggest that there is unity between the relational life of earth bound up in God's heavenly life.

Thus it is the role of Christian elders, as the apostle Paul charges Titus, to appoint elders in every town to foster and nurture the communities of Christians. Such "appointment of elders" may be exceptional in view of the apostle's strategy to plant house churches in his missionary travels of Asia Minor and beyond. The elders' character is exemplary in both family and public life: "not overbearing, not quick-tempered, not given to drunkeness, not violent, not pursuing dishonest gain. Rather he must be hospitable, one who loves what is good, who is self-controlled, upright, holy and disciplined. He must hold firmly to the trustworthy message as it has been taught, so that he can encourage others by sound doctrine and refute those who oppose it" (Tit 1:7-9). About A.D. 96 Clement of Rome writes that if necessary an elder should be even prepared for voluntary exile for the sake of the recovery of health to the community: "Who among you is noble, who is compassionate, who is filled with love? Let him cry: 'If sedition and strife and divisions have arisen on my account, I will depart, I will go away whithersoever you will, and I will obey the commands of the people; only let the flock of Christ have peace with the elders set over it'" (*1 Clement* 54:1-2).

### Elders Minister from the "Inner Person"

In the context of the church, the apostle Paul sees the offices of elder and deacon as requiring exemplary personal and public conduct. "If anyone does not know how to manage his own family, how can he take care of God's church?" (1 Tim 3:5). Elders remind the church that God has a much greater work to do in us than through us. If the faith is

---

[1]R. Alastair Campbell, *The Elders* (Edinburgh: T & T Clark, 1994), p. 40.

given and sustained through Word and Spirit, then true biblical exegesis is less a literary study of the text than an exemplification of the Spirit and Word-filled life. If we really want to understand the teaching of Jesus' Sermon on the Mount, then read and meditate upon the life of Francis of Assisi. Elders' lives should mirror the Word of God.

The Psalms view aging as a process of continual growth and fruitfulness. The psalm dedicated for the Sabbath expresses total reliance on God, promises: "the righteous will flourish like a palm tree, they will grow like a cedar of Lebanon; planted in the house of the LORD, they will flourish in the courts of our God. They will still bear fruit in old age" (Ps 92:12-14). So the old can testify: "If the LORD delights in a man's way, he makes his steps firm. . . . I was young and now I am old, yet I have never seen the righteous forsaken or their children begging bread. They are always generous and lend freely; their children will be blessed" (Ps 37:23, 25-26). "Even when I am old and gray, do not forsake me, O God, till I declare your power to the next generation, your might to all who are to come" (Ps 71:18). Perhaps inspired by such poetry, Robert Browning's "Rabbi ben Ezra" argues that youth can only express half of what God will show in the lives of elders:

> Grow old along with me!
> The best is yet to be,
> The last of life, for which the first was made:
> Our times are in His hand
> Who saith, 'A whole I planned,
> Youth shows but half; trust God: see all nor be afraid!'[2]

### Elders Enlarge Our Vision of Reality

Technology characteristically reduces our sense of reality to the technical. Secularism's egocentricity and unawareness of God is similarly reductionistic. Elders can counter these tendencies by sharing their rich and long experiences of spiritual life. William Blake (1757–1827), poet, painter and mystic, did his finest artistic work, twenty-one *Illustrations*

---

[2]Robert Browning, *Rabbi ben Ezra, The Poems and Plays of Robert Browning*, ed. Bennett A. Cerf and Donald S. Klopper (New York: Modern Library, 1934), p. 289.

*to the Book of Job,* when he was almost seventy. In this masterpiece, Blake said that we "see *through* the eyes, not just *with* the eyes." The critical eyes of Malcolm Muggeridge, the British editor of *Punch* and great lampoonist of British society, had long seen through the pretensions and follies of worldliness. But his eyes were opened to the Christian faith, and he began to see things differently still. He often quoted to me this line from Blake—seeing "through" and not merely "with" the eyes—to state that "seeing" reality is much more than just "seeing." For we have conceptions before we can receive a perception of things.

I (Dr. Houston) was on an international geographical committee in the late sixties that was asked to examine "environment perception of hazards." (For example, how frequently do floods have to occur on a river valley before building speculators avoid building on the flood plain? How many summer droughts are required before cultivators think it worthwhile to start installing irrigation practices?) One investigation was over when the San Andreas Fault in California should be deemed too dangerous to build on. Our committee found that five hospitals were actually built upon on this fault, even the emergency headquarters to deal with Red Cross responses; our geologist chairman pointed out this information to our committee with some derision. What he did not acknowledge was that his own home was on the fault line! Again, perception requires strong enough conceptions—in this case of danger—to act on what you see to be true.

The Christian faith illustrates this same principle very markedly. At Easter, we are reminded of how the two disciples, Peter and John, went to the empty tomb. While Peter glanced at its emptiness, it was John who scrutinized the evidence of how the grave clothes were no longer around the body; thus, "he saw and believed" in the reality of the resurrection of Jesus. In the story of the two disciples walking with Jesus on the Emmaus way and then seeing the stranger do a simple act of "breaking bread," "they saw and believed" that it was their beloved, now risen Lord.

Four years before he died, Ivan Illich (1926–2002), interpreted modernity as the corruption of Christianity. As Shakespeare's sonnet 94 puts it, "For sweetest things turn sourest by their deeds; / Lilies that fester smell far worse than weeds." As a Catholic priest who declaimed being called a philosopher or indeed any "professional" and yet who contributed profoundly to an understanding of Christendom, he saw that "the perversion of the best is the worst"—*pervesio optimi quae est pessimi*.[3] Today Chinese scholars are studying Christianity as the source of Western civilization so that its people can also be "modernized." But no social ideology can ever understand the illogicality of God's love in human form; it cannot be mentally understood! So Ivan Illich would challenge the popular view that the institutionalization of health care and of medicine are the outcome of Christian ethics. Rather they express the perversion of real Christianity! For in the parable of the Good Samaritan, argues Illich, "Jesus taught the Pharisees that the relationship which he had come to announce to them as most completely human is not one that is expected, required or owed. It can only be a free creation between two people, and one which cannot happen unless something comes to me through the other and by the other, in his bodily existence."[4] It is not because the needy one is a Greek or Roman citizen, an Israelite or (in our Western health care services) a pensioner but simply because the needy is a human being. This is what Jesus calls behaving as a neighbor. Ivan Illich is thus illustrating with a radical vision what it is to be a Christian elder. He or she sees with the light of the gospel, not with the spectacles of popular culture.

As Gerhard Ladner argues in his great study *The Idea of Reform*, the Roman culture knew of the natural cycle of life and death or the cycles of the seasons, but Christianity alone introduced the drama of being "born again," of *metanoia*, of indeed the reform of vision, to see reality in an utterly new way.[5] Only the advent of the incarnation has provided Christians ever since the opportunity "to see radically anew."

Too many of us, as nominal church members, see during Sunday morning services what we never see from Monday through Saturday. Instead, during the week we see empirically within a narrow, scientific/ materialistic worldview, or we see as sport enthusiasts in the stadium,

---

[3]David Cayley, *The Rivers North of the Future: The Testament of Ivan Illich as Told to David Cayley* (Toronto: Anansi, 2005), p. 56.
[4]Ibid., p. 51.
[5]Gerhard B. Ladner, *The Idea of Reform* (New York: Harper & Row, 1967), pp. 32-34.

or we see financially as business folk. To "see Jesus" alive within our hearts, all the time, requires a great deal of the experience of faith, with daily enriched biblical understanding. "Seeing," then, is not believing, unless we grow maturely in our Christian faith. The heart, the seat of the affections, is as vital as the eye for seeing and believing in the redemptive purposes of God.

The Catholic bishop of Geneva Francis de Sales (1567–1622) was a tireless letter writer as a spiritual director. On February 11, 1607, at the end of a long, cold winter, he wrote this to his mentee Madame de Chantal:

> My very dear daughter, I can see that all the seasons of the year meet their distinctive challenges to your soul. The winter you feel as being the season of sterility, disgust and even boredom. Then comes the month of May with the roses in bloom, and so too the perfumes of the spiritual flowers released by holy desires to please our good God. Then comes the autumn season, when you complain you do not see plentiful fruits. So be it because it often happens that in thrashing the wheat and pressing the grapes one finds more blessing in the harvesting and *vendage* than one would have expected. For it is natural to expect everything to happen in the spring and summer of life, but no, my dear daughter, one needs to face the inner difficulties and problems of one's inner life, as well as the apparent successes of outward appearances.[6]

What Francis de Sales would argue is that elders need to have not only a seasonal perspective of life but an eternal perspective on our temporal changes. As the apostle Paul puts it: "while the outward man perishes, the inward man is renewed day by day."

We get hints of this other way of seeing things when we have gone through a serious illness and leave the hospital to go out into the sunshine. Dramatically we see differently, grateful for small and inconspicuous things: the flowers in the garden, the bird on the tree, the simple meal we now enjoy, the visit of a friend. Why? We have, perhaps, faced death and now there is the reprieve. Perhaps through adversity we have seen the Lord in a new and revitalizing way. Indeed, it is

---

[6]James M. Houston, *Letters of Faith Through the Seasons* (Colorado Springs: Cook Communications, 2006), 1:23.

through a thousand small ways of inner struggle and yet of increasing devotional experiences of God, that we can begin to see differently. So the mature Christian elder has the advantage of increased wide-angle vision of God, by growing "pure in heart," to "see God" (Mt 5:8). This is a state that the desert fathers in the early church called *apatheia*. It is the freedom from care summarized in the Sermon on the Mount, of self-renunciation and detachment from what were once idolatrous things. It is a freedom from possessiveness in all its forms, even subtle ones that prevent a selfless attitude.

These are gradual, experienced in gentle and multivariate ways: little acts of kindness; personal sacrifices; compassion for the poor; a regular life of prayer and Bible study; neighborly concerns; a humble spirit; perhaps occasional fasting; ever deepening acts of self-scrutiny; freedom from care, in ever growing trust in God; and an increasing openness in seeking the will of God. All these help to increase one's vision of reality, where God becomes the truest source of reality in one's whole life. Ideally, godly seniors are those who have gained a balanced perspective between living in prudence and maintaining their responsibilities, whose faith grows continually—both in trusting God intimately and having wide perspectives on the kingdom of God that transcend one's family, church, denomination, profession and nation in seeking after "God's righteousness" (cf. Mt 6:33).

### Elders Are Devoted to Prayer

In the therapeutic culture we live in today, *spiritual direction* has become a new buzzword and industry. In its Ignatian origins, spiritual direction was meant to promote and deepen the prayer life of its communicants. But long before that, the spiritual fathers of the church were constantly in prayer for their children in the faith. Polycarp, before suffering martyrdom at the end of a long life of eighty-six years, prayed for two hours "remembering all who had ever come his way, both small and great, high."[7] Indeed, as long as the history of the church, believers have regularly asked a spiritual father or mother to pray for them before under-

---

[7]Polycarp, in Robin Lane Fox, *Pagans and Christians* (London: Penguin Books, 1986), p. 445.

taking critical decisions or tasks. Whereas the short vision of the peti-
tioners might be to pray for what they desire, the longer vision of the
spiritual elder will be to pray for what God deems best for them.

We live in a culture that values being busy. This activism reflects on
self-worth and self-esteem. Carrying other people's burden is therefore
not given a high priority. The life of prayer does not seem "productive
enough," and at the same time, we try to do so many things on our own
that if we need someone to carry our burdens, we view ourselves as
failures. But spiritual elders of the church, in praying constantly for
their mentees, are helping carry their burdens. This implies much listening, to gain new perspectives of the inner lives of others. As one
Eastern father, Gregory the Theologian, put it: "The norm of all spiritual direction is always to neglect one's own interest for the profit of
others."[8] This may require kindly discretion, to avoid the immature
from becoming either too dependent or too threatened by the presence
or shadow of the mentor over the immature disciple.

Just as with one's natural children, when they grow up, the relationship is more friendship than childish dependency. So too the spiritual
elder should be willing to become more a friend than an advisor, for
both people are seeking to live under God's will and service. Then mutuality, communion and reciprocity begin to widen the horizons of
trust, respect and Christian love within the fellowship of the one body-
in-Christ. There young and old, children and parents, are embraced
into a greater wholeness, all participating in the bride of Christ. For we
have only one Father, who is in heaven and only one brother, who is
Christ the Lord, and we all become "spiritual," because the Holy Spirit
pervades in all we are and do.

So the apostle Paul prays for us all: "I pray also that *the eyes of your
heart may be enlightened* in order that you may know the hope to which
he has called you, the riches of his glorious inheritance in the saints,
and his incomparably great power for us who believe. That power is like
the working of his mighty strength, which he exerted in Christ when
he raised him from the dead and seated him at his right hand in the

---

[8]Houston, *Letters of Faith*, 1:142.

heavenly realms . . . and appointed him to be head over everything for the church, which is his body, the fullness of him who fills everything in every way" (Eph 1:18-23, emphasis mine).

## Elders Live in the Face of Death

Before the last half century, loved ones died at home, and cultural and family traditions surrounding death were carried out there. It gradually became common practice to die in hospitals or (historically a bit later) hospices. Alongside this shift grew a cultural tendency to ignore death, even to deny it. This has probably resulted in greater fear of death than previous generations knew. Not only have medical skill and discovery prolonged life expectancy, but they have also attenuated the dying process. As dying has become "medicalized," death has become a scholarly subject of investigation.[9] In this field, most consider "attitudes towards death" and "fear of death" to be synonymous, also interpreting death as the last stage of human life.[10]

Often now, people fear death less than the long journey of progressive suffering, dependence, mental deterioration and most of all the loss of self-worth and autonomy. In this amoral view, which represses all spiritual value that the meaning of death may convey, euthanasia becomes the last defiant act of self-will. For those who live only for this world, with no future hope beyond the grave, death is the most terrible loss. But as the apostle Paul reflects upon the fruits of Christ's resurrection, he insists in contrast that the exchange of this mortal life for our future immortal life is incomparably better.

---

[9]David O. Moberg, ed., *Aging and Spirituality* (New York: Haworth Pastoral Press, 2001), pp. 72-73.

[10]B. Feifel and A. Branscomb, "Who's Afraid of Death?" *Journal of Psychology* 81, no. 2 (1973): 282-88. In one study, repressing thoughts of death was found to be less fearful at a conscious than at an unconscious level, and the spirituality of aging was found to be shallow in those who did not face up to their own dying (B. L. Spilka, L. Stout, B. Milton and D. Sizemore, "Death and Personal Faith: A Psychometric Investigation," *Journal for the Scientific Study of Religion* 16, no. 1 [2007]: 169-78). For all religions, facing death is the final divide of contrasted perspectives, such as Philippe Aries outlines in his well-known work (Philippe Aries, *Western Attitudes Toward Death* [Baltimore: Johns Hopkins University Press, 1974]). The Christian psychiatrist Harold Koenig has thus given a different perspective to those who deny any religious faith. What does stand out is that the actual physically dying process has now become the most universal fear (Harold Koenig, *Aging and God* [Binghampton, N.Y.: Haworth Press, 1994]).

However, many Christians do not reflect deeply enough on the connection Paul makes between the transformation our earthly life should have in the consequence of our baptism and the future life we anticipate beyond death. For the Christian, baptism is already the experience of spiritual death: the centrality of life has become Christ himself—"to me, to live is Christ" (Phil 1:21). Thus the resurrection of Christ becomes for us a personal issue. He died and rose on our account. Many Jewish contemporaries of Jesus spoke of the resurrection of the dead in terms of revivification, so that the righteous ones had hope to live on a reconstituted earth (1 Enoch 90:28-42; 2 Baruch 51:1-16).[11] But they never saw their life beyond death as only being possible "in Christ;" rather it lay inherent in their own righteousness. Likewise the Platonic philosophers hoped in the immortality of the soul, an intrinsic quality that assured life beyond death. But Paul tells the Corinthians, "just as we have borne the likeness of the earthly man [in the fall of the first Adam], so shall we bear the likeness of the man from heaven [the Second Adam]" (1 Cor 15:49). This process of transformation begins with our baptism so that the indwelling Christ within us makes the whole Christian life a progressive change. As Paul affirms, "Christ in you is the hope of glory." Our present transformation occurs within the context of the *Parousia*, of eventually receiving resurrected bodies (1 Cor 15:51-52).

Luke's account of the Acts of the Apostles emphasizes bearing witness to Jesus' resurrection as central to apostolic ministry (Acts 1:22). Indeed, the twelve were persecuted for being such witnesses, so the shadow of death was their constant companion. The physicality of this defining event receives full force: they saw with their own eyes, ate with Jesus on several occasions, and were given many "convincing proofs"—a rare word used by Aristotle as irrefutable, proven and conclusive.[12] Yet Luke also highlights the ethical consequence of Jesus' disciples being his witnesses: "with great power the apostles continued to testify to the

---

[11]Richard Bauckham, "Life, Death and the Afterlife in Second Temple Judaism," in *Life in the Faith of Death*, ed. Richard N. Longnecker (Grand Rapids: Eerdmans, 1998), pp. 80-95.

[12]Joel B. Green, "Witnesses of the Resurrection: Resurrection, Salvation, Discipleship and Mission in the Acts of the Apostles," in *Life in the Faith of Death*, ed. Richard N. Longnecker (Grand Rapids: Eerdmans, 1998), pp. 229-30.

resurrection of the Lord Jesus, and much grace was upon them all. *There were no needy persons among them*" (Acts 4:33-34). For whoever had wealth "put it at the apostles' feet, and it was distributed to anyone as he had need" (Acts 4:35). Thus Christ's resurrection released a remarkable new dynamic of fellowship, community and care for the needy. Can we imagine it being said of our churches today. "there is not a needy person among them, for they all believe in the Christian faith of the Resurrection, the Ascension of Christ from the dead"? Paradoxically for Christians, staring death in the face reveals its powerlessness over eternity, and grasping our resurrection hope turns our focus outward to those among us who are in need.

### Elders Are a Living Curriculum

Christian elders should be prepared to mentor others less advanced in the spiritual life of faith, teaching them to live in the light of the eternal. The aged apostle John praises the youth for strength to overcome, but he commends the fathers, "because you have known him who is from the beginning" (1 Jn 2:14). This life is only the beginning, not the terminus. "The high jump" is still ahead of us. This life is a training ground for the experience of the fullness of love, not just a taste here on earth, but the fullness in God's eternal presence. Love then is the key; the mark of a Christian senior should be that of a loving, caring, generous-hearted exemplar for those following on behind.

When my family of four teenage children were taken from their homeland into a distant foreign society, nothing was more important for them than having surrogate grandparents to encourage them through the big cultural adjustments they were required to make. Today as I (Dr. Houston) write, a young couple has asked my wife and I to be just that, a parental support (since they came from divorced families who did not know Christ). Christian seniors can play a subliminal role for youth coming from dysfunctional families, and the impact is more than we may ever know. This is especially true when such nurture comes personally and spontaneously; it is not just another ministry of the church. The naturally mutual interaction of youth and seniors is beneficial to both groups, helping the aged to remain young in spirit and for the young to be given a broader vision for more wisdom.

Christians look to spiritual directors as such senior exemplars who embody spiritual maturity, being both Christlike and genuine human beings, well educated and consistent in faith and practice. The countenance of a spiritually mature Christian best advertises the curriculum for further training (not the study topics our textbooks list). When we see the marks of love, joy and peace on the face of a Christian senior, we want to enroll there as both student and friend. That is the culture then that perhaps Paul is inviting us to learn in being "imitators of me, as I am of Christ."

# 8

# THE LIVED WISDOM
# OF CHRISTIAN ELDERS

...

Perhaps we have it all wrong today, when Christian leaders are esteemed primarily by their successful fundraising or by the effective business practices they exercise in their mega-churches. "Godliness" is not a category for course instruction. Even the Greek pagans coined the word *philosophia* to mean "the love of wisdom," not in the modern abstract sense of academic thought, but as exemplifying "a way of life" that determined a way of seeing the world; for behavior was primary and thoughts about it were secondary. Discourse followed life, not the reverse. Understandably then, the first Christians are described in the Acts of the Apostles as "those of the Way," where doctrine followed on discipleship. For the individual, conversion implied a total change of lifestyle, one that could be dramatic, like the experience of Saul of Tarsus, or hidden, like "the turning again" of Simon Peter. This itself is crucial to our discussion, for when we are speaking of the revitalized role of "seniors in the church," we are urging for the recovery of elders, of those who have had a long experience of the Christian life and who need to challenge the status quo of our churches, not as novices of the faith. Our advocacy is "aging is for sage-ing." We are discerning Christian elders as mature exemplars of a lifelong growth into spiritual maturity. This is in contrast to nominal church members who never seem to have been challenged to keep growing, nor see the need to pursue moral excellence in their relationships with others. Perhaps it is their self-centeredness that is paralyzing. For when we are speaking of the role of "seniors in the church," we actually have an exaggerated contrast of two categories that have gradually diverged: those in nominal church membership who may even be very active and prominent in activities but yet have never matured spiritually; and others who have never stopped growing in faith and relationships of love.

But today, novices are too readily assumed to be fully equipped because of their rapid seminary training, their musical skills or their management training. They do not need any maturity of life, only the college degree or the technical skill. A Christian senior recently told me (Dr. Houston) that he had resigned as committee chairman from his major church building project. He was a very senior engineer in his community. The youth in the church wanted more headroom in the basement basketball courts, literally demanding they "raise the roof." This would then spoil the worshipful design of the sanctuary above it, which the architect—secularist though he was—had specially designed. The change was going to be much more costly than the original estimate, which the chairman had pledged would not be changed. So the chairman was forced to resign! What the chairman had pledged would not be changed fiscally was overruled by the youth in their usurpation of power. As a Chinese immigrant culture, the youth were deemed to be more effective leaders, because of their fluency in English and with new job skills in the marketplace. Now instead of a church community that was ruled by godly elders, it was ruled by youth. This was a reversal of both Chinese and Christian values. What place will senior exemplars of the Christian life have in this new church venture? What long-term credibility will this Christian community have in the future if lifelong experiences are routinely supplanted by quick-fix technical skills? I (Dr. Houston) believe this example represents a wider phenomenon of the "progress" of secularization developing rapidly within the heart of contemporary Christianity. Perhaps the Reformation that Christian churches need today is a reorienting attitude toward how to attain wisdom.

The classical model of *paideia* education for the pursuit of excellence introduced the model of the senior as a mentor.[1] In the myth of Ulysses,

---

[1] James M. Houston, *The Mentored Life* (Colorado Springs: NavPress, 2002).

the absentee father commissions his old friend Mentes (hence *mentor*), to look after his teenage son, Telemachus, while he is absent in his travels. Seniors can act profoundly as surrogate parents to encourage young people to move forward wisely rather than impulsively, because they know the road ahead. Without the past experiences of seniors, youth can make horrible mistakes, not recognizing the consequences in the way that seniors can. Anyone who has been trained as a craftsman by a master knows this so well. As an academic tutor at Oxford University, my students learned this personally, at a level the public lectures cannot provide. The very act of learning how to learn, how to make critical judgments, how to review books, indeed how to write an essay, are all effectively developed through personal discourse and personal encouragement. Those who have been most coached personally exceed most, for there is much more to learn in life than a set of written instructions can give. Every Olympic medalist knows that a whole team of supporters is behind every accomplishment on the podium. As Christians, we all need team support!

Yet the malaise of our technological society is to make life so impersonal, even though directions for nearly every skill or lifestyle change abound. In one of his letters to his mentee Lucillius, Seneca—a contemporary of the apostle Paul—wrote: "I think there is no one who has rendered worse service to the human race than those who have learned philosophy as a mercenary trade."[2] Seeking to live according "the good life," the classical philosopher exemplified the wise way of living in teaching how he lived, not mere abstract principles. At the beginning of the Age of Enlightenment in the mid-seventeenth century, Pascal noted: "Plato and Aristotle can only be imagined dressed in the long robes of pedants. They were honest men, and like the others, they laughed with their friends; and when they amused themselves by writing their *Laws* and their *Politics*, they did it as an amusement. This was the least philosophical and serious part of their lives; the most philosophical part was living simply and quietly."[3] Even Immanuel Kant re-

---

[2]Seneca, *Letters to Lucilius*, 108, 36, quoted in Pierce Hadot, *What Is Ancient Philosophy?* trans. Michael Chase (Cambridge, Mass.: Harvard University Press, 2002), p. xiii.
[3]Pascal, *Pensees*, no. 331, quoted in James M. Houston, ed., *The Mind on Fire* (Colorado Springs:

iterated Voltaire's observation that metaphysicians are the sort of people who dream with their eyes open.[4] How much more in our day is technical or theoretical knowledge valued far more than personal example? Indeed the notion of "exemplary knowledge" is scarcely within out mental consciousness, almost unknown.

A young man just this week told me (Dr. Houston) that the condemnatory texts of the Bible stir up fears that he has been condemned to hell because of his previous manner of life. As I spoke with him, we discovered that his neurotic version of the Scriptures was built upon severe dysfunctional relations with his highly educated parents. They were always "explaining everything," instead of relating in love to him. For him all of life demanded explanations in lieu of relationships. If the explanation condemned him, then he was indeed utterly lost. His identity was a variant of Descartes's, "I explain and I am explained to, therefore I am"! How different life becomes when one walks through life with senior mentors, rather than only having a series of explanations. The pagan Greek philosophers knew this, so one entered not into an institution of education, but into the school of Epicurus or of Plato. The process of education was to imitate the master and to walk in his steps. Just as the sage perfected himself by imitating the gods, so his students perfected themselves by imitating him, in various degrees. Being like Epicurus proved that they were learning from him in so many ways. It was much more than a curriculum; it was a way of life. In this well-known cultural context, the apostle Paul could exhort: "imitate me" (1 Cor 4:16). Thus remaining sculptures of the head of Epicurus often combine the features of both Hercules the intellectual demi-god founder of culture and cities, with Asklepios, the god of healing.[5] This combination renders him primarily a father figure. The true philosopher is parental par excellence!

This analogy between classical philosophy and the Christian way of life does not stop there. For the exaggerated action-driven sense of mis-

Cook Communications, 2006), p. 211.
[4]Ann Loades, *Kant and Job's Comforters* (Newcastle-upon-Tyne, U.K.: Avero Publications, 1985), p. 16.
[5]Bernard Frischer, *The Sculpted Word: Epicureanism and Philosophical Recruitment in Ancient Greece* (Berkeley: University of California Press, 1982).

sion has tended to make evangelical Christians adopt secular attitudes, even while apparently "serving the Lord," just as modern philosophers have become much more thought-driven than the originators of *philosophia*. Both can lack a lived faith, which like vintage wine requires years of maturation. So philosophers can still be unwise individuals, and Christian activists can still be narcissists in love with themselves within their own ministries. Theory and action both need lived experiences, and that is why all too often lived behavior is being eclipsed and ignored by pseudo-intellectualism and by pseudo-activism. The new mobility of globalization and the expanding efficiency of fundraising are generating a new generation of mobile Christians, whose fluid actions does not have to—but I fear frequently does—exceed their authentic "being in Christ." Just as with the explosion of information through the electronic media, wisdom often loses out in the proliferation of knowledge.

The church must be steered away from becoming like the Sophists in the first century of the early Christian church. They were "salesmen of knowledge," teaching techniques of persuasion to attract large audiences with their wares, but they did not live the life. It appears the apostle Paul experienced the threat of such journalists of information firsthand in the great city of Corinth.[6] Whether for the Greek philosophers in the past or for Christians today, the problem is not of knowing this or that, but of *being* this or that. Christian development affects who you are as much or more than it affects what you do. It is the challenge to "walk the talk," living as a Christian exemplar for others, as "imitators of Christ." As Plutarch observed at the beginning of the second century A.D.: "Daily life gives us the opportunity to do philosophy . . . not in delivering discourses from the height of a chair, and in giving classes based on a text."[7] Likewise the early Christian apologists who demonstrated that Christ is the wisdom of God, the divine *Logos*, were inspired by the prologue of John's Gospel, that Jesus came to demonstrate to us a way of living that is the

---

[6]Bruce Winter, *Philo and Paul Among the Sophists: Alexandrian and Corinthian responses to a Julio-Claudian Movement*, 2nd ed. (Grand Rapids: Eerdmans, 2001).
[7]Plutarch, *Whether a Man Should Engage in Politics when He Is Old* 26,796d.

ultimate good. At the end of one's life this should be the mark of a Christian senior, to exemplify godly wisdom.

I (Dr. Parker) have found that elders can be encouraged to ministry though local, ecumenical conferences[8] and by inviting them to speak to younger people. One eighty-six-year-old example is Wayne Watts; he has shared his moving story as a prisoner of war and his historical wisdom about the larger context of World War II by contrasting it with other American wars.[9]

---

[8]M. W. Parker, "Building Partnerships with African American and White Churches to Promote a Good Old Age for All," *Generations* (summer 2008): 38-42; M. W. Parker, H. Koenig, J. Davis, N. Caldwell, J. Hataway and R. Allman, "A Multidisciplinary Model of Health Promotion Incorporating Spirituality into Successful Aging Interventions with African American and White Elderly," in *The Role of Faith-based Organizations in the Social Welfare System* (Bethesda, Md.: Rockefeller Institute of Government, Independent Sector, and the Roundtable on Religion and Social Welfare Policy, 2003), pp. 241-60.

[9]Wayne Watts, *From Among the Many: The Price of Freedom* (Tuscaloosa, Ala.: Self-published, 2006).

# 9

# HONORING ELDERS IN
# EARLY CHRISTIANITY

...

The recent movie *Amazing Grace* gave fuller disclosure to the life of a remarkable saint. For most of his adult life, William Wilberforce fought a courageous, enduring battle against the pro-slavery advocates of Great Britain. Like many senior saints of today, a terrible financial situation encountered him during the last decade of his life. The business in which he had helped his eldest son required more capital, and Wilberforce, always anxious to help him sold most of his stock and even his boyhood home to help. The son's business was still a failure; they lost everything. Thus in his seventies, "Wilberforce—formerly a very wealthy man—found himself nearly destitute. It was a serious blow, but those around him were deeply impressed at his equanimity and even joy in the midst of the drama. He had given away vast sums of money throughout his life, and the innumerable people and projects that had benefited from his personal generosity could never be tallied in this world. . . . [He] would end his life without a home of his own. Foxes had holes and birds had nests, but Wilberforce and Barbara were forced in old age to cast themselves upon the mercies of their second and third sons, living for alternating periods with each of them."[1]

In his own words, Wilberforce writes,

> The loss incurred has been so heavy as to compel me to descend from my present level and greatly to diminish my establishment. But I am bound to recognize in this dispensation the gracious mitigation of the severity of

---

[1] Eric Metaxas, *Amazing Grace* (New York: HarperCollins, 2007), p. 269.

the stroke. Mrs. Wilberforce and I are supplied with a delightful asylum under the roofs of two of our own children. And what better could we desire? A kind Providence has enabled me with truth to adopt the declaration of David, that goodness and mercy have followed me all my days. And now, when the cup presented to me has some bitter ingredients, yet surely no draught can be deemed distasteful which comes from such a hand, and contains such grateful infusions as those of social intercourse and the sweet endearments of filial gratitude and affection.[2]

## The Christian Within the Tensions of Family Life

When Mary was already a widow, Jesus was informed: "'Your mother and brothers are outside looking for you.' 'Who are my mother and my brothers?' he asked. Then he looked at those seated in a circle around him and said, 'Here are my mother and my brothers! Whoever does God's will is my brother and sister and mother'" (Mk 3:31-35). Jesus, it seems, establishes a new human community and with it a new personal identity, no longer based on consanguinity as in marriage and family life. Now in the radical expression of Christ's discipleship, conventional morality is no substitute for being personally committed to Jesus Christ. This is the call to a unique and transcendental relationship to Jesus Christ, as our Lord and Savior, in whom both the I AM of the Old Testament and "The Lord of Man" of the Gospels are now conjoined. It is a unique love that gives identity to the Christian community or *koinonia*, which mystically is now "in Christ."

It is the return to the creation purpose that "a man will leave his father and mother and be united to his wife" (Gen 2:24). Marriage is a sign of the covenant in the election of God, but marriage now anticipates a deeper fellowship, the fellowship of the triune God himself. Now it is the church, not the family, which reflects our true humanity, a new community into which we are bound. As Israel knew, the community was greater than the family, and its elders' role was played out within Israel itself; so too Christian seniors have their primary role within the church, not within the family. How serious it is, then, when

---

[2]Ibid., pp. 268-69.

we ostracize or neglect our elders within the life of the church. We are demonstrating (at best) an ignorance of biblical principles, unaware that our Christian identity does not come primarily from being blessed by a Christian home and Christian parents, but solely from having our own personal fellowship "in Christ."

It can be easy to confuse the Christian nuclear family with the Christian unit, the *koinonia*, which Jesus made the true relational basis. Fellowship with the Father and the Son, through the Holy Spirit is the new identity and well-being of the Christian. Thus singles and married couples are in this regard on common ground. Here the church is often gravely at fault in its segregation of singles and couples as indeed of seniors and youth. For the new parity and commonality is that when "one part suffers, every part suffers with it, if one part is honored, every part rejoices with it" (1 Cor 12:26). This affects the whole church regardless of its social composition. "Pushing singles to the fringe" or indeed "pushing seniors to the fringe" are then the antithesis of what happened in the early Christian church.

### The Care of Widows and Virgins in the Early Church

If we think the role of seniors is a great challenge to the immediate future of the church today, the role of virgins was the immense challenge to Christian society in the early church.

As in any period of history, demographics played a major role in the early church. Under Roman law, arranged marriages were the norm, with girls often betrothed as young as seven, then married at puberty to older men. Since male mortality was as young as twenty-five, many more females than males were left widows, young and old. If they did not die at childbirth, many women then went on to live into their forties and fifties. The apostle Paul, while stating his preference for celibacy, is also practical in his concern for the many single women and widows, allowing for marriage and remarriage (1 Cor 7:1-16, 25-40; 11:2-16; 14:33-35). But the church later adopted the attitude that widowhood was the preferred state—not remarriage—and the care of widows and orphans became a significant concern of Christian communities. In the mid-second century, the bishop of

Rome had charge of some 1,500 widows.

Young women then followed the saintly widows. In a large Christian community, such as Antioch in the fourth century, there were over 3,000 virgins that were under the care of the bishop.[3] As Peter Brown states, in the fourth century Roman world, Christian virgins had become "a deposit of values that were prized, by their male spokesmen, as peculiarly precious for the Christian community."[4] Such virgins were once cloistered in their homes outside the pagan society, ex voto, as if they no longer existed, and yet paradoxically they had become the backbone for the institutionalization of the church.

Ambrose recites the case of a Roman girl who rushed into the church pursued by a relative and wrapped herself within the altar-cloth. In the stunned silence of the church service, the pursuing relative shouted out: "Do you think that if your father was alive, he would have allowed you to remain unmarried?" "Perhaps he died," she snapped back, "so that no one should stand in my way." "Conquer family-loyalty first, my girl: if you overcome the household, you overcome the world."[5]

These chilling words describe what was at stake as the early Christians radically overcame Roman paganism by celibacy! The aging of our society may demand radical changes, but never anything so remarkable as the sexual revolution in reverse of the early church.

### Suffering and Medicine in the Early Church

A person's level of education has perhaps always been reflected in differentiated interpretations about sources and kinds of suffering. Generally, however, first-century persons recognized that some cases of disease were natural, others were from demons and others were divine punishment. Since the Greco-Roman culture had a "porous identity," porous in the sense that the self was then readily interpenetrable to other spirits, hence the vital need of exorcisms, unlike the modern much more "insulated self." In his ministry of healing the sick and in his exorcisms, onlookers attributed supernatural powers to Jesus, sug-

---

[3]Peter Brown, *The Body and Society* (New York: Columbia University Press, 1988), p. 306.
[4]Ibid., p. 263.
[5]Ibid., p. 344.

gesting that medical practices were little used. Yet the apostles clearly distinguished the need of exorcisms from the healing of the sick (Acts 5:16). At the same time Paul recognized some forms of sickness as divine judgment, as in 1 Corinthians 11:30-32, where some sickness and death resulted from the abuse of the Lord's table. In spite of Paul's extraordinary catalogue of sufferings he had experienced from his enemies and from natural disasters, he separated the indefinite suffering of "the thorn in the flesh" that had come from Satan (2 Cor 12:7-10).

New Testament teaching encourages comfort, encouragement, care for the sick, not necessarily that they will be healed, but that they will gain a transcendence of spirit to rise above their weaknesses and disabilities. The classic witness is Paul, who after his long list of sufferings can say, "when I am weak, then I am strong" (2 Cor 12:10). Thus too, Irenaeus in the second century recognized infirmities as endurance training, while Cyprian in the next century cites how sickness can lead some to Christ (in a homily on Ps 68:18).[6] Basil the Great suggested Christians should only seek medical assistance in some categories of suffering, for others should be directed to the priest's counsel when related to divine afflictions.[7] Thus the practices of the "laying on of hands," anointment with oil, prophecies, prayers were also part of the healing process.

Basil also realized that the art of medicine was a God-given gift to humanity, and thus to be appreciated appropriately. In some of his brotherhood communities he established the first hospitals. Around 375, he wrote to a Christian physician, Eustathius, extolling him for his combination of medical and spiritual skills: "your profession is the supply vein of health. But in your case especially, the science is ambidexterous, and you set yourself higher standards of humanity, not limiting the benefit of your profession to bodily ills, but also contriving the correction of spiritual ills."[8] The writer of the third Gospel, Luke, was him-

---

[6]Darrell W. Amundsen and Gary B. Ferguson, "Medicine and Religion: Early Christianity Through the Middle Ages," in *Health/Medicine and the Faith Traditions*, ed. Martin E. Marty and Kenneth L. Vaux (Philadelphia: Fortress, 1982), p. 98.
[7]Ibid., pp. 99-100.
[8]Saint Basil, *Letters*, trans. Sister Agnes Clare Way, C.D.P. (Washington, D.C.: Catholic University Press, 1969), pp. 25-33 (letter 189).

self a physician, so from the beginning of the Christian church, the health of the body and the soul have never been separated.

In the pagan society, suicide was considered an honorable alternative to helpless illness. Probably a majority of pagan physicians would have been prepared to assist at the suicide of their patients. But many would have refused to carry out abortions, since the potentiality of life (rather than its inherent value) was the guiding principle. Yet "child exposure" was common and no laws restricted its practice. Only the Stoics began to practice more humanitarian attitudes. Even this was nothing in comparison to the early Christian social concerns to help the helpless, care for the destitute and succor the deprived.

Like the apostle who organized "the poor relief" in Corinth for the famine relief of the churches of Jerusalem, Basil the Great lead an organization for famine relief in 364. By their vows of poverty he organized a series of "brotherhoods" in Cappadocia and Pontus to care for the sick in the first hospitals and to provide for the poor. These varied from small cottages in a village to a leper colony and large hospital within a major compound on the outskirts of a city like Caesarea. In his *Long Rules*, he dealt with the question of what recourse a Christian should have to the practice of medicine. His answer is very modern for us today: "we should neither repudiate this art altogether nor does it behoove us to repose all our confidence in it. . . . When reason allows, we call in the doctor, but we do not leave off hoping in God."[9] Always there is the double standard that it is fine for the doctor to heal the body, but God is vitally needed for the healing of the soul. Medicines and physicians' skills are also from God, so ultimately prayer as thanks, as well as prayer in petition in sickness, are all to God himself.

In the practice of medicine as in other ways, the early church took the biblical witness seriously when it came to communal life and care for those in need. The rising percentage of aged citizens in North America presents a challenge that today's church can meet with similar creativity when it is grounded in a biblical vision of human life and Christian community.

---

[9]Basil, *The Long Rule* 55, quoted in Darrell W. Amundsen, *Medicine, Society and Faith in the Ancient and Medieval Worlds* (Baltimore: Johns Hopkins University Press, 1996), p. 140.

# PART THREE

...

# SOLUTIONS FOR AN AGING CHURCH

# 10

## THE PRIMACY OF THEOLOGICAL
## ANTHROPOLOGY IN AN
## AGING CHURCH

...

We may have a biblical framework of the unique contributions Christian seniors and spiritual elders make to the church, but they fall short of explaining why the well-being of seniors—regardless of their contribution or spiritual maturity—is a Christian concern. The Bible paints an overarching picture of humanity that deserves our attention as a basis for any appeal that the elderly in our society matter.

### In the Image of God

One in two people over the age of eighty, America's (and most Western nations') fastest growing age group, suffer from dementia of some form, with approximately two-thirds being the dreaded Alzheimer's disease. When our seniors are struck down with Alzheimer's or dementia, there is still too much of their human narrative left to simply eliminate them by euthanasia, too much that still bears "the image of God," to attempt to forget or even to wipe out. God has created human beings "in his own image" (Gen 1:27). And this implies that the mystery of our humanity is unknowable outside of God's revelatory purposes.

Thus anthropology is defined by theology—not the reverse—a statement that in a secular society sounds like the greatest possible threat to human freedom. Nietzsche clearly saw things this way a century ago, that God and man appear to be inevitably on collision course as rivals. From this perspective only a low view of God can permit a high view of man. However, this is only true if our view of God is loveless, "a god who tyrannically and arbitrarily does what he wills," without a rival, as Origen quotes Celsus the pagan philosopher to have stated elsewhere. But if God is love, infinitely so, then our understanding of theological anthropology becomes radically different. Instead of viewing God as "infinite power"—as a schoolboy might see an authority figure, always there to spoil the fun—God is experienced as eternal love, always sacrificially self-giving within his triune being as each for the other: Father, Son and Holy Spirit.

If we accept the canon of biblical anthropology, that God made man and woman "in his image and likeness," then our identity is intrinsically relational. Our professions may generate the notion of being a personage only, but real persons are relationally, not functionally, defined. Seniors then do not stand around wondering what they can do. Unconditionally they "are," existing to be loved and to be a source of wisdom for the "who" they have been over a longer life-span than the rest of us. This does not negate the qualities and powers of being human; rather it legitimizes them relationally. Such legitimacy is also always for the sake of the other.

No "thing" then becomes monopolistic, when God rules in sovereign grace. In the use of reason, this definition of humanness implies that we learn not for the sake of learning itself, but to learn for love's sake. In the exercise of conscious will, this implies neither being willful nor will-less, but willing to benefit the other. As a sexual being, it then means we live in complement and mutuality, not in competitive equality, nor with inequality. Biblically then, we can never view other humans from a strictly utilitarian evaluation. But that is how we often dismiss seniors as of no use to the church; a materialistic culture can only cultivate utilitarian values. If grandmother is only a great cook or grandfather is a great handyman, are they disposable when they lose their ability to cook or do home carpentry? Likewise, in the church, how do we view our elders? Are they simply there to be entertained and humored in age segregated groups? How do we demonstrate the intrinsic value of all persons through our treatment of the oldest among us?

Western culture has forgotten that all persons are all created in the image and likeness of God. This is still true when seniors suffer from debilitating diseases. Make no mistake: Western culture can indeed become death-giving when it legitimizes abortion at the beginning of life and euthanasia at the end of it all. It loses appreciation of the incomparable value of human life, which cannot be so readily dispensable. Yet ignoring our seniors takes the first step in that direction.

## Memory as a Cultural Quality

There are obviously great cultural differences in the ways a society may value or discount the importance of seniors within their family and broader social life. Chinese generally rate their seniors very highly and include them with great respect within their extended family arrangements. This comes from their Confucian ethic of hierarchy and perhaps even more powerfully, from their ancestor worship. For example, in Taoism, a father or grandfather will be worshiped as a demi-god as soon as he dies. In Jewish and also in more traditional European societies, seniors receive significant respect from the younger.

Clearly, traditional cultures require a strong sense of the past to retain their distinctive ways. So wherever traditions matter, seniors matter too. Thus the turbulence of change—especially when a culture values change more than tradition—moves respect for a society's seniors near the vanishing point. Indeed, the association between respect for the seniors in a society has strong religious connotations which secular societies do not share. But secularism tends to be either selective or wholly in denial of the past's continuing relevance.

In the study of the past, Christians differ so radically from secularists. To speak of history is to speak of God, as the first statement of the Bible: "in the beginning God" (Gen 1:1). *Theological anthropology* means that God is the starting point of what we profess about and live out toward human beings. This is the key Christian issue for our age, and a concern for seniors is but one corollary element. For we are religious beings, and we distort the understanding of the human condition without a religious context. Humans are personal beings responsible to the "divine"—however we consider that to be—and with an afterlife. Our values and morality are shaped by our religious beliefs and practices.

The rise of Islam in our contemporary world reinforces this awareness (no doubt much to the confusion of secular humanists) that religion refuses to die and to be ignored. The Western world has begun to see that the revival of Christianity is necessary to preserve even the West's secular values. For the origins of Western culture are also religious and largely (though not wholly) Christian. Perhaps especially now Christians understand that secularism is a cultural parasite and not a true source of human values. While reforming religious corruption and the church as a social institution will continue to be valid and necessary, eliminating the Christianity of the church altogether would merely leave a void to be filled by another religion, whether it called itself by that name or not.

*Augustine and memory.* To allow secularism to remain unchallenged implies great moral losses, more than we may know. First, the loss of God in society results in the loss of a sense of history. As Henry Ford implied, if technology is all that counts, then "history is bunk!" One great shaper of Western consciousness, Augustine of Hippo, emphasized the vital role played by memory (*memoria*) in human consciousness. He views analysis of the past as never merely an exercise in remembrance. God lies behind the entire human past.

So we can go back to Augustine's *Confessions* and see how robustly he was conscious of himself, all the more as he saw himself before God. For his self-awareness was sustained by *memoria*, the mysterious memory and presence of God within. All western history is replete with self-awareness, religiously so. An amusing incident illustrates our society's lack of understanding of this. Oliver Wendell Holmes, the dean of the medical school at Harvard, once commented about the teeenage incident of Augustine: "Rum thing to see a man making a mountain out of robbing a peartree in his teens." Even for a distinguished secular jurist, breaking one of the Ten Commandments was no longer considered a matter of much moral significance, as it remained for Augustine all through his life. Holmes had no idea of how the great Augustine of Hippo could look back to his confused past and see himself in the hands of God as one sinful individual. Moreover, he failed to see how this revelation could illustrate how all fallen humanity, and indeed all history, was ultimately also in the hands of God too.

Seniors are the carriers of historical reflection and of tradition. They can reflect and see sadly missed opportunities or interpret "hinge-moments" when momentous decisions for good or evil took place, affecting all their subsequent narrative. The next generation needs to know the lessons of the past from their elders so they are not condemned to repeat the errors of the past. Later in life, Augustine realized the full horror of his youthful crime in terms of the utter depravity of the human heart as a sinner before God. This is a dimension of reality for which the great Oliver Wendell Holmes himself apparently had no awareness. He had forgotten to ask "the elders, and they will explain to you."

*The death of history.* So how many lessons from the past do we forfeit when we do not listen or pay attention to our elders? When innovation eclipses a historical perspective, we experience what has mournfully been called "the Death of the Past." Then pop culture takes over: prints of the *Mona Lisa* are on every kitchen fridge, so no one needs to visit to the Louvre anymore.[1]

If the "death of god" implies the "death of history" for the West, what happens to our sense of humanness? At best we are what the biologist Loren Eiseley described as "the cosmic orphan," looking out, alone, as the observer of the infinite universes through the Hubble telescope.[2] A similar heritage has engaged many Americans ever since, this enterprise of what Philip Cushman calls "the self-making of our identity." This is now exaggerated as a characterization of the narcissism in our contemporary culture, which implies "American life in an age of diminishing expectations," as Christopher Lasch subtitles his book *The Culture of Narcissism.*[3] Philip Cushman described what has happened in the history of psychotherapy as "the constructing of the self," a false

---

[1]Lest this sound too pessimistic, I should mention that tourism may actually be one of the forces that encourages a remembrance of past cultural heritages.

[2]Eisley coined the phrase after a conversation he had with his father as a child: "Papa, how did men get here?" "Son," he replied, "once there was a poor orphan with no one to teach him either his way or his manners." For his father had been a pioneer brought up in the hard school of the American frontier.

[3]Christopher Lasch, *The Culture of Narcissism: American Life in an Age of Diminishing Expectations* (New York: W. W. Norton, 1978).

and amoral interpretation of the self.[4] Certainly all such social critics are right to deplore the exaggerated individualism today.

But such pessimistic views overlook the long Western history of self-identity. As long as there has been autobiography there has been the individual. And what a remarkable heritage that has been since Augustine's *Confessions*, living as he did so conscious of God's presence in human affairs.

So impatience over the recollections given us by our seniors probably reflects the hearer's loss of memory, not the seniors'! Our personal narratives are only enriched when they are shared socially and, above all, enveloped by the personal experiences of divine grace. Being "an individual" then, is not the problem; the problem is being an individual without the memory of God. For then we have no ultimate relations other than ourselves to sustain our intrinsic relational nature.

Our personal narratives bore others when they are all about "me." It is a historicist notion that humans have no nature, only a history of the self. We have both "being" and a "history," for God created us and God sustains us. Bringing God within the spiritual dimension of our lives releases him to extend and envelop all other realities about ourselves. So when we speak of seniors in a Christian community, we are not dealing with, nor speaking about, "ordinary" people. "There are no ordinary people," observed C. S. Lewis, when they are recognized to carry "an eternal weight of glory." "You have never talked to a mere mortal. Nations, cultures, arts, civilization—these are mortal, and their life is ours as the life of a gnat. But it is immortals whom we joke with, work with, marry, snub and exploit—immortal horrors or everlasting splendors."

---

[4]Philip Cushman, *Constructing the Self: Constructing America, a Cultural History of Psychotherapy* (Reading, Mass.: Addison-Wesley, 1995).

# 11

## AGING SUCCESSFULLY

### Myths and Realities

...

Though researchers in geriatrics and gerontology have discovered many of the basics about how to age successfully, they are unfortunately finding it more challenging to help seniors put into practice these discoveries. Like in the area of parental caregiving, where most adult children and aging parents wait until a health care emergency to put together a caregiving plan, many older persons wait too long to make the necessary changes in their lifestyles.[1] Part of the problem is that many seniors, their families and even the church are poorly informed about the truths of aging in America.[2] This preoccupation with negative and often false stereotypes of aging has overshadowed the major importance of lifestyle in maintaining health and vigor in late life.

### The Myths of Aging

Rowe and Kahn, two leading researchers in the field of aging, developed one of the first models of successful aging that summarized dec-

---

[1]M. W. Parker, J. Bellis, M. Harper, P. Bishop, C. Moore, P. Thompson and R. A. Allman, "Multidisciplinary Model of Health Promotion Incorporating Spirituality into a Successful Aging Intervention with African American and White Elderly," *The Gerontologist* 42, no. 3 (2002): 405-15. See also M. Parker, "Building Partnerships with African American and White Churches to Promote a Good Old Age for All," *Generations* (summer 2008): 38-40.
[2]M. Parker, H. Koenig, J. Davis, N. Caldwell, J. Hataway and R. Allman, "A Multidisciplinary Model of Health Promotion Incorporating Spirituality into Successful Aging Interventions with African American and White Elderly," in *The Role of Faith-Based Organizations in the Social Welfare System* (Bethesda, Md.: Independent Sector, 2003), pp. 241-60.

ades of initial research.[3] These earlier studies by Rowe and Kahn were associated with a larger initiative called the MacArthur (Foundation) Studies of Successful Aging and were based on a series of longitudinal investigations. This early work has been expanded and has influenced current federal programs like *Healthy People 2010,* a public health initiative aimed at increasing the quality and years of healthy life and eliminating health disparities.[4] Before highlighting their model and important additions to it, the false beliefs people often hold with regard to the aging process deserve a sound critique. According to Rowe and Kahn and others, a number of counterproductive aging myths operate in our society as partial truths and fantasies, and these must be challenged because they cut at the core of why many congregations, denominations and seminaries fail to plan or act constructively about aging.[5] A review of several of the most frequently circulated myths follows.

*Myth #1: To be old is to be sick.* Dr. Robert Butler, the first director of a department of geriatric medicine and the founding director of the National Institute on Aging, was the first to employ the term *ageism* in his Pulitzer Prize–winning book *Growing Old in America—Why Survive?*[6] He described ageism as a form of prejudice in which older persons are viewed as sick, demented, frail, disabled, powerless, sexless, passive, alone or unable to learn. I (Dr. Parker) mentioned one pastor's view earlier, that his church was comprised of "no go, slow go, and fast go" categories. When these negative stereotypes were challenged, he realized that the "no go's" did indeed go; they provided needed leadership and ministry through prayer and other means. This pastor's initial views of some of his seniors were neither biblical (consider, for example, successful agers like Moses, Caleb, Abraham and John) nor scientifi-

---

[3]J. W. Rowe and R. L. Kahn, *Successful Aging* (New York: Pantheon Books, 1998).

[4]J. W. Rowe and R. L. Kahn, "Human Aging: Usual and Successful," *Science* 237 (1987): 143-49; R. L. Kahn, "Successful Aging: Intended and Unintended Consequences of a Concept," in *Successful Aging and Adaptation with Chronic Diseases,* ed. L. W. Poon, S. H. Gueldner and B. M. Sprouse (New York: Springer, 2003).

[5]M. Crowther, M. W. Parker, H. Koenig, W. Larimore and A. Achenbaum, "Rowe and Kahn's Model of Successful Aging Revisited: Spirituality the Forgotten Factor," *The Gerontologist* 42, no. 5 (2002): 613-20.

[6]Robert Butler, *Growing Old in America—Why Survive?* (New York: Harper & Row, 1975).

cally accurate. Experts in aging have also played a part in stereotyping the aging person by focusing on late life disease and disability. The truth is that most older people are experiencing less disability than ever before, reporting higher levels of health than during earlier seasons of our history, and, in general, are experiencing the highest levels of health and sustained periods of independence in our nation's history.[7]

Most elderly people today suffer from what geriatricians call chronic, long-term disease (like arthritis, diabetes, hypertension and heart disease, vision and hearing problems). However, leading experts in aging report major reductions in the prevalence of three key forerunners to chronic disease: high blood pressure, high cholesterol levels and smoking.[8] Furthermore, major reductions in the incidence of arthritis, hardening of the arteries (arteriosclerosis), hypertension, stroke and lung disease (emphysema) began to surface in longitudinal studies in the 1980s and 1990s,[9] and these findings have been increasingly confirmed in later reviews, articles and geriatric textbooks. Dental health has improved significantly as well. The percent of older individuals with no teeth (edentulous: natural teeth remaining) has dropped from 55 percent in 1957 to 34 percent in 1980, and is currently approaching 24 percent.[10]

It is possible for two older persons of the same age and with the same medical conditions to function at entirely different levels: one might be a Supreme Court Justice while the other might be a frail, dependent nursing home resident. The reason for the difference in their function-

---

[7]Kahn, "Successful Aging"; Rowe and Kahn, "Human Aging"; Rowe and Kahn, *Successful Aging*.

[8]Nancy R. Hooyman and H. Asuman Kiyak, *Social Gerontology*, 9th ed. (Boston: Allyn & Bacon, 2011): pp. 224-28. For example, see R. Kane, J. Ouslander and I. Abrass, *Essentials of Clinical Geriatrics*, 5th ed. (New York: McGraw-Hill Health Professional Division, 2004), pp. 3-119.

[9]See also S. H. Zarit, "A Good Old Age: Theories of Mental Health and Aging," in *Handbook of Theories of Aging*, ed. V. L. Bengtson, M. Silverstein, N. M. Putney and D. Gans (New York: Springer, 2009); M. Crowther, M. W. Parker, H. Koenig, W. Larimore and A. Achenbaum, "Rowe and Kahn's model of Successful Aging Revisited: Spirituality, the Forgotten Factor," *The Gerontologist* 42, no. 5 (2002): 613-20; R. L. Kane, J. G. Ouslander and I. B. Abrass, *Essentials of Clinical Geriatrics*, 5th ed. (New York: McGraw-Hill, 2004).

[10]C. A. Schoenborn, J. L. Vickerie and E. Powerll-Griner, "Health Characteristics of Adults 55 Years and Over, U.S. 2000-2003," *Advance Data from Vital and Health Statistics*, no. 370 (Hyattsville, Md.: NCHS, 2006).

ing levels is what experts call *functional status*, the capacity of a person to live and function without assistance.[11] Experts assess a person's functional capacities using two methods: Instrumental Activities of Daily Living (IADLs, such the ability to cook for oneself or manage finances) and Activities of Daily Living (ADLs, such as feeding, bathing and toileting). What does research suggest about how seniors are doing in these critical areas?

One indication of how seniors are functioning is suggested in the percent of older persons who live in nursing homes. The percent of individuals over sixty-five living in nursing homes continues to decline. Currently less than 5.0 percent reside in these institutions, down from 6.3 percent in 1982. Another indication of the health status of seniors is how they describe their own health. Surveys suggest that most seniors describe themselves as being free of disability. Research indicates that of those aged sixty-five to seventy-four in 1994, a full 89 percent reported no disability whatsoever.[12] While the proportion of elderly who are fully functioning and robust does decline with advancing age, almost 75 percent of seniors between the ages of seventy-five and eighty-four reported no disability.[13] Rather than becoming more dependent, one theory (the compression morbidity theory) maintains that the percent of seniors experiencing an active life and delayed disease and disability will continue to increase. This theory implies that premature death is minimized because disease and functional decline are compressed into a brief period of three to five years before death. Major chronic diseases like arthritis, arteriosclerosis and respiratory problems now appear ten to twenty-five years later than for past cohorts. As a result, people die natural deaths from the failure of multiple organ systems, not because of disease per se.[14] Even among the oldest (ages 85+), the majority lives independently with little disability.[15] In summarizing

[11]M. W. Parker and G. Fuller, "Successful Aging," in *Finishing Strong* (Dallas: LifeWay Publishers, 2002), pp. 63-70.
[12]Ibid.
[13]Rowe and Kahn, *Successful Aging*.
[14]W. R. Hazzard, "Aging, Health, Longevity, and Promise of Biomedical Research," in *Handbook of the Biology of Aging*, ed. E. J. Masoro and S. N. Austad, 5th ed. (San Diego: Academic Press, 2001).
[15]Ibid.; Rowe and Kahn, *Successful Aging*, pp. 13-18.

decades of research, Rowe and Kahn debunk the myth that to be old is to be sick: "We are delighted to observe increasing momentum toward the emergence of a physically and cognitively fit, non-disabled, active elderly population. The combination of longer life and less illness is adding life to years as well as years to life."[16]

*Myth #2: You can't teach an old dog new tricks.* This myth refers to the inability of older persons to remain lifelong learners. This misperception is perpetuated, unfortunately, in the negative attitudes among many older persons toward learning to use the computer and the Internet. Research suggests, however, that though seniors may require a slower pace to learn new information, they not only can do it, but they may also be able to act upon new learning more effectively than younger persons.[17] Older people can place new learning within their context of extensive experience. Organizational research suggests that seniors have an innovative advantage over youth with newly acquired information because their experience compensates for or even goes beyond the flexibility of youth.

When it comes to learning, society is age-graded. Most systems are designed for the young and operate as if there were three distinct periods of life: education, work and retirement. As a result, many of our institutions of learning (like schools and churches) do not take into consideration the slower rate necessary for optimum learning to occur with seniors. Most churches support age-graded Sunday school classes, yet the biblical model suggests that the old should teach the young (see Ps 71). Our churches need to cultivate attitudes and programs that foster lifelong learning and provide opportunities for seniors to instruct and teach the young. During pre–Desert Storm deployment, the only elder in the Heidelberg, Germany chapel proved a tremendous, calming influence to me (Dr. Parker) and to others with whom I served. As many of us prepared for war, we received news that Saddam Hussein had sent "death squads" (suicide bombers) into Europe to blow up American schools and hospitals. So anyone deploying from Europe to

---

[16]Rowe and Kahn, *Successful Aging*, p. 18.
[17]M. J. Hogan, "Divided Attention in Older but Not Younger Adults Is Impaired by Anxiety," *Experimental Aging Research*, no. 29 (2003): 111-36.

Iraq was leaving family in harm's way. This dear saint, a veteran of World War II, was able to help American soldiers facing uncertainties in battle focus on the sovereignty of God and thereby gain peace and assurance for the duties that lay before them.

One element of learning is executive function, which involves our capacity to organize our thinking (planning, decision making, avoiding distraction). Normal aging is associated with only mild declines in executive function. In one study, those aged seventy-four to eighty-one showed no mental decline over a seven-year period.[18] Though dementia, particularly Alzheimer's disease, is ever-present, many fears about memory loss are exaggerated. However, older adults suffering from dementia experience significant impairment with their capacity to organize their thinking. The reaction times of youth are generally superior to seniors, but older persons have shown significant and permanent improvements with training in cognitive reasoning, inductive reasoning and spatial orientation (for example, with practice games that enhance memory). Information about the name to be recalled (e.g., the link between the face and the name) can help older learners, whether they are given this information or they develop the descriptors themselves.[19] My colleague Dr. Karlene Ball has developed a series of cognitive training interventions that improve memory related to safer driving. The keys to her research has resulted in the development and continued investigation of a test called Useful Field of View®, which measures visual attention and identifies older drivers at risk for having traffic accidents. She also was a coauthor of a multisite study, supported by the National Institute on Aging, which found that older adults benefit from training to improve reasoning, memory and speed of processing. The keys to late-life learning are to develop a learning climate that allows seniors to work at their own pace, to provide opportunities to practice newly acquired skills, to learn memory-enhancement techniques and to

---

[18]Rowe and Kahn, *Successful Aging*, pp. 19-22, 125-42.
[19]Troyer et al., "Name and Face Learning in Older Adults; Effects of Level Processing, Self-Generation and Intention to Learn," *Journal of Gerontology: Psychological Sciences*, no. 61B (2006): 67-74.

monitor the rate of learning so that seniors are not placed in situations of comparison with younger learners.[20]

Though dementia has no cure, exercise, a strong support system and an attitude of confidence in managing problems, coupled with the acquisition of memory enhancement techniques, can greatly increase a senior's capacity to maintain cognitive function and to learn.[21] Far from the fatalism of this common myth, research suggests that the old can sharpen their intellectual capacities and avoid the cycle of mental insufficiency that stems from inactivity.

*Myth #3: The horse is out of the barn.* This myth suggests that it is too late to reduce the risk of disease and disability. If you have been smoking, not exercising, drinking too much or overeating fat-laden foods for most of your life, it is too late to change, or so this myth would have you believe. Fortunately, research affirms that lost function can be recovered, and that the risk of disease and disability can be reduced. In some cases, the level of functioning (for example, physical strength or stamina) can even be increased. Clearly it is best to begin healthy habits early and to sustain them throughout life, but this is not an excuse for continuing bad habits.

Seniors who lose excessive weight, stop smoking and begin to exercise experience significant health changes through a reduced incidence of disease and disability.[22] For example, when certain categories of older people lose weight, they reduce their risk for heart disease. Dietary changes (more grains and vegetables) can result in lower blood pressure levels for certain older persons, though medication may also be required for blood pressure management as well. Many older persons resist medications as part of this myth, but the pharmaceutical treatment of certain forms of hypertension (systolic) has reduced strokes in older men by one-third and heart attacks by more than one-fourth.[23]

Though with age the body does lose physical function, elite athleti-

---

[20]Rowe and Kahn, *Successful Aging*, pp. 19-22; K. Ball et al., "Effects of Cognitive Training Interventions with Older Adults," *Journal of the American Medical Association*, no. 288 (2002): 2271-81.

[21]Rowe and Kahn, *Successful Aging*, pp. 22-28.

[22]Ibid.

[23]Ibid.

cism is not typically needed in late life. Many reductions in physical performance are reversible. Exercise can increase physical fitness, increase muscle size and strength, favorably influence balance and help prevent falls. Lifting weights and other forms of resistance training can develop bone strength and density, limit the effects of diseases like osteoporosis and help improve balance as well.[24] Seniors and those who care for them must not buy into the myth that positive changes cannot enhance health and quality of life. It is never too late to start making healthy lifestyle changes.

*Myth #4: The secret to successful aging is to choose your parents wisely.* The role of genetics in aging has been overemphasized and overstated, according to leading researchers and geriatricians.[25] Though there is a connection between one's genetic inheritance and the ability to age well, most of the variance in understanding the aging process is associated with lifestyle. This is good news! It means older people can make choices that help determine their health-related futures. Diet, exercise and even medications may delay or completely eliminate the development of certain diseases. The longevity found in many families can be related to similar lifestyle features such as eating and exercise habits. Heredity's strongest influence appears to be in the development of genetic diseases that can shorten life (mainly certain cancers). As we grow older, the influence of genetics becomes less important and lifestyle becomes more important. The degree to which one is filled with vitality and actively engaged with life is primarily related to non-genetic factors.

*Myth #5: The lights may be on, but the voltage is low.* This myth implies that older people suffer from inadequate physical and mental capacities, and that older men and women are sexless or at least uninterested in sex. Sexuality in late life (when partners are available) is neither rare nor inappropriate. In general, sexual activity does decrease with age, but there are major individual differences among the elderly. Though chronological age is not the key factor, there are physiological changes (decline in testosterone) and certain health conditions (like

---

[24]M. W. Parker, P. Baker and R. Allman, "A Life Space Approach to the Functional Assessment of the Elderly," *The Journal of Gerontological Social Work* 35, no. 4 (2002): 35-55.
[25]Rowe and Kahn, *Successful Aging*, pp. 28-30.

diabetes, heart disease and hypertension) that can impede sexual function, especially in men. Rowe and Kahn describe one study that found that at age sixty-eight, about 70 percent of men were sexually active on a regular basis, but by age seventy-eight, the percent of sexually active men dropped significantly.[26] Overall health and the availability of a partner are major factors that influence sexual activity. Moreover, forms of physical intimacy should be distinguished from sexual intercourse: "The voltage is never too low for affectionate physical contact. Such contact may help keep the lights on."[27]

*Myth #6: The elderly don't pull their own weight.* The last myth may be the most damaging of all, implying that the elderly do not carry their fair share of society's workload. Unfortunately, much of the work completed by elders is not counted. Research suggests that approximately 3 million home care laborers would be needed if seniors stopped providing care to the sick and the disabled.[28] Such unpaid work is often hard, nonstop, grueling labor, but it is not counted except in the workbooks of heaven. Many of our religious institutions and volunteer-based programs would fail to operate without the help of seniors. Likewise, grandparenting has become part-time—and in increasing cases, full-time—parenting for many seniors. Volunteer programs provide older persons with meaningful social activities that enhance their health, and it provides churches and other organizations with experienced and reliable volunteers. As noted earlier, it is unfortunate that most of the congregations surveyed in my (Dr. Parker's) work hold to the pervasive belief that ministry is primarily *to* seniors.[29]

Seniors also play a major role in the work place. In fact, surveys suggest that over a third of those over the age of sixty-five would prefer to work, yet they are discriminated against in competing for job positions. Many seniors are forced into retirement who have both the desire and

---

[26]Ibid., pp. 31-32.
[27]Ibid., p. 32.
[28]Ibid., pp. 33-35, 167-81.
[29]Ibid.; N. Hooyman and H. A. Kiyak, "Productive Aging: Paid and Nonpaid Roles and Activities," in *Social Gerontology: A Multidisciplinary Perspective*, 9th ed. (Boston: Pearson Education, 2011), pp. 499-544.

ability to be a part of the work force.

## Aging Successfully

Which of these views of aging dominates our churches today?

> How hard and painful are the last days of an aged man! He grows
> weaker every day; his eyes become dim, his ears deaf; his strength fades;
> his heart knows peace no longer, his mouth falls silent, and he speaks no
> word. The power of his mind lessens, and today he cannot remember
> what yesterday was like. All his bones hurt. Those things, which so long
> ago were done with pleasure, are painful now, and taste vanishes. Old
> age is the worst of misfortunes that can afflict a man.[30]

> Youth is not a period of time. It is a state of mind, a result of the will, a
> quality of the imagination, a victory of courage over timidity, of the
> taste of adventure over the love of comfort. A man doesn't grow old
> because he has lived a certain number of years. A man grows old when
> he deserts his ideal. The years may wrinkle his skin, but deserting his
> ideal wrinkles his soul. Preoccupations, fears, doubts, and despair are
> the enemies, which slowly bow us toward earth and turn us into dust
> before death. You will remain young as long as you are open to what is
> beautiful, good and great; receptive to the messages of other men and
> women, of nature and of God. If one day you should become bitter, pes-
> simistic and gnawed by despair, may God have mercy on your old man's
> soul.[31]

Is it truly possible to age "successfully"? Is successful aging something
the church can promote? We believe that there is much more to aging
that waiting for our bodies to fail us, and the church can play a unique
role in teaching all its members a better way.

   *The role of faith.* In their original model based on decades of research
supported by the MacArthur Foundation, Rowe and Kahn defined the
key elements of successful aging as the avoidance of disease and dis-

---

[30]Egyptian philosopher and poet Ptahhotep (2500 B.C.), quoted in J. Viorst, *Necessary Losses*
(New York: Ballantine Books, 1986), p. 319.
[31]World War II–era leader General Douglas MacArthur, quoted in M. W. Parker, V. Call and
W. Barko, "Officer and Family Wellness Across the Life Course: A Growing Role for Social
Workers," in *Social Work Practice in the Military*, ed. J. Daley (New York: Haworth Press, 1999),
pp. 255-74.

ability, the maintenance of physical and cognitive function, and active engagement with life.[32] Christian gerontologists have argued that positive spiritual growth and development represents the fourth major category of successful aging.[33] For example, spirituality has been associated with an improvement in psychological well-being, a reduction in levels of depression and distress, a reduction in disease and an increase in life span.

Recent research is helping to renew the historical link between medicine and religious faith as doctors seek ways to help seniors age successfully. Over 850 scientific studies have shown that faith (or spirituality) enhances mental and physical health, reduces morbidity or chronic disease and contributes to long life.[34] The famous Johns Hopkins physician Sir William Osler wrote in the first edition of the *British Medical Journal* (dated 1910), "Nothing in life is more wonderful then faith—the one great moving force which we can neither weigh in the balance nor test in the crucible."[35]

Religious participation later in life has been found consistently to be associated with longer life, less disease and disability, improved cognitive and immune functioning, less depression, more freedom and less dependence, and a greater sense of meaning and purpose.[36] In our own research with 1,000 community-dwelling seniors over a ten-year period, we found religious involvement to be reliably associated with better mental and physical health.[37] Older Christians who refuse to exer-

---

[32]Rowe and Kahn, "Human Aging," pp. 143-49; Rowe and Kahn, "Successful Aging," pp. 433-40; Rowe and Kahn, *Successful Aging.*

[33]M. Crowther, M. W. Parker, H. Koenig, W. Larimore and A. Achenbaum, "Rowe and Kahn's Model of Successful Aging Revisited: Spirituality, the Forgotten Factor," *The Gerontologist* 45, no. 5 (2002): 613-20; W. L. Larimore, M. W. Parker and M. Crowther, "Should clinicians incorporate positive spirituality into their practices?" *Annals of Behavioral Medicine* 24, no. 1 (2002): 69-73.

[34]Crowther et al., "Rowe and Kahn's Model."

[35]W. Osler, "The Faith That Heals." *British Journal of Medicine* 1 (1910): 470-72.

[36]N. R. Hooyman and H. A. Kiyak, *Social Gerontology: A Multidisciplinary Perspective,* 9th ed. (Boston: Pearson Education, 2011), pp. 517-26.

[37]Fei Sun, Nan S. Park, L. Roff, D. Klemmack, M. W. Parker, H. Koenig, P. Sawyer and R. Allman, "Predicting the Trajectories of Depressive Symptoms Among Southern Community-Dwelling Older Adults: The Role of Religiosity," *Journal of Aging and Mental Health* (forthcoming); L. Roff, M. W. Parker, N. S. Park, F. Sun, D. Klemmack and R. Allman, "Transportation Difficulty of Black and White Rural Older Adults," *Journal of Applied Gerontology* 29, no. 1 (2010): 70-88; N. S. Park, D. Klemmack, L. Roff, M. W. Parker, H. Koenig,

cise, stop smoking, lose weight, alter their diet or remain active socially
are on thin ice if they take seriously the teachings of Scripture. "Don't
you know that you yourselves are God's temple and that God's Spirit
lives in you? If anyone destroys God's temple, God will destroy him; for
God's temple is sacred, and you are that temple" (1 Cor 3:16-17). "You
were bought at a price. Therefore honor God with your body" (1 Cor
6:20). "Therefore, I urge you, brothers, in view of God's mercy, to offer
your bodies as living sacrifices, holy and pleasing to God—this is your
spiritual act of worship" (Rom 12:1). Research indicates that a large
percentage of older adults suffer from depression and anxiety. Even
though these conditions are not considered to be a normal part of aging,
exercise, social connections, late life purpose and telling one's story can
help prevent depression in many older persons. Christians can be in the
forefront in encouraging the elders in their midst to treat their aging
bodies with care and also enjoy the gifts that successful agers bring to
the community of faith.

So, how do we change? We must remind ourselves that we cannot,
alone in our own flesh, correct aspects of our physical and emotional
lifestyle. We must believe God more; in faith, we hook ourselves into
God's promises, claiming them for our lives. "His divine power has
given us everything we need for life and godliness through our knowledge of him who called us by his own glory and goodness. Through

---

P. Sawyer and R. Allman, "Religiousness and Longitudinal Trajectories in Elders' Functional
Status," *Research on Aging* 30, no. 3 (2008): 279-98; L. Roff et al., "Functional Limitations and
Religious Service Attendance Among African American and White Elders," *Health and Social
Work.* 31, no. 4 (2006): 245-55; D. L. Klemmack, L. Roff, M. W. Parker, H. G. Koenig,
P. Sawyer-Baker and R. M. Allman, "A Cluster Analysis Typology of Religiousness/Spiritual-
ity Among Older Adults," *Research on Aging* 29, no. 2 (2007): 163-83; L. Roff, D. L. Klem-
mack, M. W. Parker, P. Baker and R. Allman, "Religiosity, Smoking, Exercise and Obesity
Among Southern Community-Dwelling Older Adults," *Journal of Applied Gerontology* 24, no.
4 (2005): 337-54 (the content of this article is solely the responsibility of the authors and does
not necessarily represent the official views of the National Institute on Aging or the National
Institutes of Health); L. Roff, D. L. Klemmack, M. W. Parker, P. Baker and R. Allman,
"Spirituality and Depression in African American and White Elders," *Journal of Human Behavior and the Social Environment* 10, no. 1 (2005): 175-211; M. W. Parker, L. Roff, D. Klemmack, H. Koenig, P. Baker and R. Allman, "Religiosity and Mental Health in Southern,
Community-Dwelling Older Adults," *Aging & Mental Health.* 7, no. 5 (2003): 390-97 (the
content of this article is solely the responsibility of the authors and does not necessarily represent the official views of the National Institute on Aging or the National Institutes of
Health).

these he has given us his very great and precious promises, so that through them you may participate in the divine nature and escape the corruption in the world caused by evil desires" (2 Pet 1:3-4).

*The grace of God.* As we review God's admonitions about how to age successfully, we must remind ourselves that the grace by which we were saved is the same grace by which we live. Just as Ptahhotep's view of aging contrasts sharply with General MacAuthur's, history describes two notions of God's grace. In one of Martin Luther's debates with Erasmus on the nature of God's grace, his adversary stated that God's grace was like a parent helping a child to learn to walk ("the Lord helps those who help themselves"). Luther countered passionately with a word picture. "God's grace is like being a caterpillar in a Ring of Fire. The only deliverance is from above!"[38]

Luther's view of the role of God's grace in our lives is that God does not leave us alone. "Because the sovereign LORD helps me, I will not be disgraced. Therefore have I set my face like flint, and I know I will not be put to shame. He who vindicates me is near" (Is 50:7). If we are to improve and maintain our emotional and physical health and seize God's purpose for our lives no matter how old we are, we must begin with God's grace.

God's grace is realized in part when we believe that each of us has a unique, eternal mission, "the hope to which he has called you" (Eph 1:18). What is that calling? Though I believe each of us receives a unique call from God, the mission statement for all seniors can be found in Psalm 71:

> For you have been my hope, O Sovereign LORD,
> my confidence since my youth.
> From birth I have relied on you. . . .
> Even when I am old and gray,
> do not forsake me, O God,
> till I declare your power to the next generation,
> your might to all who are to come. (Ps 71:5-6, 18)

Many Christians find God's grace revealed through the lives of older

---

[38]World Harvest Mission, *Sonship* (Oreland, Penn.: Westminster Media, 1997).

friends and mentors who share their God-co-authored biography; each story laced with testimonies of God's sustaining grace. In my own life (Dr. Parker), three of these great men for me are in heaven; two remain. One faces a chronic condition called *polymyalgia rheumatica* or PMR, pain involving many muscles. PMR can produce an extremely painful swelling of the artery walls that restricts blood flow. When this happens in the blood vessels that supply blood to the head, the condition can cause blindness or result in a stroke. Though there is no current cure, a high dosage of corticoid steroids can provide symptomatic relief, which unfortunately can contribute to osteoporosis. Charles, my older friend who lives with PMR, not only suffers from chronic, intense pain, but he also has bones that are so weakened that he could sustain a fracture just by turning over in bed. What is his mental state? "[His] heart is glad and [his] tongue rejoices; [his] body also will live in hope" (Acts 2:26). How is he fulfilling God's purpose for his life? Just recently, he returned to full-time missionary service where he played a role in the release of two missionaries held captive by the Taliban in Afghanistan and led a ninety-five-year-old woman to Christ.

If we are to avoid preventable disease and minimize disability in our aging bodies, we must maximize our physical and mental fitness and remain true to our spiritual mission by believing God's grace and promises. "I have told you these things, so that in me you may have peace. In this world you will have trouble. But take heart! I have overcome the world" (Jn 16:33). The role of faith in our lives opens up a new dimension to the aging process. It enables us, enriches us and empowers us to live beyond what we, alone, could achieve. "May God not find the whine in us any more, but may He find us full of spiritual pluck and athleticism, ready to face anything He brings. . . . God never has museums."[39]

When one thinks of elders, one should not think of frail, dependent people. On the contrary, the hope of our nation and perhaps of the world rests on the shoulders of those who comprise the aging church. The most frail and physically dependent person may also be the most

---

[39]Oswald Chambers, *My Utmost for His Highest* (New York: Dodd, Mead, 1935), p. 136.

ardent prayer warrior or the most wise or courageous member of a congregation. Legions of seniors in churches nationwide can lead the way to a spiritual transformation of America and even the world. Elders can leave us a multitude of legacies, including how to live sacrificially, how to appreciate traditions that teach us to value history, how to treasure the moment, how to confront our materialistic tendencies, how to value life from the womb to the grave, how to maintain a robust health and intellect for as long as possible, how to live successfully with and learn from chaos and difficulty, how to live courageously, how to persevere, how to express faith in love, how to genuinely worship, how to live on a budget, how to forgive, how to live in unity with other Christians, how to share one's faith, and how to glorify and enjoy Christ now and forever.[40]

---

[40]Appendix B provides questions that might help pastors and lay leaders to assess their ministry *to* and *from* older persons.

# 12

## CAREGIVING

### The Twenty-First Century's
### Greatest Test of Character

. . .

When Jesus saw his mother there, and the disciple whom he loved standing nearby, he said to his mother, 'Dear woman, here is your son,' and to the disciple, 'Here is your mother.' From that time on, this disciple took her into his home" (Jn 19:26-27). Though Jesus' long-term care plan for his mother might seem like a last-minute one, it was of course divine in nature. He knew who was best suited to care for his mother. When we consider the suffering Jesus was experiencing at the time, his command serves as a stark reminder of the importance he placed on the fifth commandment. Though we are not encouraging people of faith to get Ph.D.s in caregiving, we are saying that, in most cases, caregiving requires considerable preparation, because people are living much longer with a variety of health challenges.

The twenty-first century will see elder caregiving as the single most important human resource issue in the church and the workplace.[1] Na-

---

[1]D. Caruso and C. Bonney, "Productivity for Caregivers Who Take Time from Their Work Responsibilities," *Mature Market News*, July 11, 2006, pp. 1-2; M. W. Parker and J. Houston, "A Theology of Dementia and Life Review," paper presented at the Southeast Regional Alzheimer's Dementias' Conference, Hope: Prevention, Care and Cure, University of Alabama, Tuscaloosa, Ala., August 25, 2010; D. Myers, L. L. Roff, H. W. Harris, D. L. Klemmack and M. W. Parker, "A Feasibility Study of a Parent Care Planning Model with Two Faith-Based Communities," *Journal of Religion, Spirituality and Aging* 17, no. 1/2 (2004): 41-57; M. W. Parker et al., "Parent Care and Religion: A Faith-Based Intervention Model for Caregiving Readiness of Congregational Members," *Journal of Family Ministry* 17, no. 4 (2004): 51-69.

tional, state and local governmental programs will play a role in addressing this challenge, but even with their increased involvement, most communities are not equipped or prepared to help meet the growing need.[2] Most people spend less time planning the last season of their life than they do organizing their next two-week vacation. This is particularly true in the area of elder caregiving. Though elderly people rely on their families more than any other entity, aging adult children and their parents simply do not plan ahead. The church, with a few exceptions, has been relatively silent despite the fact that most churchgoers will be involved in elder care decisions at some point, and despite Jesus' obvious concern for the care of his mother even in the midst of excruciating circumstances.

Jesus' concern for mother's care reminds us to examine our own personal parent care plan. For reasons not fully understood, Jesus entrusted the care of his mother to John, one of his disciples, perhaps his closest friend and a member of his religious family. Though we are not privy to the factors behind Jesus' decision, we know that the admonition to "honor thy father and mother" existed within the Judaism of Jesus' day. Based on a Judeo-Christian model of family life (Ex 20:12), Jesus affirmed the importance of caring for parents by his own example on the cross and through his teachings on the subject (Mt 15:3-9; Mk 7:9-13). The apostle Paul restated the fifth commandment (Deut 5:16) and emphasized the importance of parental caregiving and the benefits that accrue to those who fulfill parental responsibilities (Eph 6:1-3; 1 Tim 5:1-4).

Despite the consistency of these instructions, most churches do not provide practical parent care guidance to adult children and their older family members.[3] In part, this reflects the general paucity of applied gerontological research and training with faith-based communities in the area of parent care or late life planning. For these and other reasons, conscientious professional and lay religious leaders have increasingly

---

[2]MetLife Foundation, "The Maturing of America: Getting Communities on Track for an Aging Population," 2001, www.n4a.org/pdf/MOAFinalReport.pdf.

[3]H. Holstege and R. Riekse, eds., *Focus on the Family's Complete Guide to Caring for Aging Loved Ones* (Wheaton, Ill.: Tyndale House, 2002).

found themselves largely unprepared to address the growing needs of older persons in their faith communities and their families.[4]

Communities of faith are, however, in excellent positions to help American families plan for the care of their older members. In fact, Americans are more likely to rely on their own faith and on advice from their clergy in addressing family problems than they are to rely on social service or other community agencies. This trust and faith in clergy are particularly true for underserved groups.[5] Further, research evidence also demonstrates the strong positive association between faith, religious attendance and good health, particularly in the later years.[6] This chapter cannot describe the entire parent care readiness program that is available for church communities, but it does provide resources and a description of a workable model. Leaders in communities of faith can use this conceptual model to help develop comprehensive parent care training programs for their own congregations. The model below presents an empirically tested, community-based framework that uses a faith-sensitive, ecumenical approach for parent care training.[7] Above all, it aims at improving the well-being of older persons. This chapter also adapts (for faith-based communities) an evidence-based, parent care intervention program informed by prior research.[8] Ultimately, I (Dr. Parker) hope this can, for churches, provide effective preparation for families who will face the developmental task and religious duty of "honoring mother and father."

---

[4]M. Parker, "Building Partnerships with African American and White Churches to Promote a Good Old Age for All," *Generations* (summer 2008): 38-40.

[5]R. S. Jackson and B. Reddick, "The African American Church and University Partnerships: Establishing Lasting Collaborations," *Health Education & Behavior* 26, no. 5 (1999): 663-75; E. J. Jackson and C. P. Parks, "Recruitment and Training Issues from Selected Lay Health Advisor Programs Among African Americans: A 20-Year Perspective," *Health Education & Behavior* 24, no. 4 (1997): 418-32.

[6]H. G. Koenig. *The Healing Power of Faith* (New York: Simon & Schuster, 1999); W. L. Larimore, introduction to *Focus on the Family's Complete Guide*, pp. v-vii.

[7]M. W. Parker, J. Bellis, M. Harper, P. Bishop, C. Moore, P. Thompson and R. A. Allman, "A Multidisciplinary Model of Health Promotion Incorporating Spirituality into a Successful Aging Intervention with African American and White Elderly Groups," *The Gerontologist* 42 (2002): 406-15.

[8]The research was sponsored by the Hartford Foundation and the Gerontological Society of America at the U.S. Air War College. M. Parker and J. Martin, "Introduction to Special Edition," *Geriatric Care Management* 13, no. 1 (2003): 1-2.

## An Overview of Parent Care in the United States

The care of the elderly in the United States is largely a family affair. Among older people in U.S. communities, less than 10 percent receive formal help, but nearly 80 percent receive care solely from family, friends and neighbors. The availability of informal help can determine whether older people remain in their homes. On average, family caregivers provide care for more than twenty hours a week and for more than four years, with over a third providing care for five years or more. Increases in life expectancy particularly the oldest old (ages 85+), growth in female labor-force participation, increases in blended families, decreases in fertility rates, expansion of family mobility and geographic separation and development of more diverse, multigenerational family structures affect the capacity of families, including those in communities of faith, to care for older family members.[9] Reviews of related research on family caregiving suggest that both proximate and long distance care providers are not prepared for typical care needs their family members and close friends will have as they age.[10] Instead, many individuals at midlife find themselves reacting to health care crises of their elderly family members.

Caregiving roles have increased in importance as the population has aged and as older persons who live at home and in other community settings require assistance because of functional limitations associated with chronic disease and disability.[11] These demographic imperatives are having a dramatic impact on family, organizational and congregational life in the United States. Family caregivers experience adverse

---

[9]P. Dilworth-Anderson, S. W. Williams and T. Cooper, "Family Caregiving to Elderly African Americans: Caregiver Types and Structures," *Journal of Gerontology: Social Sciences* 54B (1999): 237-41; C. V. Baldock, "Migrants and Their Parents: Caregiving from a Distance," *Journal of Family Issues* 21, no. 2 (2000): 205-24.

[10]Parker and Martin, "Introduction"; M. W. Parker, V. R. Call, R. Dunkle and M. Vaitkus, "'Out of Sight' but Not 'Out of Mind': Parent Care Contact and Worry Among Military Officers Who Live Long Distances from Parents," *Military Psychology* 14, no. 4 (2002): 257-77.

[11]S. Pandya and B. Coleman, "Caregiving and Long-Term Care: Fact Sheet #82," (Washington, D.C.: Public Policy Institute, 2000); R. Toseland, G. Smith and P. McCallion, "Helping Family Caregivers, " in *Handbook of Social Work Practice with Vulnerable and Resilient Populations*, 2nd ed., ed. A. Gitterman, (New York: Columbia University Press, 2001), pp. 548-81; M. W. Parker, P. Baker and R. Allman, "A Life Space Approach to the Functional Assessment of the Elderly," *The Journal of Gerontological Social Work* 35, no. 4 (2002): 35-55.

physical, mental and financial burdens. Women continue to provide
most of the care, and many experience the tension of being "in the
middle," juggling multiple roles. Elder care giving should be more and
more an intergenerational undertaking, and the church can help promote the necessity of sharing this predictable role by providing workshops and caregiver support programs that cut across denominations.

Though employers and service organizations are increasingly aware
of the potentially adverse impact of parent care on productivity, most
churches and denominations remain taciturn on the topic.[12] The national economic value of informal family caregiving has been estimated
at almost $400 billion per year, approximately 18 percent of the total
national health care spending in the United States.[13] Although the
costs of caregiving to religious organizations have not been studied
(e.g., inability of members to donate time and money because of caregiver responsibilities), parent care is costly to employers and employees.
One national study has estimated the costs of replacing employees, ab-
senteeism, workday interruptions, eldercare crises and supervisors' time
at $1,142 per employee, and the annual, aggregate cost to U.S. business
of decreased productivity of employees with caregiving responsibilities
at $11.2 billion.[14]

Reviews of caregiving intervention studies indicate that participation in individual and group intervention programs with caregivers and
the use of day care and other community resources for care recipients
can be effective in supporting family caregivers' efforts to maintain
cognitively and physically impaired older persons in community settings.[15] In fact, recent studies indicate that caregiver support programs

[12]National Alliance for Caregiving, *The 1997 National Alliance for Caregiving/AARP National
Caregivers Survey* (Bethesda, Md.: National Alliance for Caregiving, 1997); M. Neal,
M. Chapman, B. Ingersoll-Dayton and A. Emler, *Balancing Work and Care Giving for Chil-
dren, Adults, and Elders* (London: Sage, 1993).

[13]P. Arno, C. Levine and M. Memmott, "The Economic Value of Informal Caregiving," *Health
Affairs* 18, no. 2 (1999): 182-88.

[14]Metropolitan Life Insurance Company, *The MetLife Juggling Act Study: Balancing Caregiving
with Work and the Costs Involved* (Westport, Conn.: n.p., 1998).

[15]Although numerous books, journal articles and Internet sites are available to assist those faced
with filial responsibilities, the effects and potential benefits of these informational sources
have not been thoroughly investigated. M. W. Parker, L. Roff, R. Toseland and D. Klemmack,
"The Hartford Military Parent Care Project: A Psycho-Social Educational Intervention with

can delay nursing home placement and reduce health care costs for care recipients.[16] The reported change in only some variables reinforces the conclusions of many review studies over the last fifteen years: while such programs mainly benefit the recipients of care, caregiver support groups also tend to have a mild impact on caregivers themselves.[17] While caregivers generally report high satisfaction with and subjective benefit from interventions, most research projects found that caregiver support groups had small to moderate effects on caregivers' general well-being, burden and depression.[18]

Preliminary findings from research with one of the largest employers of persons who live great distances from their parents, the U.S. military, has suggested that a lack of preparedness for parent care has placed senior ranking military members at higher risk for vocational, family and health-related problems.[19] This research lends robust, quantitative support to previous qualitative findings by concerning long dis-

---

Long Distance Parent Care Providers," poster session presented at First National Gerontological Social Work Conference, held in conjunction with Council Social Work Education Annual Conference, Atlanta, Ga., March 2003; R. Schulz, *Handbook on Dementia Caregiving, Evidence-Based Interventions for Family Caregivers* (New York: Springer, 2000); S. H. Zarit, J. E. Gaugler and S. E. Jarrott, "Useful Services for Families: Research Finding and Direction," *International Journal of Geriatric Psychiatry* 14 (1999): 165-81.

[16]See, for example, H. Brodaty and K. Peters, "Cost Effectiveness of a Training Program for Dementia Caregivers," *International Psychogeriatrics* 3, no. 1 (1991): 11-23; T. Peak, R. W. Toseland and S. M. Banks, "Impact of a Spouse-Caregiver Support Group on Care Recipient Health Care Costs," *Journal of Aging and Health* 7, no. 3 (1995): 427-49.

[17]D. W. Coon, D. Gallagher-Thompson and L. W. Thompson, *Innovative Interventions to Reduce Dementia Caregiver Distress: A Clinical Guide* (New York: Springer Publishing, 2003); J. Kennet, L. Burgio and R. Schulz, "Interventions for In-home Caregivers: A Review of the Research 1990 to Present," in *Handbook on Dementia Caregiving, Evidence-Based Interventions for Caregivers,* ed. R. Schulz (New York: Springer Publishing, 2000), pp. 61-125; P. McCallion and R. Toseland, "Supportive Group Interventions with Caregivers of Frail Older Adults," *Social Work with Groups* 18, no. 1 (1995): 11-25; S. Zarit and L. Teri, "Interventions and Services for Family Caregivers," in *Annual Review of Gerontology and Geriatrics,* ed. K. W. Schaie (New York: Springer Publishing, 1991), 2:241-65.

[18]M. Bourgeois, R. Schulz and L. Burgio, "Interventions for Caregivers of Patients with Alzheimer's Disease: A Review and Analysis of Content, Process, and Outcomes," *International Journal of Aging-Human Behavior* 43, no. 1 (1996): 35-92.

[19]M. W. Parker, V. R. Call, R. Dunkle and M. Vaitkus, "'Out of Sight' but Not 'Out of Mind': Parent Care Contact and Worry Among Military Officers Who Live Long Distances from Parents," *Military Psychology* 14, no. 4 (2002): 257-77. Two hundred twenty-seven military officers were surveyed in this study. For the officers surveyed, their satisfaction with the "parent-care plan" (PCP) they had devised was inversely related to their level of worry, even when a variety of other variables were introduced into a structural equation model.

tance caregiving,[20] and it further indicates that officers' satisfaction with a realistic PCP reduces their worry about their parents and further indicates that realistic parent care plans can go a long way in easing the worry adult children experience over the care of their elderly parents.

This finding in particular underscores how important it is for parents to make and discuss future plans with their children. According to preliminary research, only 8 to 17 percent of the population actively plans for their end-of-life care by talking with their children about their wishes and completing an advance directive.[21] Worries about being a burden on their children and difficulty coping with the unknowns of dying or end-of-life care cause many parents to avoid making plans or having discussions of plans with children. Further, contemplating the loss of a parent is traumatic for most children (even adult ones), and initiating a discussion about a parent's end-of-life plans is difficult, more so if a parent insists that no plans are needed.

When the family lacks a sense of what the content of a plan should include or parent-child relationship problems exist (or both), adult children often encounter resistance from their aging parents if they try to develop a plan with them. Moreover, many adult children lack the motivation to participate in parent care training when their parents are healthy.[22] Unfortunately most of the tasks associated with the proactive development of a parent care plan are best completed when the parents are able to participate fully in the process.[23] Some parent care tasks legally require the parents' full understanding, participation and sanction.[24] A tested parent care planning process, if effectively presented, provides adult children with an opportunity to engage parents in this seemingly awkward yet critical topic. The process elicits the parents' wishes and desires about medical, legal, environmental and emotional preferences

---

[20]J. Climo, *Distant Parents* (New Brunswick, N.J.: Rutgers University Press, 1992).
[21]J. Anthony, "Your Aging Parents: Document Their Wishes," *American Health*, May 1995, pp. 58-61, 109; A. M. Cugliari, T. Miller and J. Sobal, "The Cardiopulmonary Resuscitation-Not-Indicated Order: Futility Revisited," *Archives of Internal Medicine* 155 (1995): 1893-98.
[22]Parker, "Preparing for Parent Care."
[23]Larimore, introduction to *Focus on the Family*, pp. v-vii.
[24]L. Campisi, M. Parker, D. Marson, S. Cook and F. Moore, "Legal-Insurance-Financial Tasks Associated with Parent Care in Military Families," *Geriatric Care Management* 13, no. 1 (2003): 8-14.

before the insidious and/or rapid onset of diseases and disabilities that often render parents unable to represent themselves. Adult children and their parents need encouragement and assistance in becoming more intentional in the creation of this individualized family planning guide.

## The Potential Role of Faith Communities in Elder Care

Clergy and other pastoral professionals are uniquely qualified to reinforce the importance of proactive parent care preparation. Like ministers who have been on the forefront of advocacy for premarital counseling, religious leaders can employ their moral authority and utilize religious teachings to underscore the need and methods for families to prepare for the normal, developmental responsibility of parent care. Adult children, spouses and other family and non-family caregivers involved in faith-based communities can play key roles in maintaining the health and independence of older persons. Religious leaders need adequate training and access to proven resources and methods in order to develop and promote exemplary programs that address these issues.

Though it is impossible to prepare fully for the consequences of unforeseen events (e.g., acts of terrorism like the events of 9/11), military families have already taken steps through intergenerational family care plans to reduce the long-term consequences of these and other traumas on their families. In like manner, religious leaders can help their congregations to be more prepared for the unpredictable (acts of terrorism, auto accidents, health crises, power outages during extreme weather changes) by being more prepared for the predictable, important challenges of life, like parent care.

The unifying framework described below and the theoretical basis for the intervention, coupled with the demographic imperative for faith-based parent care interventions, marks a needed reversal in the trend towards separation of spirituality, organized religion, non-faith-based institutions, academia and health care professionals that has occurred over the past several years. As we move from a three-generational to a four-generational family structure, our fastest growing age group has become the "oldest old" (85 and older). Lower percentages of our population are working and contributing to social security and other entitlement programs, which makes even less likely our government will come to the rescue in parental caring. Caring for an elderly family member often hits dramatically at midlife, when caregivers are typically employed and at the top of their careers. The primary caregivers of our aging parents in the past were stay-at-home daughters, who have since entered the full-time workforce. As parents live longer, the working "woman in the middle" and a growing number of employed sons are feeling the pinch associated with the increasing demands of family and work. All the while, our nuclear families have grown smaller, so there are fewer caregivers available to help. Researchers are confirming that the primary caregivers of today are more isolated and unprepared than ten years ago. Despite these trends, the upward spiraling costs of long-term care, and the increasing financial incapacities of older people to meet them, the American family remains at the core of caring for aging parents.[25]

Despite their membership in a local church, many caregivers fly solo as the primary caregiver. At the most basic level, we encourage the family and the church to be involved, and we encourage the development of professional relationships that might enhance the quality of care provided, "to make ready" the family caregivers of today—most of whom already love their parents more than any professional could. We recognize that if we over professionalize the care provided to older loved ones, we could undermine our nation's greatest strength in facing these challenges—the loving convoys of prepared families and congregations. Our research with congregations indicates pastors and lay leaders are already concerned about how to meet the needs of their aging congregations, while late-life diseases like Alzheimer's disease and multiple chronic morbidities are challenging the fabric of how health care is provided. Legal and financial complexities associated with increased longevity are affecting the economic stability of our families, congregations, communities and the nation. Even the capacity of our military to fulfill its mission is affected when our most experience and seasoned personnel are

---

[25]M. W. Parker et al., "Parent Care and Religion: A Faith-Based Intervention Model for Caregiving Readiness of Congregational Members," *Journal of Family Ministry* 17, no. 4 (2004): 51-69.

troubled about their service to country when it conflicts with their notions of honoring their aging parents, which is more complicated when care is provided from a distance.[26] We have developed a program that has had some initial success with civilian and military congregations.[27] Our interdisciplinary team of professionals has developed a parent-care educational program that includes an assessment and tailored intervention program that takes into consideration factors like information overload, the work demands of employed caregivers and the complexities of the long-term care system. Our model of caregiving is aimed at applying twenty-first century information and service technologies in preparing families to honor their mothers and fathers (or other relatives) in late life with intelligent and loving care. In addition, improved caregiving readiness will allow members of faith-based organizations to remain productively employed or engaged in volunteer services and activities, while the effects of their parent care plan will result in a higher quality of life for their older loved ones.

## Parent Care Intervention Program

The following parent care intervention program is based in part on a military parent-care program aimed at increasing officers' readiness to care for parents.[28]

---

[26]M. W. Parker, V. R. Call, R. Dunkle and M. Vaitkus, "'Out of Sight' but Not 'Out of Mind': Parent Care Contact and Worry Among Military Officers Who Live Long Distances from Parents," *Military Psychology* 14, no. 4 (2002): 257-77.

[27]D. Myers, L. L. Roff, H. W. Harris, D. L. Klemmack and M. W. Parker, "A Feasibility Study of a Parent Care Planning Model with Two Faith-Based Communitites," *Journal of Religion, Spirituality and Aging* 17, no. 1/2 (2004): 41-57; M. W. Parker and J. Martin, "Introduction to Special Edition," *Geriatric Care Management* 13, no. 1 (2003): 1-2; J. Martin and M. W. Parker, "Understanding the Importance of Elder Care Preparations in the Context of 21st Century Military Service," *Geriatric Care Management* 13, no. 1 (2003): 3-7; M. Crowther, P. Baker, W. Larimore, H. Koenig and M. W. Parker, "Military Families: Spiritual and Emotional Tasks Associated with Elder Care," *Geriatric Care Management* 13, no. 1 (2003): 15-22; L. Campisi, M. W. Parker, D. Marson, S. Cook and F. Moore, "Legal-Insurance-Financial Tasks Associated with Parent Care in Military Families," *Geriatric Care Management* 13, no. 1 (2003): 8-14; L. Roff, R. Toseland, J. Martin, C. Fine and M. W. Parker, "Family-Social Tasks in Long Distance Caregiving with Military Families," *Geriatric Care Management* 13, no. 1 (2003): 23-29; G. Fuller, P. Baker, W. Larimore, R. Allman and M. W. Parker, "Helping Military Families Establish a Medical Care Plan for an Elderly Parent," *Geriatric Care Management* 13, no. 1 (2003): 16-22.

[28]Parker and Martin, "Introduction," pp. 1-2.

All military personnel with dependent family members are required to complete, prior to deployment, a family care plan that makes provision for the medical, legal and spiritual welfare of surviving family members if the service member—soldier, sailor, airman or Marine— does not return. I (Dr. Parker) served as the lead author in the program, and I have advocated before Congress that the traditional composition of the military family care plan must be expanded to include provision for the aging parents of military personnel. The family care plan that the U.S. military uses to assist surviving family members is being modified in clinical studies to include older and disabled loved ones.[29] Leaders from faith-based communities can benefit from lessons now being learned from military families as they strive to help their members develop a family care plan that includes older loved ones.

Under the sponsorship of the John A. Hartford Foundation and The Gerontological Society of American, I (Dr. Parker) and my interdisciplinary team developed tools to help military officers and their parents complete a parent care plan.[30] The purpose of the study was to test the efficacy of the assessment, the workshop and educational materials in helping adult children complete specific parent care tasks and thereby improve their readiness to meet current and future parent care responsibilities. A Parent Care Readiness Assessment (PCRA) instrument was developed to determine the degree of preparedness of military personnel. Preliminary results from ongoing field trials suggest that those who participated in the workshop and received the support materials completed more parent care tasks and exhibited higher levels of parent care confidence than the control group. Earlier research found that military families with an elder-care plan had less stress and anxiety than those without a plan.

Communities of faith have successfully adapted the parent-care-intervention program for congregational families to make conscious, informed choices related to the completion of specific and critically important parent care tasks. Though the program is currently being

---

[29]M. Parker, "Commendation for Research and Service," *U.S. Congressional Record* 148, no. 135 (October 15, 2002): E1872-73.
[30]Ibid.

automated for a website (some of the content of the program has been placed in appendix C), it is intended to connect leaders in communities of faith and families with resources and information related to parent care. The tasks of parent care are organized into four domains or categories: medical, legal-insurance-financial, family-social and spiritual-emotional.[31] Each domain reflects a set of real life challenges (or specific parent care tasks) that potentially comprise an important aspect of a parent's care plan. Time management and problem-solving strategies recommend that complex challenges be broken down into essential elements so that realistic progress can be made and so that the person completing the tasks is not overwhelmed with the breadth of the job.[32] This model underscores the importance of assessment in all four domains and the necessity of a tailored intervention strategy that provides assistance in completing the high priority tasks. The tailoring process minimizes the overwhelming "smorgasbord" approach because only information and resources appropriate for the task at hand are provided. The primary focus of the intervention is the completion of highest priority tasks in a timely manner. In this context, timely professional consultation adds additional precision to the assessment and intervention process. This process accentuates the preferences of mother and father because the goal is preparation and readiness. Further, the model is best understood as an ongoing process that involves reassessment of completed and uncompleted tasks as the functional and health status of the elder changes.

We have provided a detailed list of the caregiving tasks for each of the four domains (medical, legal-financial, emotional-spiritual and familial) in appendix C, and we have provided some web links for each task by domain. In addition, we recommend the following three organizations for locating information about local agencies: Area Agency on Aging, <www.aaa1b.com>, or call 1-800-852-7795; Department of Human Services, <www.eldercare.gov>; or Administration on Aging,

---

[31]M. Crowther, P. Baker, W. Larimore, H. Koenig and M. Parker, "Military Families: Spiritual and Emotional Tasks Associated with Elder Care," *Geriatric Care Management* 13, no. 1 (2003): 15-22; Roff et al., "Family-Social Tasks," p. 2.
[32]Parker and Martin, "Introduction," p. 2.

<www.AOA.gov>, or call 1-800-677-1116.

Before closing out this chapter, we want to briefly review the results from a feasibility study of our model with participants from two church communities. Members of Protestant congregations in Alabama and Texas attended a parent-readiness workshop, where they completed a structured Parent Care Assessment. Following completion, they were given information on how to complete salient tasks through lectures provided by local gerontologists and geriatricians, and through access to a list of resources like the one provided in appendix C. At the Texas site, adult children and aging parents participated together. The parents thought differently about the importance of the tasks, but by participating jointly, communication gaps were closed and planning was possible. The finding from these two studies highlight the significance of developing an educational approach to parent care that is closely tailored to the specific needs of each family. The Parent Care Readiness Program model offers a comprehensive map for developing an effective ministry innovation to congregational leaders who want to strengthen the family in later life and promote care readiness. It integrates spirituality and faith practice into the caregiving process, because the program is built on the fifth commandment. Use of this program legitimized the promotion of conversations and mutual planning between parents and their adult children. The outcomes from these two studies, employing the Parent Care Readiness Program demonstrated that congregations can be powerful venues for enabling adult children and older parents to honor one another through an intentional ministry of care preparedness.[33] Our more recent research confirms that faith-based organizations can provide computer access and computer training as an incentive to participate in the program.[34]

---

[33]Parker and Martin, "Introduction," pp. 1-2.

[34]D. Myers, L. L. Roff, H. W. Harris, D. L. Klemmack and M. W. Parker, "A Feasibility Study of a Parent Care Planning Model with Two Faith-Based Communities," *Journal of Religion, Spirituality and Aging* 17, no. 1/2 (2004): 41-57.

# 13

## LOCAL SENIOR MINISTRY
## ASSOCIATIONS AND ECUMENICAL
## PARTNERSHIPS

### • • •

Despite religious edicts and demographic realities that accentuate the need for faith-based initiatives to deal with a rapidly aging population, communities of faith have not responded up to their tremendous potential. In general, the professional communities (scientific and practice) have not had access to congregations, and this lack of collaboration has continued because unifying frameworks in successful aging and caregiving have not incorporated spirituality into their evidence-based models of intervention.[1] We have found senior ministry associations to be invaluable in overcoming these obstacles. In the past, we have linked our work with denominations and national ministries like the Christian Association Serving Adults (www.gocasa.org), which seek to build networks of pastors and other age fifty-plus ministry leaders in churches and parachurch organizations.

Senior ministry associations are ecumenical organizations with three primary goals: to challenge seniors to God-inspired ministry and leadership; to support and encourage individual church "ministers" to the elderly and their caregivers in local churches; and to foster church-

---

[1]M. W. Parker, "Building Partnerships with African American and White Churches to Promote a Good Old Age for All," *Generations,* summer 2008, pp. 38-42; W. L. Larimore, M. W. Parker and M. Crowther, "Should Clinicians Incorporate Positive Spirituality into Their Practices?" *Annals of Behavioral Medicine* 24, no. 1 (2002): 69-73; M. Crowther, M. W. Parker, H. Koenig, W. Larimore and A. Achenbaum, "Rowe and Kahn's Model of Successful Aging Revisited: Spirituality, the Forgotten Factor," *The Gerontologist* 42, no. 5 (2002): 613-20.

medical partnerships that help seniors age successfully God's way. To start a senior ministry association, we recommend that a large, respected church host an initial luncheon for discussing the possibilities with other local professionals, clergy and lay leaders. Invitations should be as diverse and inclusive as possible.

Over the past twelve years, I (Dr. Parker) and an interdisciplinary team have successfully conducted over twenty community-based interventions in five different communities, targeting local congregations, older persons and their caregivers. Dr. Houston was strategically involved in the most recent program on the topic of dementia. All of the interventions, ranging from successful aging conferences with large audiences to smaller, parent-care training programs, have been organized and supported by local congregations and scientific communities.[2]

As a result, much of what is known about how people age successfully is not being applied effectively by scientific and religious institutions. The following "town and gown" model for organizing community-based, senior ministry associations uses a paradigm that relies primarily on the collaborative synergy that can be harnessed between academic institutions and congregations.

Churches are often untapped resources to help our growing population of older adults to age well. The Alabama town and gown model for organizing community-based, senior ministry associations relies primarily on the collaborative synergy that can be harnessed between academic institutions and congregations. As noted in the preface, our team consists of Christian professionals in nursing, law, geriatric medicine,

---

[2]D. Myers, L. L. Roff, H. W. Harris, D. L. Klemmack and M. W. Parker, "A Feasibility Study of a Parent Care Planning Model with Two Faith-Based Communities," *Journal of Religion, Spirituality and Aging* 17, no. 1/2 (2004): 41-57; Parker, "Building Partnerships," pp. 38-40; M. W. Parker, J. Bellis, M. Harper, P. Bishop, C. Moore, P. Thompson and R. A. Allman, "Multidisciplinary Model of Health Promotion Incorporating Spirituality into a Successful Aging Intervention with African American and White Elderly," *The Gerontologist* 42, no. 3 (2002): 405-15; M. W. Parker, L. Dunn, J. Goetz, S. Ousley, M. Rogers, M. Piper, R. Harrell, H. Lee, N. S. Park, S. MacCall, J. Williams, C. Spencer and X. Li, "Helping to Unite an Aging Southern Community: An Internet Directory Project and Telephone Survey of Location Congregations," *Journal of Community-Based Partnerships* (forthcoming); L. Dunn, M. W. Parker, D. Li, M. Piper, R. Harrell, H. Lee, N. S. Park, S. MacCall, S. Martin, J. Williams and C. Spencer, "Building Sustainable Community Parnerships to Promote Successful Aging: A Preliminary Study of Local Congregations and Agencies," *Journal of Community-Based Partnerships* (forthcoming).

neurology, psychiatry, kinesiology, psychology, social work, primary care, internal medicine, neuropathology, theology and other disciplines who have remained committed to discovering solutions for translating systematically what we know scientifically and professionally to our target group: older persons and their caregivers. Throughout this chapter, *we* and *our* refers to this team of researchers with whom I had the privilege of conducting studies, running programs and analyzing research.

We discovered the possibilities for these types of collaborations with the help of elderly mentors in African American churches in the south. These underserved elderly helped us to face the challenges of developing religious-academic partnerships: religious bases of community power that blocked ecumenical work; pejorative thinking among academics about organized religion; resistance to town and gown collaborations; and institutional racism and ageism. As we experienced their love and forgiveness, we began to see the staggering needs and possibilities through their eyes for all older people, and they have served as living examples of how added years are a basis of hope and not despair.

We believe that partnerships between the church and academia, grounded in human relationships at a community level, can help to answer the demands and challenges of prolonged life. We further believe that something good can come out of the "buckle of the Bible Belt" and out of congregations across the world today. Religious Alabama's remaining glaring hypocrisies are prime opportunities for experiencing the transforming leadership our elders can provide.[3]

Our model involves developing sustainable community-wide organizations which serve as the focal point for healthy aging conferences, senior volunteer activities, cooperative ventures to protect seniors from natural disasters, gerontological libraries of health and a variety of church-based programs linked to research that promote evidence-based practices (e.g., falls prevention, proactive eldercare planning, drivers as-

---

[3]Alabama has some of the nation's highest rates of chronic disease and disability, high levels of congregational membership among seniors, and two academic centers of aging that offer a sufficient density of interdisciplinary researchers willing to partner with the church.

sessment, caregiver support services).[4] The overall goal of our community based model has been to promote ongoing partnerships that advance the status, purpose and health of older persons by promoting successful aging practices and by encouraging older members of faith-based communities to volunteer and to pursue positions of community leadership as an outgrowth of their faith.

Senior ministry associations consisting of local area churches representing all denominations and races should pursue partnerships with one another and with researchers to host specific initiatives that help elders to avoid disease and disability, maximize cognitive and physical fitness, remain actively engaged in life through volunteerism and continue to learn and grow spiritually. The process can begin with something as simple as an invitation to lunch from one church leader to other church and community leaders and interested academics.

## Our Model

- utilizes an interdisciplinary, multi-institutional collaborative synergy (religious congregations, academic institutions and local, state and federal programs)

- targets a specific population (seniors and their adult children) for services

- encourages research and the evaluation of interventions

- affirms sequelae of sustainability that includes local nonprofit governance, accountability and financial partnership with academic researchers and churches across denominational lines

In addition, our model promotes a planning-organizational process that

- maintains an equitable distribution of leadership positions across all racial/ethnic and denominational groups

- identifies academics and practitioners who are willing to serve as

---

[4]M. W. Parker, "Building Partnerships," pp. 38-42; Myers et al., "A Feasibility Study of a Parent Care Planning Model," pp. 41-57; M. W. Parker et al., "Parent Care and Religion: A Faith-Based Intervention Model for Caregiving Readiness of Congregational Members," *Journal of Family Ministry* 17, no. 4 (2004): 51-69.

experts in developing programs for seniors that address gaps in service

- adheres to the broad goals of Healthy People 2010, a program managed by the U.S. Department of Health and Human Services (www. healthypeople.gov)

- offers programs to recipients without a faith-based test

Recent efforts to organize senior summit discussion groups following conferences with faith-based communities have attempted to underscore the importance of being sensitive to what seniors want. In a recent conference held in a large city (250,000+), the participation rates were relatively small compared to a similar conference in a much smaller community (90,000). The attendance rate among seniors in the smaller community was approximately six times greater than that in the larger city. Some of the differences in attendance appear to be related to thinking about seniors as a uniform demographic and allowing a diverse group of seniors the right to self determination through enhanced leadership roles in planning activities. Also, the absence of an ongoing senior ministry association consisting of Protestant and Catholic congregations in the larger city many have negatively affected the turn-out rate. Those involved in planning senior summits and conferences report that older people in congregations have a difficult time admitting their difficulties and struggles to the clergy and lay leaders (e.g., finances, transportation, health issues, loneliness), and many seniors are skeptical of "free" services, like the broad ranging programs available through many area agencies on aging in the United States. Our work suggests that many seniors think about federal and state programs as "welfare." Respite services for caregivers was identified as a major need, along with more affordable day care for seniors experiencing dementia and functional limitations. Jewish and Islamic leaders have reported a sense of isolation from Christian faith-based conversations, so local senior ministry associations need to discuss the level of partnership with other world religions. In my (Dr. Parker's) work, no faith-based test or financial charge was a condition of attendance at conferences. Instead, the faith-based communities underwrote the conference and insured that it was Christ-centered. They provided transportation and made certain that major ethnic groups were represented. At conferences, booths were provided for a charge to local agencies, and agency representatives were often scheduled as speakers.[5]

This model was put into action, for example, when the senior ministry association in Tuscaloosa, Alabama, sponsored and coordinated a conference where lifestyle changes and individual and corporate forms of spirituality were affirmed using an expanded Rowe and Kahn model of successful aging that includes spirituality.[6] Faculty from academic, medical, government and religious institutions presented a variety of workshops at a multi-church sponsored conference that hosted over six hundred older people. Post-conference surveys indicated extremely high levels of satisfaction across all groups represented, and approximately 90 percent of conference participants made commitments to change unhealthy lifestyles. The African American religious community provided critical leadership in achieving excellent African American participation rates.

In implementing this Alabama town and gown model of community-wide senior ministry activities, we encountered a number challenges to university-community relationship building. Also, because Christians tend to worship in predominantly white or predominantly black churches in Southern communities, we had to develop trust among members of the two racial groups. However, town-gown and racial

---

[5]M. W. Parker, H. Koenig, J. Davis, N. Caldwell, J. Hataway and R. Allman, "A Multidisciplinary Model of Health Promotion Incorporating Spirituality into Successful Aging Interventions with African American and White Elderly," in *The Role of Faith-Based Organizations in the Social Welfare System* (Bethesda, Md.: Rockefeller Institute of Government and Independent Sector and the Roundtable on Religion and Social Welfare Policy, 2003), pp. 241-60; M. W. Parker, J. Bellis, M. Harper, P. Bishop, C. Moore, P. Thompson and R. A. Allman, "A Multidisciplinary Model of Health Promotion Incorporating Spirituality into a Successful Aging Intervention with African American and White Elderly," *The Gerontologist* 42, no. 3 (2002): 405-15.

[6]M. Crowther, P. Baker, W. Larimore, H. Koenig and M. Parker, "Military Families: Spiritual and Emotional Tasks Associated with Elder Care," *Geriatric Care Management* 13, no. 1 (2003): 15-22; M. Parker, H. Koenig, J. Davis, N. Caldwell, J. Hataway and R. Allman, "A Multidisciplinary Model of Health Promotion Incorporating Spirituality into Successful Aging Interventions with African American and White Elderly," paper presented at the meeting of the Rockefeller Institute of Government Conference on Faith-Based Initiatives, Bethesda, Md., March 6, 2003.

challenges were successfully overcome, due in large part to the efforts of African American pastors who modeled forgiveness and resiliency for the community at large.

Part of the appeal of our model is that it challenges churches to assist communities in working collaboratively across institutional and racial barriers. Our collaborative approach capitalizes on the common bonds of spiritual devotion and practice among different denominational groups and academic researchers. Our model has united cultural and denominational groups of elderly people by focusing on health and successful aging and by fostering inclusive and collaborative relationships among historically separate cultural and spiritual communities.

We are optimistic that the model we have begun to develop is transferable to other communities. Its appeal continues to grow nationally among leaders of academic institutions, religious denominations, communities, national lay volunteer programs, national religious organizations, urban and rural communities and state government prevention programs. At present, senior ministry associations based upon the Alabama model are being organized in cities located in Alabama, Louisiana, Texas, Kansas, Michigan and California.

The model summarized above is one proven approach with the potential to unite Christian seniors across racial and denominational lines.[7] Churches serve the Lord on a community-wide level by making available to seniors some of the most recent, effective aging strategies. The Alabama Town and Gown strategy involves the formation of partnerships across denomination lines with academic and governmental leaders to meet the needs of our older church members and to challenge them to significant living.

Models like this are just beginning to surface, which also means that a lot of hard data about how people age successfully is not being applied effectively by scientific and religious institutions. Using a similar model,

---

[7]M. Parker, "Building Partnerships," pp. 38-40; Parker et al., "Multidisciplinary Model of Health Promotion," pp. 405-15; Crowther et al., "Rowe and Kahn's Model of Successful Aging Revisited," pp. 613-20; published proceedings: *The Role of Faith-Based Organizations in the Social Welfare System* (Washington, D.C.: Independent Sector, 2003), pp. 241-60.

Krause argues that though African Americans are often distrustful of medical authorities, they are generally very trusting of their faith community.[8] Our work corroborates Krause's perspective that the faith-based community has a unique opportunity to make a difference in the physical, emotional and spiritual health of older African Americans, particularly when the congregation is perceived as cohesive, optimistic, and emotionally and spiritually supportive. With the vulnerable community of the book of Nehemiah as an inspiration, we began cultivating partnerships between state of science aging researchers and congregational leaders of all denominations with idea that older, successful aging persons can lead the way in "rebuilding the walls" of communities across America—one at a time, from Katrina-affected cities to rural, underserved communities. We found that many leading scientists in the field of aging are willing to provide their services (teaching at conferences, designing medical interventions) gratuitously motivated by their own faith in Christ. We contend that organized Christianity has a moral obligation to confront the common thinking that older persons are more of a burden than a gift and to assist clergy and lay leaders' in preparing their congregations for filial responsibilities in ways that reaffirm the value of all older persons irrespective of their health status. Finally, we maintain that our model can help restore intergenerational connections and help older people age more successfully.

In developing the relationships so necessary for the success of ecumenical—academic work, our team has found mentors in the African American and white churches of the South and in the professional community who have taught us the value of our personal faith and the power of prayer in overcoming obstacles like religious bias, pejorative thinking among academics about organized religion and institutional racism.

Just as Nehemiah challenged his congregation to "arise and build" (Neh 2:18 NASB) because "the God of heaven" would "give us success" (Neh 2:20), today's church is in a position to answer the demands and

---

[8]N. Krause, "Church-Based Social Support and Health in Old Age: Exploration Variations by Race," *Journal of Gerontology* 57B, no. 6 (November 2002): S332-47.

challenges associated with prolonged life. The entire book of Nehemiah is about how to rebuild and change a community and a nation. It begins with Nehemiah's confession and repentance (Neh 1), his prayer, God-dependent boldness in seeking assistance from powerful leaders (Neh 2), and his willingness to "do battle" (Neh 3–6) in order to rebuild a wall and a nation (Neh 6–12).

Several of our studies and initiatives faced similar challenges to the multiple voices of opposition to Nehemiah's work. From the heart of the deep South, we have heard it whispered, "What possible good can come out of 'sweet home' Alabama, where Sundays remain the most segregated day of the week?" We found that the right answer is, "Plenty good!"

Alabaman culture has many strong religious undertones, meaning that despite some visible problems, one does not have to look far for opportunities to join faith, race and community forces. Alabama hosts two academic centers of aging that contain a sufficient density of interdisciplinary researchers who are willing and able to partner with the church. One prime example of this partnership involves women of color in Alabama, who have one of our nation's highest rates of diabetes. Researchers from both centers helped plan and initiate a National Institute of Aging longitudinal study of approximately 1,000 community-dwelling Alabamians ages sixty-five and over. Among other findings, researchers learned that diabetic African American women have limited mobility. However, most manage to attend church with regularity, opening up the perfect scenario for establishing an effective faith-based intervention program for them. Similarly, using senior ministry associations, churches can partner with leading researchers to host specific initiatives that help elders avoid disease and disability, maximize cognitive and physical fitness, remain actively engaged in life (volunteerism) and continue to learn and grow spiritually.

Each of our interventions operates on the foundational principal that each senior, like a modern-day Nehemiah, wants and needs to be invited to participate fully in helping "rebuild the walls" of all that is good in their community, county, state or nation. While the underserved receive material benefit from state-of-science interventions, the rich and the educated are motivated as well to be actively involved because the information represents the latest research on topics of interest (how to live with arthritis). Planners and participating experts benefit largely through the lessons learned from sacrificial giving and translating what they know for the common good. In learning to give and receive, all benefit in the spiritual realm. Loving, selfless service provides the professional with an anti-narcissistic inoculation. Using senior ministry associations, senior volunteers can share lessons learned, helping to organize evacuation strategies for older persons living in hurricane prone communities; using retired teachers to assist high school dropouts; using gerontologists to develop church-based, computer gerontology centers in local churches; developing caregiving support groups; helping state of science and practice researchers to share information about brain health and driving; and developing aging-in-place community and congregational planning.

The appeal of this model continues to grow nationally among leaders of academic institutions, religious denominations, communities, national lay volunteer programs, national religious organizations, urban and rural communities, and state government prevention programs.[9] Just recently, I (Dr. Parker) have been approached by leaders in the academic and faith-based worlds in New York, Kansas and California to organize a national summit on the role of congregations in addressing the long-term care needs of Americans in their local communities. While responsiveness to special health needs and concerns of minority populations has its benefits, a result of the ensuing ethnically targeted

[9]M. W. Parker et al., "Evacuation of the Frail Elderly During Katrina: Lessons and Solutions," paper presented at Forensic Psychiatry Post Katrina Conference: Lessons Learned Post Disaster, New Orleans, March 5, 2007; M. W. Parker et al., University of Alabama Center for Community-Based Partnerships grant proposal, funded for 2008-2009, the Tuscaloosa Senior Ministry Association and graduate students with the University of Alabama's Center for Mental Health and Aging and the School of Social Work (2008). L. Roff et al., "Functional Limitations and Religious Service Attendance Among African American and White Elders," Health and Social Work 31, no. 4 (2006): 245-55. L. Roff et al., "Religiosity, Smoking, Exercise and Obesity Among Southern Community-Dwelling Older Adults," Journal of Applied Gerontology 24, no. 4 (2005), 337-54. L. Roff et al., "Spirituality and Depression in African American and White Elders," Journal of Human Behavior and the Social Environment 10, no. 1 (2005): 175-211.

approaches is an implied emphasis on the differences between various groups and communities. We present an alternative and perhaps more collaborative approach that capitalizes on the common bonds of spiritual devotion and practice among different denominational groups and professionals using this approach. We continue to seek members for our growing "band of brothers and sisters" across the country who seek to answer the question "What if an army of spiritually inspired, successfully aging seniors arose to 'rebuild the walls' of your city?"

# 14

## IMPORTANT STEPS TO UNIFYING
## OUR COMMUNITIES

...

I (Dr. Parker) commend three common and easily adaptable resources for churches wishing to increase participation of and care for seniors in church congregations. Often these unifiers enable the formation of mutually beneficial relationships between the young and the old. If successful aging includes meaningful relationships, and if functioning well as the body of Christ means honoring the hard-earned wisdom of our elder members, everyone stands to benefit from investigating how these unique opportunities can benefit local persons and local congregations.

### Technology as a Community Unifier

As we have noted earlier, research suggests that most communities in America are not prepared to meet the needs of their rapidly aging populations. Yet religious congregations represent an underutilized community-based system through which older adults can receive health promotion messages, learn about available local services, gain access to important Internet resources and establish a vibrant convoy of social relationships of all ages. The tradition of parish nursing, which is rooted in the Judeo-Christian tradition of caring for others as an expression of God's love, combines professional nursing and health ministry; however, most congregations cannot afford such a program for meeting the needs of older adults and their caregivers. The Internet may offer some solutions that tap into community programs that target seniors.

*Internet technology.* In two studies funded by the University of Alabama's Office of Community Affairs, an interdisciplinary team of researchers and students developed an accurate Internet e-mail distribution list of local congregations, as well as extensive electronic and hard copy directories of over 600 congregations in the area that contained up-to-date contact information (address, telephone number, e-mail address and website).[1] This information was provided to area congregations and to over twenty-one local agencies to enhance interagency and faith-based communication. Undergraduate students also completed a telephone survey of pastors and lay leaders about the services offered to older adults in the community, while other student teams developed state and national directories of resources in aging that can be accessed via the Internet. Findings revealed that even though a broad range of services were offered by local agencies and congregations, major service gaps, areas of redundancy and communication problems between agencies and area congregations existed. Hard copies of the directories were distributed to the larger congregations and some underserved churches that did not have Internet access, and electronic copies of all the directories were sent using the Internet. Community meetings were held, and participating congregations and agencies discussed future opportunities for improving interagency and interdenominational collaboration and communication. The results indicated that congregations are willing to serve as conduits through which older adults can receive health-promotion messages and learn about available programs offered by local, state and national agencies and organizations that specialize in the care of older persons.

Initial outcomes suggest that the Internet can serve to connect the community through sharing state of science information across denominational, agency, congregation and age barriers. We learned that di-

---

[1]M. W. Parker, L. Dunn, J. Goetz, S. Ousley, M. Rogers, M. Piper, R. Harrell, H. Lee, N. S. Park, S. MacCall, J. Williams, C. Spencer and X. Li, "Helping to Unite an Aging Southern Community: An Internet Directory Project and Telephone Survey of Local Congregations," *Journal of Community-Based Partnerships* (forthcoming); L. Dunn, M. W. Parker, X. Li, M. Piper, R. Harrell, H. Lee, N. S. Park, S. MacCall, S. Martin, J. Williams and C. Spencer, "Building Sustainable Community Partnerships to Promote Successful Aging: A Preliminary Study of Local Congregations and Agencies," *Journal of Community-Based Partnerships* (forthcoming).

rectories of resources (see appendix C) can be used to improve agency access of faith-based organizations while fostering ecumenical, agency and university collaborations at the community level.

Overall, interviews with local agency and pastoral leaders confirmed that religious congregations are largely unprepared to address the challenges associated with living longer and to challenge the ageism of that exists in most organizations and community-based systems, including congregations. We discovered that many churches are simply too small and under-resourced to address the challenges associated with aging congregations and communities, like technology, elder care, late life significance, aging in place, grandparenting, epidemic-like incidences of Alzheimer's disease, depression and chronic disease, home health care, late life planning, securing life histories, access to geriatric care and the promotion of successful aging. Ninety-five percent of the churches in our sample of over 650 churches had fewer than two hundred members, and many of the pastors of underserved communities worked two or more other jobs in order to secure an adequate income for their own families.

On the positive side, however, research studies like this have accumulated a growing body of evidence to support the viability of community-based partnerships across denominational lines. These partnerships must include existing community agencies (for example, Area Agencies on Aging) that already provide viable programs to address some of these challenges. Furthermore, our longitudinal research with over one thousand community-dwelling older people continues to underscore the resiliency of health enhancing aspects of vibrant spirituality in late life. Giving underserved communities access to state of science information through the Internet may prove to be an increasingly viable way to help older persons age successfully. Larger churches can help smaller congregations by helping to underwrite the costs of Internet access and by providing computers, printers, fax machines and other technologies.

*The vital role of churches.* In a recent presentation regarding the results of a survey of representatives from a large group of faith-based organizations and agencies in Birmingham, Alabama, Claire Parker summarized the "service needs" or older adults and ways in which faith-based communities could help meet the growing needs of older persons.[2] The following represents the prioritized list of "service needs" based on the input of over one hundred respondents from local agencies and faith-based organizations: (1) health/medical issues; (2) financial and income challenges; (3) transportation; (4) social opportunities; (5) in-home services; (6) food and nutrition; (7) access to services; (8) suitable living arrangements; (9) caregiver support; (10) raising grandchildren; (11) dementia; (12) safety; and (13) legal/estate issues. Can you image any one church meeting these needs? Missing dramatically from this list is the clear notion of ministry *from* elders, though one can easily shift the focus with this in mind to see wonderful opportunities for ministry (e.g., grandparenting, safety, home care) for seniors to make a difference in practically every area listed. It is clearly a matter of perspective.

Our vision includes ministry *to* and *from* seniors, and it is highly likely that some elders involved in ministry might very well be the recipients of the same ministry down the road. The evidence is clear cut, and it confirms that the vast majority of older persons are vibrant and quite able to design and support ministries that address all of these specific needs and other programs that target other age groups. Our "town and gown" model underscores the reality that no one church or person can do it alone. As in Nehemiah's day, a strong vision is needed, but the community must work together to rebuild the wall.

We think that every community that considers establishing a senior ministry association needs to identify existing programs and services to avoid duplication of effort and the depletion of existing resources. After identifying the existing programs, each community must identify the gaps in service (e.g., most communities have a shortage of transportation capacities for older and disabled persons, inadequate in-home services, and limitations of proper housing and living arrangements). Our direct work with congregations regarding health and medical issues

---

[2]C. Parker, "Survey of Organizations Phase I: Identifying Resources and Challenges Serving the Senior Community," unpublished research, February 16, 2010, UAM Center for Aging, Birmingham, Alabama.

and caregiving has been described already, and we refer the reader to these sections and to appendix C, which addresses specifically a broad range of medical, legal-financial, spiritual-emotional and familial needs of older persons and their caregivers. Many of the websites recommended address the full range of service needs identified in this recent survey, and we recommend that clergy and lay leaders use these resources in developing programs that address these concerns. We think it is impossible for any single church to assume responsibility for meeting these needs; however, we maintain our vision that the church can partner to meet these needs, but we have also found in our work that every community is different and the range of services vary greatly. For example, in general, rural communities have fewer services, which underscores the importance of the church in providing transportation help and other services that would otherwise not be available.

Though we address the epidemic of cognitive and intellectual impairment associated with dementia in our chapters on caregiving, dementia and disability (and in appendix C), we must emphasize how critical it is for pastors and lay leaders to ask some of the following questions: who are the cognitively impaired in our congregation? Do they live alone? If our cognitively impaired members live in an assisted-living facility or nursing home, are they visited regularly by people who have some understanding of the cognitive and psychiatric symptoms of dementia? For example, during an initial greeting of a member suffering from memory loss, visitors should know that the person being visited may not remember their name; however, they can recognize whether a visitor has a kind, gracious countenance or whether the visitor is frustrated or angry because his name was not remembered. For frail or disabled members living at home, should the congregation consider putting a team of volunteers together to address uncompleted or ongoing responsibilities (e.g., helping with home repairs)? Should the church or a group of churches provide an ongoing educational support group to caregivers? Should church leaders make an active commitment to visit cognitively impaired and other disabled, frail members? How can the church build and sustain relationships with local professionals in aging?

Congregations can play a more active role in helping people prepare and anticipate life transitions at mid- and late-life—roles that affect a person's purpose in the family, in the church and in society—such as launching young adults, elder caregiving, "retirement" and late life. Cultural factors that influence the way people understand diseases, such as hypertension and diabetes, need to be addressed. The church could offer a countercultural vision about retirement: provide a clear perspective through classes on how to transition from work to other duties, by encouraging prayer for God's call on their late life, and by exposing them to service opportunities related to their gifts, education and availability. Work, education and leisure are lifelong, cradle-to-grave structures for the Christian, while society seems fixed on an ageist, age-graded view of education, work and retirement. Churches must learn to partner about these theological issues with other congregations using senior ministry associations. Larger congregations need to adopt a strategy of inviting smaller, underserved congregations to be a part of senior programs that could involve education, counseling, nutrition, computer and Internet skills, exercise (family life centers), end-of-life issues (durable powers-of-attorney, end-of-life directives, etc.; see appendix C) and transportation. Churches need to be sources of information about existing community programs while developing relationships with the professional community.

Primary caregivers are more isolated than ever, and most are working women who belong to congregations. Rather than speaking out and offering scientifically proven programs for elder caregivers that are based on Scripture, our research in over twenty communities has found only one viable caregiver support programs in the nation that are housed in and managed by congregations. Despite the good news about the overall health status of elders, little is being done to help older persons plan for probable periods of dependency. Aging-in-place initiatives (community planning, home health and home design) are rarely church initiated or promoted, though the vast majority of older persons would prefer to live in their homes rather than transition to a series of expensive, long-term care facilities. Many elders are unprepared to face catastrophic events like power outages, hurricanes, tornadoes and other severe events, and while many congregations have visitation programs, most fail to address these life-threatening challenges. Similarly, elders face transportation issues, and though many churches offer assistance to church, many elders experience a growing isolation that contributes to depression and late life insignificance.

As noted earlier, the average woman who reaches the age of sixty-five can expect to live nineteen more years and, on average, five of those years will constitute a time of dependency. Men who reach sixty-five can expect fifteen more years with three years of dependency. It should be noted that men tend to have partners late in life, while women tend to have more sustained periods of widowhood. The church could play a significant role in reducing these periods of co-morbidity and dependency by promoting successful aging themes that help older persons to engage in spiritual growth and lifelong learning, avoid disease and disability, maximize their cognitive and physical fitness and otherwise remain actively engaged in life through volunteerism, grand parenting and other forms of community and family leadership. (See chapters 12 and 14 for more information on such programs.)

Many national ministries aimed at older persons have struggled financially or have not been sustainable, and as the church suffers financially during hard economic times, more cuts in senior programs can be anticipated. This is all the more reason for churches in local communities to develop partnerships. How many family life centers are needed in one community? Despite these concerns, our research indicates that even small under-resourced churches continue to minister to older people with traditional ministries. The presence of a small group life through home Bible studies may provide the single best opportunity for reciprocity across the generations as people of all ages live out their faith on a regular basis.

### Small Group Life in a Community of Believers

During the course of his twenty-year military career, my family and I (Dr. Parker) have experienced firsthand the benefits of intergenerational fellowship made available by and through participation in home Bible study groups. As members of Officers' Christian Fellowship, home Bible studies were considered integral to a vital expression of faith particularly while serving overseas. My family was also active in establishing, promoting and managing small groups in different churches and denominations while we lived in a variety of communities in the United States—from California to Alabama. In particular, I remember my church life in Ann Arbor, Michigan. Dr. Bartlett Hess, who helped found the Evangelical Presbyterian Church in the United States, was my pastor. At the age of eighty-five, Dr. Hess was busily starting his twenty-seventh church at the same time I began post-doctoral studies in aging at the University of Michigan. Three of Dr. Hess's twenty-seven churches had over five thousand members, so we might say that he was doing something right related to church growth.

At the heart of Dr. Hess's successful, lifelong ministry was his advocacy for small Bible study groups that fostered fellowship between young and old alike. Dr. Hess, an avid swimmer up until his death, never really thought of himself as old, nor did those who knew him, and this was reflected in his specific passion for developing the small group life of congregations. At the core of his strategy was the home Bible study group where members of all ages were encouraged to belong to a weekly home Bible study group consisting of a singing, short Bible study, time for sharing, prayer support and usually a dessert. He also encouraged the development of specific support groups that aimed at those overcoming addictions, grief and other life-course themes. I remember that he had plans for developing caregiver support groups, and I remain certain that Dr. Hess would have been open to a life review support group that sought to capture a person's history. People of all ages flocked to his churches because their needs for fellowship, faith and hope were met in an atmosphere that encouraged participation in regular forms of personal fellowship not typically possible during worship services or age-graded Sunday school dominated by (appropriately) a focus on teaching.

### Intergenerational relationships.

It is very sad to realize how difficult this creative interaction among the generations has become. When we see how many new university campuses are bring erected in the middle of deserts and cornfield, we become painfully aware of the counter-educational effects of isolation among generations. In these new "halls of learning," thousands of students are packed together, and their sheer numbers make meaningful contact with their teachers practically impossible. Numerous students spend most of their four years of college education almost exclusively with their peers, unable to play with a child, work with a teen-ager, talk with an adult, or have any human contact with the elderly. Those who are separated in order to be educated find themselves in a situation in which the educating context of life is taken away from them. Being in close contact with peers during your formative years is extremely valuable, but when there is no world around you as a reminder of where you came from and where you will go, that closeness might become stagnating instead of mobilizing. And that is a real tragedy.[3]

Small groups allow and foster the development of friendships across age barriers and provide for an opportunity of reciprocity. Perhaps more today than ever, those at early and midlife have been hurt by a lifestyle that promotes and encourages achievement. Often, the church becomes just another place to look for compensation, recognition and significance in a culture that defines significance by our function in life—what we do and by our position on the tribal totem pole. Vibrant small group life in a church can bring young and old alike together in ways that challenge the premise that significance can be achieved singularly by performance. Those who have lived longer have often been humbled by life. The achiever might ask, "Doesn't the Lord help those who help themselves?" Often it is the older member of small group who can lovingly challenge these and other false, unbiblical doctrines that have led many a achievement-oriented believer down a slippery slope of destruction, failed relationships and reputation building.

While our conscious and unconscious drives often work against the Holy Spirit, older persons are uniquely suited in a small group atmosphere to encourage younger people to seek God's will and purpose with an attitude of prayerful stillness. In a world full of the narcotic of busyness, made worse by inappropriate reliance upon modern technol-

---

[3]H. Nouwen and A. Gaffney, *Aging: The Fulfillment of Life* (New York: Image Books Doubleday, 1990), p. 120.

ogy, elders can affirm from their own experience, "My soul finds rest in God alone." This signals death to a spirit of self-importance or of restless ambition. Elders can serve as living examples of the how we must not listen to the world's claims on achieving significance through performance.

Such youth-age connections have the potential to significantly benefit both old and young. There is a growing body of research that suggests that senior support systems consist, primarily, of other seniors and that the opportunities of connecting with younger people (both within and outside the church and family) are not being realized. This failure to connect across generations is a problem that can be answered, in part, by church leaders at the local and national level. Programs that mandate connections, like forcing young children to visit in nursing homes, have met with limited success. However, tailored, personal introductions between the young and the old through sustainable programs have fared much better. As colleges and universities go more and more to online curricula, students will be in greater need of the face-to-face fellowship available to them in small groups.

> It is indeed the task of everyone who cares to prevent people—young, middle-ages, and old—from clinging to false expectations and from building their lives on false suppositions. If it is true that people age the way they live, our first task is to help people discover lifestyles in which being is not identified with having, self-esteem does not depend on success and goodness is not the same as popularity. Care for the aging means a persistent refusal to attach any kind of ultimate significance to grades, degrees, positions, promotions, or rewards, and the courageous effort to keep men and women in contact with their inner self, where they can experience their own solitude and silence as potential recipients of the light. When one has not discovered and experienced the light in Christ that is love, peace, forgiveness, gentleness, kindness, and deep joy in the early years, how can one expect to recognize it in old age?[4]

Nouwen summarizes the truth that living out biblical principles early on in life can yield a bounty of blueprints to our youth and adults

---

[4]Ibid., p. 137.

on just how to accomplish this. On the conviction that simply exposing young people to their elders can be transformative, I (Dr. Parker) was delighted to see it happen in a freshman seminar on aging that I taught at a major university. Undergraduates majoring in prelaw, premed, English, Spanish, psychology, social work, communications, business and religion made a meaningful connection with an eighty-year-old, rural-dwelling, childless widow. The students gained respect for this elder who lived alone on seven hundred acres, cut her own grass, managed a small country church and cemetery, and this senior saint gained some new friends and had a renewed sense of connectedness with young people.

During the writing of this book, one of the top U.S. collegiate football coaches took a leave of absence, acknowledging that coaching had become a form of worship and that he needed to reestablish his priorities of God first, family second and work third. Like many successful people, it is easy to be deceived by arguing that we are over-achieving types or that our work is motivated exclusively by God's call while ignoring God's priorities for a loving family. As Dr. Houston has suggested in other writings, the church is full of people who argue in this way and who secularize the Christian message by infecting it with a spirit of busyness, defining themselves and their faith by their activities. If we are addicted to activity, how can we hope for meaningful relationships grounded in prayer and Christian accountability? Small group life that includes a ready exchanges between young and old may prove to be the single best way for a church to develop a program that cuts across the generations.

Intergenerational small groups should be a major part of all church life. Like the cell life of the body, small groups, consisting of all aged persons, provide vital opportunities for the establishment for truly meaningful friendships. Mentorship from a trusted elder can help a younger person in developing non-achieving ways of handling relationships. As Dr. Houston has suggested, behind our struggles to change and to be changed may be the fact that we have never learned to be gentle with ourselves, let alone with others in our social convoy of relationships.

*Barriers to small group fellowship.* Certainly it is absurd to think that God will do great things for us and through us if we are unwilling to allow him to interfere in the ways we manage our lives and how we relate to other people of all ages. "I just like people my own age!" "I can't stand the young people of today." These discussions surface in disagreements about music, the traditional use of hymns and in other matters. These prejudices can be challenged as we learn to fellowship with regularity in small groups.

Our wounds in relationships keep us from experiencing a more abundant Christian life. What if we were wounded emotionally in childhood? What if we suffer from perfectionist tendencies? Are we are full of anger and controlling tendencies? Are all of us in need of a psychiatrist or the latest pharmaceutical remedy for the challenges of life? For many, the cycle of woundedness, loneliness and rejection can be broken through the establishment of a church-related small group ministry that by design cuts across all generations.

Another barrier to fellowship is the "cult of personality." For many within the church, our personalities are simply masks we wear. And unfortunately, others within the church have become more comfortable dealing with our personality than the real person underneath the mask. Each of us is rich in the biological, spiritual, psychological and sociological aspects of personhood. Though research suggests that aspects of our personalities are quite enduring, we would argue that this is, in part, the result of our own fears of rejection that might come if our masks of personality were removed. Small group life in the body of a local church can help us to overcome the powerful influence of the cult of our personality. Seniors are just as vulnerable to the dance of personality and to mask-wearing in the social dance of life. Small group life can help us to hope in God's capacity to change us into more loving people, who in fact are more genuine, vulnerable and real with others. Senior saints can help the process through their unconditional love and acceptance, while speaking the truth lovingly when needed.

*The benefits of small groups.* God has created us as relational beings. Despite what many may think, there are people able and willing to love us and accept us because they have experienced the first love of Christ.

As we open ourselves up to friends in small groups, we can mutually encourage one another to greater levels of faith and prayer to God, who first loved us. We can learn to have deeper emotions of acceptance because of how deeply God has accepted us in Christ. His love for us is infinite.

Small group involvement provides a time to listen, serve and learn to be quiet before God and others. Elders have likely learned the hard ways of Christian discipleship. Rather than encouraging self-reliance, something Martin Luther called the opposite of faith, older Christians are more likely to promote God-dependency and to share the powerful messages of the prodigal and elder sons, the necessity of the preaching the gospel first to yourself and then to the world and the belief that he who began a work in us will see it to completion. Healthy elders are good listeners and are therefore more likely to encourage appropriate interpretations of a young person's dreams and hopes.

Small groups provide younger people with a support system for getting answers to their spiritual questions apart from their parents. UCLA conducted a series of surveys of over 100,000 students representing forty-six colleges throughout the United States. In this investigation, supported by the Templeton Foundation, researchers found that today's college students have very high levels of spiritual interest and involvement.[5] Many are actively engaged in a spiritual quest and are exploring the meaning and purpose of life, and they are thirsty for answers. Sociological-longitudinal surveys of the social support systems of older persons clearly show an absence of young people, while mid-lifers are busy trying to make a living. All three generations lose out: the old because they must deal with the continual loss of members of their age cohort to death; the middle-aged because they need their parents' and grandparents' help in parenting their children; and the young because of the lost wisdom and love available through older persons.

Elder-youth-connecting small groups ultimately allow others and ourselves more time and opportunity and space to become the person

---

[5]UCLA Student and Faculty, "The Spiritual Life of College Students: A National Study of Students' Search for Meaning and Purpose," *UCLA Student and Faculty Research* (Los Angeles: Higher Education Research Institute, 2005).

God created us to be and to live a life characterized by abundant service. My lifelong testimony has been of the powerful influence elders have had on my personal and professional life. These senior saints have affirmed my worth, competence and sense of belonging to the family of God, and these elders have supported me in pursuing a variety of Spirit-led vocational callings. Modeling a life characterized by resilience and a capacity to endure victoriously the storms of life, senior saints can help a younger person not to lose sight of their dreams in the midst of life's difficulties.

The reciprocity of social exchange that can occur in the small group life of a church can bring about profound, efficacious changes in the relationships of a congregation as the gospel is preached in word and deed. Small churches can band together in offering support groups to elder caregivers and by organizing teams or groups of people who might be able to provide more substantive support to those who are immobile or suffering from cognitive deficits and other functional incapacities. Some rather remarkable work has been accomplished by congregations who work hard to provide a variety of services to older, less mobile seniors (yard work, home repair, transportation, etc.).

I (Dr. Parker) pray with a small group of African American pastors every Saturday morning. Over time, I have learned more and more about segregation in many of the communities of the South. One of my friends intentionally visits predominately white churches with regularity. Though he would say that he always feels welcomed, he would also say emphatically that he sees the same pain in the congregational halls of the wealthy as he has sees in pews of the underserved. Small groups provide all congregations, rich and poor, served and underserved, with real opportunities for fellowship and for emotional and spiritual healing. Small group life allows for the mysteries of life to be shared and discussed, a process that in turn reminds all of us of our helplessness and need for fellowship.

One of the mysteries of life includes the presence of evil in this world. Small group members can remind us that we are not alone in our respective journeys, but that we are members of a company of Christians passing through this world. Small groups provide us with opportunities to share our hope and faith in dealing with these mysteries. We are encouraged to share our faith even when our work atmosphere might be contrary to such a witness. After 9/11, only the members of the WWII generation could site a similar experience with evil, the attack on Pearl Harbor. I recall a conversation I had with one of my non-Christian colleagues on campus after 9/11. As I passed, the colleague bemoaned with all of America, "That attack was simply evil!" "Ah," I said, seeing an opportunity to share my faith, "If there is evil in the world, then you must say the reverse is true. Perhaps there is a good God as well!" Our brothers and sisters in Christ can remind us that we are not orphans, but children of the living God. Like these older saints, we can cry "Abba Father!" Elder saints, through small groups, can help us to cope courageously with life as it is because God has proven himself strong in their lives over their lifetimes.

### The Life Review

"If any man builds on this foundation using gold, silver, costly stones, wood, hay or straw, his work will be shown for what it is, because the Day will bring it to light. It will be revealed with fire, and the fire will test the quality of each man's work. If what he has built survives, he will receive his reward" (1 Cor 3:12-14).

Everyone has a personal story to tell. As a specific aspect to small group life, churches can help to establish life review and life reminiscence groups that capture the life histories of elder-saints for posterity. Completing one's life review (or what some call an *oral history*) can help prevent late life depression, connect different age groups, provide older people with an opportunity to share their story of faith and capture a family's heritage. Life review is the act or process of recalling the past, but it can also involve the evaluation and resynthesis of past experiences precipitated by the need to resolve conflicts and achieve a sense of meaning to one's life. Orderly reminiscing is a necessary part of coming to terms with one's life and should be encouraged in faith-based communities. Partnerships across denominational lines could be formed for this purpose, and churches could help to identify and promote life review programs developed by local skilled and trained oral historians.

The goals of reminiscence are typically achieved with the use of themes, props and triggers (e.g., music, photographs or items from a person's past) to stimulate memories. A life review usually involves a period of reminiscence and self-reflection. A variety of methods can be employed. They include: written or taped autobiographies, pilgrimages (in person or through correspondence), reunions, construction of a genealogy, the creation of memorabilia through scrapbooks, photo albums or a collection of old letters, a verbal or written summary of life work, preservation of ethnic identity and the transmission of family values.

Life Review was developed for older adults and is based, in part, on Erickson's psychosocial developmental theory. The primary goal is to facilitate recall of past experiences and to promote interpersonal functioning and thereby improve well-being. It helps preserve the past and gives a personal legacy to the future. Life reviews and oral histories can be captured on DVDs, VCRs, in writing, on a tape recorder and/or as a codicil to a person's will. The life review is generally considered to be a normal developmental task of the later years characterized by the return of memories and past conflicts, which can result in resolution, reconciliation, atonement, integration and serenity. It can occur spontaneously or can be structured. The process helps conserve life stories, including everyday experiences and special events. Getting to know a loved one through reminiscing helps families discover many positive qualities about an older relative, enhances his/her self-understanding and provides a source of personal continuity that contributes to a sense of meaning in one's life.

Internet sites have been established that allow for a person who served during World War II to have that record of service recorded in official WWII archives (see appendix B). A variety of specific methods associated with life review and reminiscence are available and include: a life story book, structured reminiscence, positive core memories, life review and experiencing and a life challenge interview. Some methods will require the additional training of church staff and lay members, but the most important thing is to get started. The last American soldier to serve in World War I just passed away, and as previously noted, members of the WWII generation are rapidly dying off. Also, Alzheimer's disease and other dementias are stealing some people's capacity to share life stories. The church must act now if it is to establish programs that honor elders with someone who will take the time to listen and capture their unique stories. Congregations can creatively expand the concept of small groups to help provide a supportive atmosphere for older persons to tell their stories. Local oral historians and others skilled in computer technology can provide input into the creative process of capturing their stories. (A list of questions and other ideas for initiating and completing a life review are given in appendix A.)

# PART FOUR

...

# LATE LIFE
# SIGNIFICANT LIVING

# 15

## Faith Is All About Relationships in a Culture of Disability and Depression

*What good to us is a long life if it is difficult and barren of joys,*
*and if it is so full of misery*
*that we can only welcome death as a deliverer?*

Sigmund Freud

• • •

The social unacceptability of the aged is usually related to the rather ageless, non-acceptability of disabled people in general. Dr. Parker and his family experienced this directly when his older son, a football and basketball star—who played guitar beautifully by ear—suffered a C-5/C-6 spinal cord injury (SCI) while diving into the Gulf of Mexico his senior year in college. Despite the many advances in science with SCI research, Dr. Parker's young pastor quickly informed him that "God had not healed a SCI in 2,500 years of church history." Certainly the well-intentioned pastor meant to encourage a level of caution regarding the hoped-for recovery. After trips to SCI treatment centers at Johns Hopkins, The University of Miami and other state of science programs, the Parker family learned that this was not always the case, and they were taught to remain somewhat hopeful in the science. Later, after Dr. Parker met a young man who experienced spontaneous recovery of function after his conversion to Christ some eight years post-injury, the family could hope for recovery spiritually and scientifically, knowing that all scientific truth is of the Lord.[1]

The more technologically advanced we become, the more intolerant we seem to be regarding the notion of disability. We appreciate greatly the new mobility given to those in wheelchairs, the feats of those in the Para-Olympics and the possibility of a paraplegic sailing solo around the British Isles. Having power—or even regaining power—puts such disabled persons in a special category. But usually this refers to younger people, for as we grow old our handicaps multiply, and so the category of being "handicapped" is closer to a death sentence for the old than it is for those who are younger. The youngest among us are the exception: medical technology now routinely tests for prenatal evidence of such genetic disabilities as Down's syndrome to check if a pregnancy should be aborted. Such practice casts a shadow over the living who are disabled, particularly the elderly. As Malcolm Muggeridge told me (Dr. Houston) thirty years ago, "I stand against child abortion, for you will also need to stand against euthanasia in your generation." His prediction was true. "Eugenics" is concealed yet culturally acceptable in our culture.

*Eugenics* comes from the Greek word *eugenes*, meaning "well-born." Francis Galton, who coined the word in 1883, was living in the age of "social Darwinism," optimistic of "improving society" and of genetic improvement of the human race. The Jewish Holocaust was the horrendous Nazi state practice of cleansing and improving the pure Aryan blood. Now eugenics must be covert; no political state can afford to make it public policy. But parents are allowed and often encouraged in most prenatal testing today, to abort any "unfit" fetus. The birth of children with Down syndrome has actually declined because of such measures, even as the potential for its incidence has grown since women are risking later pregnancies, when a professional career is prolonged rather than the lower priority of family. When a pregnancy becomes unwanted because of the threat of mental retar-

---

[1]It is worth noting that despite the theological and scientific inaccuracy of the young pastor's comment, the congregation lovingly embraced the Parkers, even their son, in real and practical ways.

dation, this sends a signal to those at the end of life: "Why then should you continue to exist because of your disability?" Yet we all have disabilities. Some of us wear spectacles, others have a hearing aid and others need a walking stick. Why do we glorify having "the perfect body"? Anthropologists will tell us how varied are the expressions of beauty in a woman or of manliness in a man among the diverse ethnic groups. Advertisers lead us to discover that we can have poor sex or bad breath depending on which product we are not buying. But the introduction of genetics into the cultural narrative gives us all a new dread of genetic disorders.

A current article in the medical journal *Lancet* predicts that children now being born can anticipate a life span of a hundred years. The question raised by Freud will haunt us even more than when he wrote it: "what good to us is a long life . . . if it is so full of misery?" Three basic disabilities are facing seniors today: depression, dementia and Alzheimer's disease, and general senility. Megatrends are taking place in medicine and health care; many dramatic changes can be anticipated. What the medical profession does not predict is that any major breakthrough is likely to occur any time soon for these three major challenges.[2] No matter how many changes are made possible, we shall still all die. Disease still lies ahead of the human race. As the population ages, such diseases will become more prevalent, not less. Depression is also increasing as a cultural malaise, reflecting the reductionist trends of our technological society.

### The Reductionism of Specialization

The Duke University Christian psychiatrist Dan Blazer has written openly about the present impasse we seem to be in. In his book *Freud versus God*, provocatively subtitled *How Psychiatry Lost Its Soul and Christianity Lost Its Mind,* Blazer says psychiatry has been functioning without a soul since the 1960s, when it moved away from the context of social or community mental health to embrace a more specialized embrace of neuropsychiatry. Some even interpret religion

---

[2]Stephen C. Schimpff, *The Future of Medicine: Megatrends in Health Care That Will Improve Your Quality of Life* (Nashville: Thomas Nelson, 2007), p. 248.

within the context of psycho-pharmacology, suggesting that personality and even spiritual sentiments are biological phenomena which can be stimulated and even changed.[3] As Peter Kramer claims in *Listening to Prozac*, our choice of drugs will lead us "to conduct our lives differently." Such medication will become "an important agent for personal transformation."[4]

Little did we realize that the predictions of Aldous Huxley's *Brave New World* in 1932 would become popular sentiment today. North Americans have become so fearful of pain—not just physical, but emotional and social as well—that they will accept medicine for its prevention without ever questioning its use. They refuse to believe in the moral benefits that suffering can give us. Instead they will accept whatever drug is necessary to change their emotions and even their personalities, regardless of the consequences. Medicine, psychopharmacology, and psychoanalysis leap in to solve problems in ways that disregard the complexity of the human person. (Even Freud in his generation was far more holistic in linking psychoanalysis with civilization, society and family life, and Carl Jung attempted to link personal malaise with religious needs.)

By Christianity "losing its mind," Blazer refers to a similar reductionism within Christianity, a failure to engage every discipline with the light of the gospel. What is left is the vacuum of professional specialization, which the baby boomer generation has largely created. Thus a relational reformation of the church in the twenty-first century will require theologians and other professional Christian disciplines to embrace and include—far more holistically than they have to this point—geography, history, sociology, psychology, psychiatry, medicine, economics, politics and indeed all the growing new arts and sciences of the human condition. The loss of the Christian mind is the loss of the holism of knowledge, as all "being in subjection to Christ." Yet all our Christian knowledge must be assimilated and applied personally, recognizing our place in the world and within our culture and before God in terms of each one's own and whole personal being.

---

[3]Dan Blazer, *Freud versus God* (Downers Grove, Ill.: InterVarsity Press, 1998), pp. 113-15.
[4]Peter Kramer, *Listening to Prozac* (New York: Penguin, 1993), p. 300.

## Disabilities Are Our Permanent Condition

No one wants to be disabled, which leads us unto denial and ignorance about ourselves. This denial can be our worst enemy. We go too late to the doctor, and we fail to make the kinds of decisions about our life style that will help us to avoid late life disease and disability. So our bodies suffer. Our natural aging process affects our bodies more than we may know. We lose approximately 1 percent a year of many of our bodily functions after we have entered our third decade of life, such as lung and kidney function and our bone strength.[5] Exercise, nutrition, mental exercise and social skills will help to slow these aging processes, especially when we also lower stress and cultivate our souls.

But the second source of self-ignorance is more profound, the denial that we are all sinners, having inadequate relationships with those around us, but most of all with God. For while we may know and repent of sins done to others, we live in an ontological state of "sin before God." Our mortality has then a double dimension, within our bodies and before God. That is why we need a new paradigm to see medicine and theology more fully integrated, a "relational reform" of Christianity in our secular society.

Most people do tend to ossify in their worldviews or ideologies, secular or religious, the older they get. We have accumulated prejudices, habits of thought, negative experiences, mental and emotional reinforcements; these make us less flexible to viewing life more openly and allowing for debate. Each profession, medical or religious, has become increasingly specialized, while at the same time it is more apparent than ever that holistic thinking is interdisciplinary. Not only this, but human emotions are being recognized as increasingly more significant for understanding the human condition. Yet at the same time the emotional suffering of aging becomes more like a straitjacket for many seniors. It gives them no hope of escape, no increasing faith to grow deeper in understanding, nor richer in spirit, nor wider in relationships. Instead it seems as if they have been placed in a social box more and more like the coffin that will take them eventually into the cemetery.

---

[5]Ibid.

Living holistically also means that we not deny nor disown our weaknesses and handicaps, at whatever level they may occur. Yet denial is in our DNA: the denial of our mortality, of our status as a sinner before God, of our wrongdoing to others, of our addictions, of our basic weaknesses within our inner life.

Due to the rise of paraplegic injuries among young athletes and extreme sports devotees, society is now accepting appropriate redesigns of buildings and walkways for youth as well as seniors living out of a wheelchair. However, the public symbol of the wheelchair remains a form of social apartheid that raises the question "what's wrong with you?" We do well to recall that we all have disabilities, the most debilitating of all being that we are all sinners.

The medical profession operates within the universality of human pathology, that we are all subject to the handicap of disease, yet the secular paradigm is blind to this universal handicap of morality. In consequence the medical notion of "handicap" is itself being narrowed in interpretation and acceptance. It is okay to have and treat accidental injuries, but it is going to become taboo—perhaps, someday, forbidden—to have genetic disabilities, such being born with Down syndrome or a genetic disease such as cystic fibrosis. Scientists in biotechnology will reintroduce eugenics, argues Richard Lynn and many other advocates.[6] The temptation for new authoritarian states to revive eugenics will intensify as genetic medicine expands, as it is quietly doing presently.

Medicine and theology meet at the critical juncture of accepting or rejecting "human perfectibility." As John Passmore points out, *perfection* can connote mastery of technical skills, subordination to God's will, attaining a natural end, freedom from moral defect, a metaphysical state, living a perfectly ideal life or even becoming godlike.[7] It is the classical legacy of metaphysical perfection bequeathed to Western culture by the Greeks. Early Christianity rejected this ideal, as Augustine's debate with Pelagius exemplified.[8] Sinners need God's grace to

---

[6]Richard Lynn, *Eugenics: A Reassessment* (Westport, Ind.: Praeger, 2001).
[7]John Passmore, *The Perfectability of Man* (New York: Scribner's, 1970), pp.43-45.
[8]Michael Hanby, *Augustine and Modernity* (New York: Routledge, 2003), pp. 106-33.

cope with how we do bad things even when we seek to do good things. John Wesley forgot this when he pursued the impossible ideal of "Christian perfectionism"![9] It is no accident that in the earlier part of the past century, liberal Methodist advocates of eugenics based their medical ideals on faith in human perfectibility.[10]

This idea of perfection parallels the changing foci of the medical community. In the early twentieth century, notes doctor Stephen C. Schimpff, his grandfather's paradigm of medicine was limited however to "diagnose and predict outcome." Shimpff's own early medical paradigm became "diagnose and treat"; now after a long life he sees medicine taking on the paradigm "predict and prevent."[11] Revolutionary technology is now introducing genomic medicine that will create "personal medicine." Genetic testing will predict the potential developments of a "personal disease" later in life and offer "designer vaccines" to suit one's own DNA profile.

There are three medical conditions that still force us to accept aging gracefully. First, the natural aging of our bodies can begin in the prime of youth—late twenties through the thirties. This is particularly true for bone health if we do not have a healthy lifestyle that includes proper diet and exercise. Osteoporosis, a disease that affects bone density in late life is often referred to as a pediatric or young adult disease with a geriatric outcome because bone density is largely determined at a younger age by lifestyle (proper diet, exercise). Still, for many of our bodily senses and functions, we lose some capacity over time as a natural part of the aging process. As we noted in earlier chapters on successful aging and the myths of aging, we can avoid or minimize the effects of some diseases and therefore retain more of our capacities over time. In the past, scientists relied primarily on cross sectional work that failed to control for the effects of diseases. Second, there is no sign yet that dementia and Alzheimer's disease will not increase as fast or faster than

[9]John Wesley, "A Plain Account of Christian Perfection" in *John Wesley and Charles Wesley*, ed. Frank Whaling (Ramsey, N.J.: Paulist Press, 1981), pp. 297-376.
[10]*Methodist Quarterly Review* 84 (1929), quoted in *Theology, Disability and the New Genetics: Why Science Needs the Church*, ed. John Swinton and Brian Bock (New York: T & T Clark, 2007), pp. 87-91, 201-13.
[11]Schimpff, *Future of Medicine*, pp. 4-5.

the demographic increases of an aging population. Third, as a mental and spiritual condition that biomedicine can only affect in a limited way, emotional depression is on the rise with senility. These three challenges we shall consider in reverse order in this and the next.

## The Growing Suffering of Depression
## by an Aging Population

Psychiatrists now recognize that depression causes more disability than any other psychiatric disorder. It is dramatically rising in Western societies to become the third major pandemic after heart diseases and cancers. But unlike them it cannot be so readily named, although it is now fashionable to "medicalize" depression as *clinical* (or *major*). Dan Blazer critiques this trend in his recent work, *The Age of Melancholy*; the retreat of psychiatry from its social context to identify problems in the individual alone, he says, overlooks "the complex interaction of people's symptoms with the social and cultural environment in which those symptoms emerge. The end result is to sterilize emotional suffering."[12] The unhappiness so many may feel intensifies because their own social situations are not being seriously enough understood.

A primary symptom of depression is sadness. Striving for happiness is the reaction of so many, and the intense episodic pleasure/happiness most sought as its antidote is sexual. Yet as Freud, a sadly depressed man all through his life, admitted, "we are never so defenseless against suffering as when we love, never so helplessly unhappy as when we have lost our loved object or its love."[13] Whatever promiscuous youth may think of sex as an anti-depressant, seniors learn to experience its illusionary promise. The fleeting excitement and happiness of sex cannot compete with our long-term need for loving relationships with others, and most important, with God.

Another popular approach today is to view depression as chronic unhappiness which cognitive therapy can change. Buddhism (under

---

[12]Dan G. Blazer, *The Age of Melancholy: "Major Depression" and Its Social Origins* (New York: Routledge, 2005), pp. 31-33.
[13]Quoted in Armand Nicholi, *The Question of God: C.S. Lewis and Sigmund Freud Debate God, Love, Sex, and the Meaning of Life* (New York: Free Press, 2002), p. 101.

the leadership of the Dalai Lama) is linking secular neuroscientists and cognitive therapists to explore the skills of Tibetan monks with their meditative exercises. The Himalayan state of Bhutan has made "happiness" its gross national product, not money. As the West becomes satiated with materialism, the themes of worthlessness, of self-blame, emptiness, meaninglessness, isolation, inadequacy, fatigue and sleep problems are leading to changes in behavior, to diminishing social contacts and (with religious people) to a loss of faith.

New spiritualities are now arising such as the text of Piero Ferrucci, *The Power of Kindness: The Unexpected Benefits of Leading a Compassionate Life*, which the Dalai Lama calls "a book after my own heart."[14] It argues that the kindest people thrive most, all without any need of a Christian life. Instead, it suggests, we can engender within ourselves all the utopian values we desire: honesty, warmth, forgiveness, contact, trust, mindfulness, empathy, humility, generosity, respect, flexibility, memory, loyalty, service, yes, and you can even be "an expert in joy" itself![15] This kind of thinking is that predictable pendulum swing from a the rationalism of our previous modern culture, which ignored our emotions altogether. We repressed awareness that our feelings are a significant source of personal knowledge about ourselves. We did not understand our changing moods very much. We chided or repressed them—"What's wrong with me?" Our aging population now reaps the consequences of our seniors having few insights to cope with increasing bouts of sadness, depression and a sense of worthlessness. Perhaps our view of Christianity has been so strongly activist that when one can do very little, one's citadel of faith also begins to dissolve. Perhaps our faith was doctrinaire and rationalistic, so seniors begin to doubt whether their Christian faith amounted to very much after all, since now they feel prayerless and God seems so far away from their present needs.

How different it is for those who do not put hope in their own stoicism or faith in their ability to increase their happiness, but who embrace the Christian beliefs and practices that draw us near to God daily.

---

[14]Piero Ferrucci, *The Power of Kindness*, trans. Vivien Reid Ferrucci (New York: Penguin, 2007).
[15]Ibid., p. 253.

How different are the habits of the heart gained by a biblically meditative, prayerful way of living, which leads to the redemptive and transformed emotions of "love, joy, peace, patience, kindness, goodness,
faithfulness, gentleness and self-control" (Gal 5:22-23). These are the
fruit of the Holy Spirit of God, not of self-achievement but as his gift
to us. But it requires the cruciform life, of "those who belong to Christ
Jesus," having "crucified the sinful nature [i.e., the natural human life]
with its passions and desires" (Gal 5:24).

### Depression as Reflective of Our Way of Life

Depression can range from the universal feeling of sadness, to feelings
of low mood, despondence, self-criticism, low-esteem, self-hate, to
specific psychiatric conditions of melancholia, manic-depressive illnesses and even suicidal tendencies. The continuum suggests that
"things are falling apart" either emotionally or worse. Old age com-
pounds these negatives in our lives to give the sense of a final judgment. Other seniors can experience the opposite, enjoying "the fruit of
the Holy Spirit" as never before. One Christian senior, Peter Green,
wrote in 1950 about his old age. He noted that seniors often would tell
children that the best years of their life would be their school days,
implying that things were not going to get better as they grew older.
"How much better if one could tell them with conviction," he reflected,
"that life rightly lived goes on getting better and that God's promise to
those who love Him and whom He loves is that at evening time it shall
be light."[16]

The Christian psychiatrist Armand Nicholi, comparing two great
voices of the twentieth century, Sigmund Freud and C. S. Lewis, notes
that in their youth both were depressed. Lewis finally reconciled suffering with faith, but Freud never could do so. Lewis lost his beloved
mother at nine years old, lived with a pessimistic father and suffered
horribly from his first boarding school years. He confessed that as a
child "he had the gloomiest anticipation of adult life."[17] But after he
came to Christian faith in his adult years, joy became a new reality and

---

[16]Peter Green, *Old Age and the Life to Come* (Oxford: A. A. Mowbray, 1950), pp. 13-14.
[17]Nicholi, *Question of God*, p. 111.

he eventually died serenely. Freud was in his seventies, faithless and melancholic all his life, when he welcomed death as a deliverer from a life full of miseries. He appeared from correspondence to know that his worldview offered little hope of happiness, and he felt powerless to do anything about it. He died by euthanasia administered by his doctor, having dreaded death all his life.

### Relating with Seniors in Depression

Certainly, contrasted ways of living have different relationships to the experience of depression. A Christian like Lewis found his identity not in himself but "in Christ"; he turned outward instead of inward. He gained a new understanding of love as expressive of God, not as derived from his own sexual drive or other bodily needs. This changed also his attitude towards others, seeing them as destined to an eternal destiny, not just limited by their mortality to die. As he stated in a famous sermon I (Dr. Houston) heard him give: "No one ever talks to a mere mortal . . . it is immortals who we joke with, work with, marry . . . your neighbor is the holiest object presented to your senses."[18] Persons transcend everything on this earth, and therefore all the foibles, weaknesses, trials of senility, yes, and death, too, are not the end of their story.

But to relate truthfully with depressed seniors, we need to challenge the mores of our culture. We are aware that we live with rapid change, with increased mobility and with intensified technology. It is "high modern" society if we approve of it, or it is "post-modern" if we feel disenchanted by it. The cultural pessimism of the latter frames the context in which depression is reaching epidemic proportions today. A complex web of factors fosters depression, and the following four aspects are especially a threat if unrecognized or ignored.

*Taking our personal emotions seriously.* Since depression is itself an emotion, ignoring it intensifies its experience. The aged are particularly vulnerable to this happening, since their very existence can easily be ignored. Surviving World War II, many grew up ignoring their feel-

---

[18]See C. S. Lewis, *The Weight of Glory* (New York: HarperCollins, 1980), p. 46.

ings and lived life in "survival mode." Absentee fathers, both in war time and later in economic recovery, the new role of mothers in the work-force, later high divorce rates and ignorance of what later became a therapeutic revolution separated the old from the current youth in major ways. One scarcely knew oneself, let alone others, if one suppressed personal feelings as an unnecessary luxury. Behind this is the strong Stoic influence that has characterized Anglo-Saxon culture. It affirms emotions as trivial, untrustworthy and false. Bryon's character *Faust* expresses the consequence, "To feel for none is the true social art / Of the world's stoics—men without a heart."[19]

Asian cultures are even more pronounced in this regard; one never discloses feelings at all. In Chinese culture, respect for one's elders is a form of personal suppression. Family wounds cannot be acknowledged, the complete opposite of the way our therapeutic culture in the West now makes uncovering family wounds a way of life! In South Korea, *chong*, I am told, are the warm family feelings that tend to suffocate all personal feelings within the home setting. Such socialized cultures are also "shame cultures," where losing face with one's friends is far more frighteningly than feeling inward guilt within one's self. As a Chinese proverb puts it, "A man needs face like a tree needs its bark."[20]

We can only anticipate the explosive consequences in such shame cultures, when Western awareness of individual guilt—for which one can only blame one's self—is compounded by looking into the mirror to look within one's protective sense of "face," to be ashamed of "myself"! After that there is nowhere to hide. A healthy understanding of shame and guilt recognizes both as having positive as well as negative values: on one hand, they can encourage a true sense of sin, but on the other, they can deny what is right and wrong. Thus the depression of aging souls may be the long undisclosed burden of sins committed that were never confessed and never forgiven. Angry people are often those who have never had their stories heard in empathy.

Need we be surprised then that an aging population will express

---

[19]Lord Byron, *Don Juan* (New York: Penguin Books, 2005): canto 5.25 (p. 225).
[20]Quoted in Wong Fong Yang, *Discipline or Shame?* (Selangor, Malaysia: Kairos Publications, 1998), p. 20.

more and more anger, when sentiments and feelings were never discussed, never exposed, never healed? The emotions of seniors should never remain bottled up, allowing them only to die in further bitterness. No longer can the post-modern individual, believer or non-believer, look at our life as "a detached self, disengaged from personality and historical contingency," to be merely a thinker, Christian or otherwise.[21] Writers like Kierkegaard urge us to become "passionate thinkers," indeed passionate Christians! These are persons who reflect and live out from their whole inner life how Christ has entered so deeply inside them, so that like the apostle they confess "Christ in you, the hope of glory" (Col 1:27).[22] Merely detached thinkers only reflect the current opinions of the culture, with no real passion of their own that they can share with others.

*Overcoming loneliness.* If many seniors suffer depression because their own emotions are stifled for multiple reasons, then many others are sadly depressed because they feel so lonely. Older populations suffer from the lack of deep relationships because they are not emotional enough, but the generation after that group suffers because they have had ambiguous relationships with others. They need deep, unambiguous relationships, but such lonely people are themselves incapable of establishing such deep and lasting relationships. Their loneliness becomes a vicious cycle, full of contradictions and often of chronic conflicts with others. Just as depression has become blurred between deep/clinical depression and other more pervasive forms, so also the distinction between loneliness as a neurosis and as social affliction is unclear.

I (Dr. Houston) have myself explored what one might call, "the continent of loneliness," as if one were alone in the vast emptiness of Antarctica.[23] It reflects the social experiences of a lifetime—of innumerable causes for feeling lonely, being misunderstood, falsely judged, envied, depressed—that are common to all of us. These causes are rooted in all of our differing narratives, and yet when we view a lonely aged person,

---

[21]Fergus Kerr, *Theology After Wittgenstein* (Oxford: Basil Blackwell, 1986), p. 25.
[22]Rick Anthony Furtak, *Wisdom in Love, Kierkegaard and the Ancient Quest for Emotional Integrity* (Notre Dame, Ind.: Notre Dame University Press, 2005), pp. 109-10.
[23]James M. Houston, "Exploring the Content of Loneliness," *Crux* 46, no. 4 (Winter 2010): 2-13.

we tend to flatten out the rich narrative that person may have had into a clinical phenomenon we observe, as just being "lonely." For some, being lonely is akin to helplessness. For others, irrational fears generate feelings of hostility that results in loneliness. Some cultivate an idealized self that fantasizes poor relationships. It appears as if the therapeutic revolution in America has created a narcissistic culture that has now in turn generated a culture of depression. Others who know us do not share our grandiose sense of self-importance, so then we feel unknown because we are unrecognized for what we think we are.

Dejected and brooding, some lonely people mourn over a defeated self, an unsuccessful self or even a dead self. With such helplessness, paralysis sets in; everything appears to be fatal, all in a state of flux. For without hope that reaches into the future, the present closes in upon a depression in which today is a temporary blur, the past forgotten and the future blocked. This time distortion induces a dominating sense of meaninglessness. Boredom spreads its anonymity, and we no longer have any inducement to be innovative, creative and venturesome.

The sociologist Richard Stivers has attributed these "shades of loneliness" as "pathologies of a technological society."[24] He concludes, "How is the technological personality related to these psychological disorders? The technological personality allows one to internalize some of the visual and auditory stimuli of the technological society, thereby creating a kind of stimulus shield; but it offers no help with the problem perpetual loneliness. Indeed it reinforces and deepens loneliness because the technological personality militates against establishing sincere relationships. One is left with role-playing and shallow emotions."[25]

Yet loneliness can be a force for good. It can be reinterpreted as solitude where we can create an inner space for God, for the cultivation of a contemplative life. This can deepen our inner persons, energize our creative intuitions, give empathy for those lonelier than ourselves and above all demonstrate that the real Christian is never alone, when God's

---

[24]Richard Stivers, *Shades of Loneliess: Pathologies of a Technological Society* (Lanham, Md.: Rowman & Littlefield, 2004).
[25]Stivers, *Shades of Loneliness*, pp. 142-43.

nature as "Immanuel" is truly "God with us." This is profoundly and eternally "a social life" in its fullest possible meaning.

*The faith to "belong."* A characteristic of depression is to forget that we all belong together as human beings. We only experience loneliness because we have also experienced relationships. Various disabilities of age, disease or infirmity, we have seen, may make us feel excluded. These do depress us. Seniors have long memories that may induce nostalgic loneliness which others cannot share, yet our uniqueness at whatever age induces this too. So seniors need to avoid the temptation of feeling themselves to be a special category.

Our primary faith rests upon the reality God has created us all "in his image and likeness." Theological anthropology is the only basis for considering ourselves human. Otherwise "human" is a will o' the wisp. Naturalists can only speak of the clever ape, an evolutionary achievement of one species over others in a Darwinian struggle. But our faith in relating with God interprets our being as having an eternal destiny, so that death is not the end of the story. Death is a great cause of depression, since having no prospects beyond the grave makes our mortal life so ultimately meaningless. Freud, as we saw, hated the process of growing old, because death was the final reality. But Lewis enjoyed growing old, writing to a friend a month before he died, "Yes, autumn is the best of seasons, and I'm not sure that old age isn't the best part of life."[26] It is this profound sense of belonging to God that makes all the difference in how we go on living.

Søren Kierkegaard startled many religious people in his day when he wrote in his *Concluding Unscientific Postscript*: "Christianity is not a doctrine."[27] By this startling statement he meant it is not speculative but relational, an existential way of living. We are to live out what we believe, reforming our unhappy way of life into another way of being. For Christian beliefs actually make us Christlike, not leaving us merely arguing about their validity. They help us integrate our whole life, to find it meaningful, even with disability and depression, as we grow

---

[26]Quoted in Nicholi, *Question of God*, p. 232.
[27]Søren Kierkegaard, *Concluding Unscientific Postscript*, trans. Walter Lowrie (Princeton, N.J.: Princeton University Press, 1941), p. 339.

older. We see our life as given by God, not just a human series of achievements and failures. It has a meaning beyond our decaying body of eternal value. As the apostle Paul affirms: "Though outwardly we are wasting away, yet inwardly we are being renewed day by day." As a result, "we do not lose heart" (2 Cor 4:16).

Our focus upon actions changes, since we can do less. Instead our focus increases the importance of relationships, with God and with others. We pray and contemplate more. We become more attached, not less, to loved ones. We become more involved in the inner lives of others, to encourage, nurture and love them. Our commitment to daily duties finds new faithfulness in supporting an infirmed spouse or in the care of older people, particularly in congregational life. We live more for the present day, with fewer dreams about the future. All in all, our sense of reality, of living a truthful life, indeed of living "Christianly," should transcend all disabilities and even suffering from depression. Christian seniors should be seeing and affirming the need to be the reformers of contemporary Christian life.

# 16

## FACING ALZHEIMER'S DISEASE AND OTHER DEMENTIAS WITH HOPE IN GOD'S REMEMBRANCE

*Human ecology is the understanding and care of human beings*
*as whole persons in light of their relationship with God,*
*themselves, their families and the society in which they live.*

MISSION STATEMENT OF LUTHERAN GENERAL HOSPITAL,
PARK RIDGE, ILLINOIS

• • •

I received the news of my son's injury and life-sustaining surgery late in the evening of the 4th of July. I had no real idea of what the implications of a spinal cord injury were for my son and family. Over the next several months I learned the hard way what many of the tasks of caregiving were. No one provided me with a coherent look at the full landscape of caregiving tasks ahead, let alone the state of science and practice information I needed about how to meet these challenges. All caregivers need hope . . . hope perhaps from an informed theological perspective that provides a sense of purpose in the face of the injury, hope perhaps from a therapist that sees return of function not just adaptation as a feasible treatment goal, or perhaps hope in the form of someone willing to simply listen, to get into the deep water with us. These are examples of the real "cups of cold water" needed that bond us to professionals of all disciplines.[1]

---

[1]T. R. Elliott, M. Parker and L. Roff, "Family Caregivers and Health Care Providers: Developing Partnerships for a Continuum of Care and Support," in *The Multiple Dimensions of*

Contrary to popular opinion, most American families do not abandon family members with disabilities, diseases and conditions to paid professionals and paraprofessionals. Yet most health-care-service practitioners and some church leaders fail to acknowledge and affirm the central role families play in extending health care services, because most pastors and lay leaders lack the necessary skills to encourage and enable families to do their Herculean jobs more effectively. In this chapter, we emphasize that pastors and lay leaders need to acknowledge and support family caregivers in their vital caring role as a first step toward dealing with the growing phenomenon of caregiving and facing the unique challenges of family members caring for individuals with disabling conditions.

Many people who live in community settings who belong to churches require assistance at some time because of chronic disease and disability, and dementia is clearly an example of a common, chronic, progressively disabling condition that affects the person and the family. The term *dementia* (or *senility*) indicates progressive, marked decline in intellectual or cognitive functions associated with damage to brain tissue; this may affect personality and behavior, and it may be of a reversible or an irreversible type. In the aging process, once there is loss of memory, the immediate popular judgment is, alas, this must be the onset of the dreaded brain disease, Alzheimer's, which leaves the body still alive after the brain is dying or dead. We may call this a *neuropathic ideology*, reflecting our scientific culture in which thought is more valued than love.

Ray Smith cared for his wife, Grace, until she died with Alzheimer's disease. As trained nurses, he and his wife respected the critical use of drugs, which were then still experimental, but he wanted to show the medical profession there was a wonderful alternative to drugs, namely diet and love given in personal care. So from 1991, when the disease was first disclosed in Grace until her death in 2003, Ray and Grace explored an alternative and remarkably rich journey together, in tender loving care. Afterward he wrote a book, *Amazing Grace: Enjoying Al-*

---

*Disability* (New York: Springer Press, forthcoming).

*zheimer's*, whose message he had already given to the press of several countries.[2]

Also in gentle protest, Lisa Genova, who holds a Ph.D. in neuroscience from Harvard, wrote a moving novel titled *Still Alice* from a chillingly deterministic paradigm of genetics.[3] The subject, Alice, has a genetic deficiency that induces Alzheimer's disease, which then means one or more of her three children are also doomed to repeat her fate.[4] The book's setting is Genova's alma mater, Harvard, where the victim is (ironically) the William James Professor of Psychology in the discipline of psycholinguistics. She has a brilliant mind and is as professionally successful as her husband, a biological scientist. But in mid-life her world suddenly crashes when she is diagnosed with an early onset form of Alzheimer's disease. The book narrates Alice's tortuous relations with her daughter Lydia, who refuses to go to college, lives with her boyfriend and has no other ambition than to become an actress. Alice and Lydia fight every time they meet. Genova skillfully narrates Alice's progressive deterioration until she can no longer recognize her husband and is unaware she is staying in her own Cape Cod holiday home. At this point, Alice's inner world has become as empty as a wintry snowfield. But when Lydia places her baby on Alice's lap and squeezes her mother with all the intimacy she can give, Lydia asks her mother: "Okay, what do you feel?" "I feel love. It's about love." Squealing with joy, with every crease in her face filled with delight, Alice asks: "Did I get it right?" "You did, Mom. You got it exactly right."[5]

Even the story of Alzheimer's from the patient's own point of view, biological determinism and all, is softened and made human when readers encounter this personal narrative. *Still Alice* leaves readers wondering about the values of our culture, questioning which is the worse atrophy: the loss of love in pursuit of academic ambitions or the loss of brain abilities from disease?

---

[2]Karem Gram, "This Is What Love Is," in *The Vancouver Sun*, August 16, 2007, B3.
[3]Lisa Genova, *Still Alice* (New York: Simon & Schuster, 2009).
[4]Ibid., p. 292.
[5]Ibid.

## An Embodied Patient or a Socialized Person?

There is a tension between an unrelenting disease and human care, encapsulated well by the statement of Olive Sacks, professor of neurology and psychiatry at Columbia University in New York, "In examining disease, we gain knowledge about anatomy and physiology and biology. In examining the person with disease, we gain wisdom about life."[6]

Yet new philosophers now use neuroscience to redefine philosophy as merely the function of embodied minds, the body being everything.[7] Increasingly, even the larger culture struggles to come to grips with the common fallacy that "the mind" is only the brain. The brain is a remarkably flexible organ of the body, which, since the 1960s, has been studied and understood more completely by the science of neuropathology. Its circuitry is not static, but dynamic, slowly changing according to both organic and also environmental conditions, themselves in flux.[8] The brain's extraordinary ability to remember is like the recording archangel Gabriel, reputed in the Middle Ages to have written down every committed human deed for all time. But "the mind" and indeed "consciousness" are wider categories, socialized by many more external stimuli that shape the entire human narrative of what it means to be created as a unique person.

Whereas Alzheimer's may be specified as a brain disease, dementia is an encompassing concept that can be used theologically to reflect upon the deterioration of a much greater realm of personal stimuli, including one's social environment. A "dementing person" may be said to have two forms of deterioration going on at the same time: a deterioration of the capacities of the brain to direct bodily functions and a diminishing social environment consisting of friendships, social contacts and self-significance. These are indeed a multiplicity of personal losses. For Christians, dementia may also involve a loss of faith, a distancing or seeming absence of God, an empty prayer life and other experiences.

---

[6]Olive Sacks, *The Man Who Mistook His Wife for a Hat* (New York: Summit Books, 1985), p. 1.
[7]For example, see George Lakoff and Mark Johnson, *Philosophy in the Flesh: The Embodied Mind and Its Challenge to Western Thought*. (New York: Basic Books, 1999).
[8]A. R. Damasio, *Descartes' Error* (London: Picador, 1995).

Such a broad interpretation of *dementia* requires a paradigm shift like that introduced by early Christianity into the Greco-Roman world. For the incipient credibility of Christianity in the first century was that it was countercultural: it included Gentiles as well as Jews, slaves as well as Roman citizens, women as well as men. Jesus even included lepers, perhaps the equivalent of social outcasts that the demented have now become in our modern culture. All categories of people were treated as persons in Christ. The church, as in days of old, must take a countercultural stand in the twenty-first century regarding the unborn child and the senile alike, to treat all as persons, not cultural artifacts, as wanted or unwanted, useful or useless, legacy or burden. We would argue that even if a demented person requires burdensome care, Christ is able to provide meaning for such care and the courage and capacity to set correct boundaries that protect the caregiver and recipient of care. But we must be grounded in certain scriptural principles. We are all persons, all created "in the image of God," whatever our religious or ethnic origins. Yet between the first century and now, little help was given to the helpless, the insane and the other vulnerable categories of humanity. Admonition to love the least of these helps give biblical purpose and meaning to the hard work of caring for someone who might not recognize or appreciate the care. With earlier diagnosis, the church may need to move into position to prepare those affected by the disease and those who choose to be lovingly present. Though the term *caregiver* is helpful, it represents a rather modern application of words that leaves out the word *love*.

Barbara Tuchman, who has studied carefully the upheavals of the fourteenth century, notes that Western society in the late Middle Ages made virtually no organized provision for the vulnerable members of society other than within a few religious communities.[9] To be fair, church leaders and doctors have historically been confused about innovative medical practices until modern times.[10] And yet the concept of

---

[9]Barbara Tuchman, *A Distant Mirror: The Calamitous Fourteenth Century* (Harmondsworth, U.K.: Penguin, 1979).

[10]Ronald L. Numbers and Ronald C. Sawyer, "Medicine and Christianity in the Modern World," in Martin E. Marty and Kenneth L. Vaux, *Health/Medicine and the Faith Traditions* (Philadelphia: Fortress, 1982), pp. 133-60.

personhood could have better informed even antiquated medical care. Only gradually from the seventeenth century onwards did institution-alized care begin to take place. But even in the beginning of the nine-teenth century, the great innovator of medical care for those suffering from mental distress, Samuel Hahnemann, could still condemn the way doctors treated "the insane," as worse than prison guards might treat criminals.[11] Most of these mental institutions still remained de-personalizing until the past two or three decades.

I (Dr. Parker) was an eyewitness to such institutional care. While working on my doctorate, I conducted, in contract with the Alabama Department of Mental Health, suicide assessments of inpatients at Bryce Hospital during the infamous, precedent-setting Wyatt-Sticky court case in which a mental patient successfully sued the state of Ala-bama for providing inadequate mental health care, a case that later served as the basis for federal standards of inpatient psychiatric care. Years after the successful court action was enacted at Bryce, I was asked to accompany a local pastor to visit a hospitalized member of his con-gregation. Afterward, even after all the changes had been enacted, it seemed to both the pastor and me that the friendliest person we met during the entire experience was the patient. Despite the many im-provements in inpatient psychiatric care, the experience left me all the more convinced of the importance of kind-natured family and church visitation in elder caregiving.

Today, far better diagnostic skills are in place for dementia. In the past few decades, the Diagnostic and Statistical Manual, used to di-agnose psychiatric or psychological disorders, has literally tripled in size and content. Most professionals admit that labeling a person is not equivalent to cure, but an accurate diagnosis constitutes a neces-sary step in the right direction. Even so, major cultural modifications are still needed. For example, how do we discuss memory loss with seniors? Many are confused about the terms *dementia* and *Alzheimer's disease.* The latter is still associated with "no help, no cure and no hope." It is a neurological condition of brain degeneration. But de-

---

[11]Samuel Hahnemann, *Organon of Medicine,* trans. J. Kunzli and P. Pendleton (London: Victor Gollanz, 1983).

mentia, while suggestive of a lessening of cognitive faculties (including memory loss) suggests, we would posit, also a dementing environment—a culture of dementia—of being socially considered "growing old." It is thus a prevalent condition of all seniors—of becoming conscious of the loss of self-significance, of a weakening of self-identity, of becoming "a social burden," with the conscious awareness of the growing loss of previous abilities. Thus a senior will now enter into a pattern of life that could include emotional and mental disarray, where it is often difficult to distinguish between cause and effect. Does depression occur from brain disease or from social alienation? Does the speed of dementia indicate the collapse of social support, whereas neurological decline usually moves much more slowly? Rarely does a senior ever have the reflective powers or the advice from others to face up to such issues.

Categories of identity such as "senior," "patient" and "mentally ill," are all demeaning, yet they are consistent with a biological model of the human being. Some of the first psychiatric studies with dementia patients were done in Sweden by I. Karlsson, and the results were published in 1988. Karlsson demonstrated that where there had been intensive personal care and more social interaction, measurable neurological improvement occurred in the brains of dementia sufferers.[12] Prior to this clinical experimentation, another researcher made provisions to house such sufferers in smaller residential units as fully part of the local community but with additional caregiving.[13] The first issue of a medical journal devoted to the care of dementia appeared in the United Kingdom only in 1992.[14] In contrast, the U.S. journal *Ageing and Society* began in 1980. Pioneering work on dementia care has been conducted and published by Tom Kitwood in such works as *The New Culture of Dementia Care* and *Dementia Reconsidered: The Person Comes*

---

[12]I. Karlsson, G. Brane, E. Melin, A.-L. Nyth and E. Rybo, "Effects of Environmental Stimulation Biochemical and Psychological Variables in Dementia," *Acta Psychiatrical Scandanavica* 77 (1988): 207-13.

[13]L. Annerstadt, *Collective Living for the Demented in Later Life* (Lund, Sweden: Gerontologiskt Centrum, 1987).

[14]*Journal of Dementia Care*, since 1992.

*First.*[15] And the U.S. journal *Alzheimer's Care Quarterly,* issued since 1999, focuses on loss of memory merely as a physical disease of the brain, which medication may slow it's degenerative process. But this deflects attention from the preventive, social measures, which are ameliorating of the much broader personal disabilities of the afflicted. Stronger, more intentional personal relations are required, by and for seniors, as a preventive measure against the rate of memory loss.[16]

The care needs of dementia sufferers encompass three distinct dimensions. First, in dementia we can and should apply state of science findings from neuroscience and other specialties. Second, we must consider whether our whole culture may be showing signs of being "a dementing society" that contributes to widespread senior experiences of dementia. Third, we must face up to the magnitude of ethical tasks required of our caregivers. All three approaches are needed, suggesting that the growing challenge of dementia in an aging society can become a blessing in disguise by changing our cultural paradigm and fostering a more caring society.

### The Neuroscience of Dementia

*Dementia* (Latin *de mens,* "out of mind") is used to describe a group of symptoms, a syndrome characterized by multiple cognitive and functional deficits of sufficient severity to interfere with daily activities and social relationships.[17] The loss of functioning in dementia is due to the death of brain cells, which can be caused by a variety of diseases. It is important to distinguish between treatable and potentially reversible causes of dementia, but nonreversible dementias like Alzheimer's disease predominate in the geriatric population. Although progressive, the course of dementia symptoms varies depending on underlying disease processes. Caregivers especially (most of whom have no medical train-

---

[15]T. Kitwood and S. Benson, eds., *The New Culture of Dementia Care* (London: Hawker, 1995); Tom Kitwood, *Dementia Reconsidered: The Person Comes First* (Maidenhead, U.K.: Open University Press, 1997).

[16]What we have not been able to find is evidence whether ethnic groups such as the Chinese, Koreans or Japanese—who generally practice more traditional family care of the aged—have less incidence of the cultural dementia discussed above.

[17]American Psychiatric Association, 2000.

ing) need to understand that dementia can mean different things for different people. It may express itself many ways according to its diverse effects upon varied individuals. It may even be that further research will indicate what we now call "Alzheimer's" is an umbrella term that turns out to have diverse pathological processes.

Vascular dementia is widely considered the second most common type of dementia. It develops when impaired blood flow to parts of the brain deprives cells of food and oxygen. It is estimated that some 10 to 20 percent of cases of dementia occur in this way or from mild strokes. Thus it is becoming apparent that mixed causes may account for later forms of dementia. More recently, it has become apparent that mixed causes may account for dementia, including neurological disorders such as Huntingdon's and Parkinson's diseases, together representing another 5 to 10 percent of cases of dementia. Reversible and partially reversible dementias may comprise 10 to 20 percent. But the prevalence of reversible dementia is much less than it was previously thought.[18] Earlier in life, illnesses tend to be more clear-cut and definitive. But with senility so many factors have accumulated that causes become less available to explain the pathology. The prevalence of dementia increases rapidly with age; it is perhaps 5 percent for those aged seventy-one to seventy-nine, but over 37 percent for those ninety or older. Because of the aging of the populations of the industrialized countries, the prevalence of dementia is expected to increase dramatically.[19] Recent testimony by California's first lady Maria Shriver (daughter of Sergeant Shriver, who served with President Kennedy and was diagnosed with Alzheimer's in 2003), former House Speaker Newt Gingrich and Supreme Court Justice Sandra O'Conner (March 2009, Washington, D.C.) was intended to raise awareness about the disease and promote community support, citing a new study from the Alzheimer's Association that found more than five million Americans suffer from the disease, treating the disease costs nearly

---

[18]A. Clarfield, "The Decreasing Prevalence of Reversible Dementias: An Updated Meta-analysis," *Archives of Internal Medicine* 13 (2003): 2219-29.

[19]R. Katzman, "Epidemiology of Alzheimer's Disease and Dementia: Advances and Challenges," in *Alzheimer's Disease: Advances in Etiology, Pathogenesis and Therapeutics*, ed. K. Iqbal, S. Sisodia and B. Wimblad (Chichester, U.K.: Wiley, 2001), pp. 11-21.

$150 billion a year, and indicating that one in two persons over the age of eighty will suffer from dementia. Currently, research suggests that two-thirds of those with dementia will suffer from Alzheimer's disease, which means the whole of society will soon be facing a challenge of epidemic proportions.

Dementia causes profound changes in a person's functional abilities. Sustained loss of memory and impairment of other intellectual functions cause dysfunction in daily living. At least one of the following cognitive disturbances must also be present: (1) *aphasia*, vague or empty speech, (2) *apraxia*, impaired ability to execute motor functioning, (3) *agnosia*, failure to recognize or identify objects and (4) *disturbance in executive function*, failure to think abstractly and to plan, initiate, sequence, monitor and stop complex behavior.[20] Because the assessment is therefore complex with wide ramifications, a whole team of experts is needed both to diagnose and to provide the appropriate caregiving skills. This is one area in which a church community can provide referral sources to utilize the appropriate specialists and agencies within the community, which a single caregiver may have no way of knowing nor of coordinating but church members may have personal experience with. While a primary caregiver such as a spouse is vital, very soon many secondary caregivers are required also, something that in aging congregations is already becoming a necessary or even central pastoral task.

### Living in a "Dementing Culture"

Our physical illnesses are, to some extent, also borne in the context of a socially sick society. City life, intense professional pressures, financial worries, technical alienation, competitive colleagues, jealous neighbors and dysfunctional family life take a toll not only on our spirits, but also upon our bodies. Bereavements, loneliness, disempowerment, ignoring, withholding love, disparagement, stigmatization, labeling, disruption and many other negative traits of an alienating culture of ageism intensify malignancy for seniors. Their morale

---

[20]R. Kane, J. Ouslandr and I. Abrass, *Essentials of Clerical Geriatrics*, 5th ed. (New York: McGraw-Hill, 2004).

too often dips into a downward spiral to the point that tragically, some want simply to turn their face to the wall and die. Dementia in its earlier stages seems itself to cruelly mock the sufferer: while immediate memory disappears quickly, long term memory often remains intact and so engenders great comparisons and the connections between past and present.

Dementia is a significant challenge to the Cartesian assertion "I think, therefore I am!" A senior may not be able any longer to think as lucidly as in the past, nor to remember in ways that satisfy one's sense of order and precision. But the older years are a time to be loved more than ever before, to dwell in the security of "I am beloved, therefore I am." The house may now be much more messy, the cooking may sometimes be weird, the day's program may become less predictable—so what? These are no longer as important as one previously thought to be essential. A "homey home" is what really counts, not a showpiece. It is not dementia that necessarily entails a radical disintegration of the person, but the lack of care for that individual who might no longer experience any love. It is the death of "the person" that is most deadly!

Many non-churchgoers have a personal narrative that explains their later lack of religious support. In the novel *Still Alice*, when the main character was in the early stage of her disease, the thought of no longer being a Harvard professor terrified her. Almost instinctively one day, she stumbled into All Saints' Episcopal Church, only a few blocks from her house. She was relieved to find no one there, because she could not explain why she had come. She sat in a pew, looking at the stained glass windows of Jesus, as the shepherd and as the healer performing a miracle. A banner to the right of the altar read, "God is our Refuge and Strength, a Very Present Help in Trouble." She could not be in more trouble than now, so she remained long, waiting for indefinable "help." But her mother had been a secular Jew and she was raised Catholic by her father, so the validity of her childhood faith was never supported by her mother and she had received no satisfying answers from the church or her father. So now in Alice's trouble "she felt like a trespasser, undeserving, unfaithful."[21] Similarly, many in our society could find the early stage of dementia a critical opportunity to come to faith, to receive comfort and support when their loss of independence might direct them to a new dimension of hope and comfort. But somehow they come at the wrong time when the church is empty or with undisclosed barriers of a negative narrative. Or it could be that with senility they cannot bear to confess as did Nicodemus, "how can a man be born [again] when he is old?" (Jn 3:4). Is it not too late?

### The Character of the Caregiver(s)

The great and complex challenges of the onset of dementia become a day of reckoning within a family and for all concerned. The character of the caregiver(s) plays a vital role in dementia. As the author of *The Alzheimer's Sourcebook for Caregivers* has observed, "If we do not deal with our own issues of love and grief around the failures of love, we cannot live with Alzheimer's disease."[22] It is as if we need all of our own life, in all its maturation and fruition, to stand up to the final test of our own personal resources and meet the challenges we will face with the dementia of the loved one(s). How do we love the "no goes" in our congregations and families?

Thus the onset of dementia may also induce a bio-psycho-social-spiritual crisis within the inner lives of family members now faced with unprecedented emotional challenges. For the emotional life of the demented is itself heightened with uninhibited bouts of frustration, anger, fear and loss of significance and of identity. The natural responses of caregivers will often be negative when they should be positive. Coming to terms with the illness may be a long, slow process requiring growing understanding and patience. Previous conflicts within the family tend to be exaggerated further, everyone interpreting from their own wounded narrative. The church could lead the way in helping its members lovingly prepare for the care of aging parents, rather than simply

---

[21]Genova, *Still Alice*, p. 98
[22]F. Gray-Davidson, *The Alzheimer's Sourcebook for Caregivers* (Los Angeles: Lowell House, 1993), p. 161.

reacting in crisis.[23] Such preparation might help shore up scriptural admonitions to honor mother and father. "No goes" provide the family and the church with an opportunity to learn how to love unconditionally, and perhaps there are no greater gifts than a skill set of love that is able to meet the most difficult of tests and a learned dependence upon the Holy Spirit for the capacity to love in a Christlike manner.

All positive responses are summed up in one concluding need, love. Providing five basic needs of human personhood unpacks the meaning of love: comfort, attachment, inclusion, occupation and identity.

*Comfort.* One's first instinct when a loved one begins to lose coping abilities is to put one's arms around him or her and whisper comfort. Literally, comfort provides inner strength when one's world is falling apart. The emotional life becomes raw and the oscillations of anger and distrust, together with dependence and gratitude, create swinging moods of strong dialectics. These can change suddenly and unexpectedly, like a sudden storm on a placid lake. One early victim of dementia, Diana Friel McGowin, in her book *Living in the Labyrinth* vividly describes her struggles to remain a person, despite her disabilities: "My every molecule seems to scream out that I do exist, and that existence must be valued by someone! Without someone to walk this labyrinth by my side, without the touch of the fellow-traveler who understands my need of self-worth, how can I endure the rest of this uncharted journey?"[24] The sense of loss requires empathy and immediate response of support in sudden moments of personal loss. As an old friend wrote me recently about his own situation, "senility is experiencing a series of bereavements."

*Attachment.* The medical pronouncement "the patient has Alzheimer's" is like the pronouncement of the Israelite priest in the Old Testament, "this is a leper." There is the immediate feeling of separation, of distancing one's own cognitive skills from the one now going "crazy." One does not live together as "one flesh" in a long, happy marriage without becoming sensitive to the slightest sense of being now somehow separated. One no longer remembers all the telephone calls, all the mes-

---

[23]Ideas for such preparation are discussed in more detail in chapter 12.
[24]D. F. McGowin, *Living in the Labyrinth* (Cambridge: Mainsail Press, 1993), p. 124.

sages of friends, the times of appointments, and more. Thus the deepening sense of being cut-off from loved ones, of new threats of loneliness,
makes the importance of attachment a vital gift of the caregiver. *Attachment* implies the vital need of bonding, as is most often discussed with
respect to childhood. John Bowlby's creative studies of the needs of a
child to be bonded can be extended to explain the ongoing importance
of attachment throughout life.[25] When a senior's world grows progressively uncertain, maintaining family bonds may be as vital for seniors as
it is for children. People with dementia are continually finding themselves in situations they experience as strange. Providing a familiar and
consistent environment that includes the underlying loyalty of the
caregiver(s) allows the senior to remain stronger in spirit.

*Inclusion.* Our intrinsic need of belonging, of not being exiled and
alone, can be called *inclusion*. We are created to be social beings, "made
in the image and likeness of God." Having close family ties, enjoying
good friends and living in community should all be norms of personhood. Individualism itself is a cultural defect, not a human benefit.
Inclusion comes poignantly into the foreground when those with dementia feel the threat of being cut off as sensitively as those who are
deaf or blind. Thus the more deterioration sets in; the more they seek
attention. In older institutions this need was not met, and seniors were
often left terribly alone. Tessa Perrin has described vividly "the bubble
of isolation" in which seniors with advanced dementia can dwell.[26]
When such needs for inclusion are not met, the downward spiral may
quickly end in death. But in reverse, when treated as a person, the senior may once more have hope and be given space and dignity.

*Occupation.* In the novel *Still Alice*, as soon as the professor of cognitive psychology is diagnosed with Alzheimer's, she has to give up
her prestigious career. It's all over! Or is it? In actuality, occupation is
much more than one's job. It reflects upon our creativity and need for
self-esteem through actions that enhance our significance in many
different ways. A mother who has cooked and entertained hospitably

---

[25]John Bowlby, *The Making and Breaking of Affectional Bonds* (London: Tavistock, 1979).
[26]Tessa Perrin, "Occupational Need in Severe Dementia: A Descriptive Study," *Journal of Advanced Nursing* (1997).

all her life cannot suddenly be told no longer to do these things. (It is bad enough to be told your driving days are over!) A father may have to relinquish some professional and other public duties, gradually perhaps, but he can still pursue hobbies he loves. Gradual relinquishment is kinder, more affirming and therapeutic. When we are deprived suddenly of our accustomed occupations, we readily atrophy in our giftedness. So caregivers must know seniors well enough to know what gives the deepest satisfaction and sense of significance. Other factors are already attacking self-esteem; there is no need to further compound the loss.

*Identity.* All of us have a name that distinguishes us from everyone else. This mirrors our need to have an identity, which is also our narrative. Our stories make each of us unique, giving unity and meaning to our continued existence. This link between past and present gives us courage to face the unknown future even in the presence of death. (Even on our tombstone, if we are rich enough to have one, we have inscribed our name, date of birth and relationship with others.) Loved ones have always remembered our birthday, and family lore has placed us within a specific set of relationships. It becomes crucial with dementia to know that even when we may forget our own identity, with memories fading away about many things, we are not forgotten. For others now hold our memory instead as the loving recorders of our own past. Caretakers who take the time to learn about the personal history of dementia sufferers, or friends and family members who can play a part in recalling the life stories of those to whom they provide companionship and care, offer a great gift to those whose self-identity is in peril.

When caregivers can put themselves into the shoes of those they care for, they experience more empathy for the sufferer and can more easily respond by meeting the needs discussed here. Yet the natural reactions of caregivers commonly contribute the opposite of these primary needs. The wounds of the demented wound them as well, as if the caretaker needed the most comfort. The human response is to feel repulsed when kind intentions are misunderstood, and then anger alienates caregiver and the demented further. Caregivers often interpret their roles as requiring them to take charge and "do the job properly," which only generates more helplessness for the unemployed sufferer of dementia. This results in a further sense of worthlessness and a further loss of personal identity for the victim of dementia. Further spirals into depression follow suit, and the fall into deeper alienation.

**Preventative Action**

What about family members who want to help their parents and themselves avoid the dreaded condition altogether? Does science offer any hope? Will there be a cure and are there preventive precautions to the much-feared Alzheimer's disease? Our current understanding of the latest research suggests earlier and more definitive diagnostic scenarios, and it confirms that proactive brain health (healthy body—healthy brain) maintenance before and during the early stages of Alzheimer's and other dementias may slow the process of deterioration.

While medical science would distinguish between genetic causes of dementia, such as found with Alzheimer's disease, we have seen too that there are many other causes as well. The website <www.alzbrain. org> raises questions that may indicate our own risk factors for dementia, whatever our age: Do I have untreated high blood pressure? Am I overweight? Or do I have evidence of obesity? Do I eat a poor diet? Do I have severe bouts of depression? Do I have poorly controlled diabetes? Do I exercise very little? Do I watch too much television and do not use my mind very much? Is there a strong history of dementia in my family? Do I smoke or drink alcohol a lot? Is my social and spiritual life very limited? Positive responses to any of these questions will suggest a poor brain lifestyle that may contribute to dementia later in life. Since our brain is part of our body, dementia is not just a concern for seniors but for everyone, young or old.

Our colleague and friend Dr. Richard Powers serves on the Alzheimer's Foundation Board and is a neuropathologist and geriatric psychiatrist. As such, he is a leading spokesperson and educator on the topic of prevention, having advised both presidential campaigns on policy matters in the 2009 election. Dr. Powers would be quick to share that there is a great deal of misinformation about a cure for Alzheimer's disease and other dementias. Though a cure is unlikely in the next five years, much can be done to help caregivers anticipate and plan care. Also, in his *Handbook for Spiritual Communities on Helping Members with Memory Problems*, Dr. Powers alerts the baby boomer generation on "ten ways that *recognizing* dementia may help your parents"[27] Recognizing dementia:

1. corrects treatable causes of memory troubles

2. slows the progress of some dementias

3. improves medical and hospital care

4. reduces risk for accidental injuries

5. avoids complications from over-the-counter medications

6. allows the parent to organize and safely manage their personal business

7. reduces risk of avoidable problems that cause a parent to move from their home

8. protects against financial exploitation

9. protects against abuse by others

10. improves the quality of everyone's life by reducing anxiety and stress

Informed adults can make healthy lifestyle changes that decrease their risk of developing dementia. But even in the presence of a diagnosis, simple lifestyle and safety modifications can lessen the unpleasant impact of dementia on both seniors and those who care for them.

Another colleague in neurology and member of our team Dr. Daniel Potts has become a unique advocate and champion of dementia patients and their caregivers. Born out of his experience as an Alzheimer's caregiver, Dr. Potts promotes the expressive arts to improve the lives of dementia patients and their caregivers through his foundation, Cognitive Dynamics. Lester Potts, his father, has become a local celebrity; he is a seventy-eight-year-old end-stage Alzheimer's

---

[27]Richard E. Powers, *A Handbook for Spiritual Communities on Helping Members with Memory Problems* (Tuscaloosa, Ala.: Bureau of Geriatric Psychiatry/DETA, 2007).

patient and has been the subject of a book and several media articles because of his art, art that he started creating *after* his diagnosis and by a man *who had never painted before.*[28] Dr. Potts is involved in bringing expressive art therapies to Alzheimer's patients in the underserved, rural areas of Alabama.

## Memory Reflects God's Character

In a scientific culture like ours, is there any greater threat to a senior than being told through all sorts of innuendos, "You're losing your mind!" For four primary reasons, the loss of memory is a new universal fear among our society as we age. First, cognition is of primary importance in our technological society. Second, personality changes clearly occur as a result of memory loss and its emotional consequences. Third, we have become a society in which people consciously value their self-made identity and exaggerate the value of the role their professional careers define them. Fourth, contemporary living is complex. (This becomes painfully apparent when we lose our wallet with all its plastic cards so vital to our day-to-day welfare. We have so many more things we say we cannot afford to forget!)

Into this setting, a Christian response speaks profoundly. Memory is far more intrinsically God's business than a human concern. As Julian of Norwich took up a small hazel nut into her hand, she said "God made it; God cares for it; for God loves it!" A dear friend of mine (Dr. Houston) died with a hazel nut still tucked inside his pillowcase. For the God who created us will take of us even beyond the shadow of death. Søren Kierkegaard observed: "life can only be understood backwards; but it must be lived forwards." If we know we came from a loving, healthy family we can live confidently into the future. Biblically we are assured we were created "in the image and likeness of God," and that his purpose was to be Immanuel, "God with us." Israel was assured God had made a covenant with them, to be "their God," who stipulated his bond with them as "the God who remembers" them. We can only fundamentally understand the category of person as a theological cat-

---

[28]Daniel C. Potts, *The Broken Jar* (Tuscaloosa, Ala.: Word Way Press, 2006).

egory, of being intrinsically relational in our creation by the triune God of grace.

When therefore "God remembered Noah" and saved him from the flood (Gen 8:1), "remembered Abraham" in saving Lot from destruction (Gen 19:29), opened Rachael's womb to bear a child in her barrenness (Gen 30:22) or heard the groaning of the afflicted Israelites in their bondage in Egypt (Ex 2:24), God had much more than a good memory. The term reflects God's divine character in both redemption and judgment, his redemptive history of Israel. God's remembrance expresses his attentiveness towards us personally, whether in grace or in judgment. Unlike human memory, which is corrupted and diverted to other loyalties, God's active remembering is identical with his actions and his character of love. It is his creative and redemptive power. Our powers of memory may not be sustained, but he is "the same yesterday, today and forever."

The prophets, then, strongly urge us "to remember the LORD thy God," and indeed to "remember his statutes" (stipulations of the covenant life). Within the Hebrew context, states Brevard Childs, "an act of remembrance is not a simple inner reflection, but involves an action, an encounter with historical events."[29] The past will not disappear so that we operate only presently, as God too will not go away just for our rebellious desires. Such remembrance implies confession, contrition and conversion. Above all it calls our attention to the exclusive attention we should give of ourselves to God, since our uniqueness reflects upon the universal human need of God, of a relationship with him that no one else can ever rival. Such remembrance then is the equivalence of "choosing life," eternal life, over all else.

Biblical memory is always associated with the *heart*, which is the most important anthropological term of the Old Testament. It functions to control all physical, mental, emotional and spiritual functions, so no English word is like it, making it difficult to translate. As my (Dr. Houston's) friend and colleague Bruce Waltke has described, it is "the inner forum of the soul," the center of one's personal being in both its

---

[29]Brevard S. Childs, *Memory and Tradition in Israel* (London: SCM Press, 1962), p. 34.

inner and outer realities.[30] Such "remembrance within the heart" is therefore far deeper and richer than merely having a good memory. Christians in a state of advanced dementia, having lost mental memory, can remain secure in the Father's everlasting arms. God's memory of us qualifies us as human persons, even if we are in an advanced state of dementia. My niece with Down's syndrome has a love for Jesus that is genuinely central to her inner emotions; within her mental handicap, she can still solemnly obey Christ's invitation at the Eucharist to "do this in remembrance of me" (1 Cor 11:24-25).

Christian memory therefore is unlike classical memory, which is merely the recall of reflective reason and at its best, recalling the existence of the gods, or even the belief that the soul is itself divine. Conjoining memory with the heart, the great Christian father of the church, Augustine of Hippo (354–430) sees memory as "the eye of the heart," and "the love of God" as the purpose of memory. In the beginning of his great classic *Confessions*, "remembering the Creator" is the act of conversion and in the praise of the heart, as knowing the proper relationship to God. This then leads to the proper relationship with the neighbor, or "the other," to love socially as well. While memory plays a cognitive part in Augustine, as it must do, this is subsidiary to the interiority of personal relatedness to and with God, which lies at the heart of biblical faith.

Following further into the biblical role of memory, the other great father of the Reformation, John Calvin (1509–1564), interprets the Scriptures not as timeless truths but as the participatory engagement of God with human persons. It is by having a heart submissive to God, in the light of Christ, by the operation of his Holy Spirit, that we properly exercise the role of memory. So memory is not the simple deposit of information we can recall later, but it is more truly the inward formation of the person by being brought into a relationship with the Trinity. Thus there is no true memory for Calvin, without God being its object in spiritual attentiveness. Thus the autonomous self, which today is so threatened by the calamity of dementia, is itself

---

[30]Bruce K. Waltke, *An Old Testament Theology* (Grand Rapids: Zondervan, 2007), pp. 225-27.

"demented," for it has no true knowledge of one's self, nor indeed any knowledge of God.

In his commentary on the book of Deuteronomy, Calvin thus reminds us of God's remedy of remembrance: "Nothing but the recollection of [the Israelites'] deliverance could tame their arrogance; for what could be more unreasonable than that *they* should be insolent who were formerly the slaves of a most haughty nation [Egypt], and who had not acquired their liberty by their own efforts, but contrary to their hope and deserts had obtained it by God's mere favor."[31]

Christian families dealing with dementia and other forms of mental deficiency can be assured and comforted that Christian faith is not undermined nor destroyed by the losses of cognition. Primarily, God is mindful of us—not the other way around—as the psalmist exclaims with gratitude and wonder in Psalm 8. Since our memory of God is much more a "soulful affair" than a matter of brain chemistry, the findings of neuroscience will never threaten our faith.[32]

---

[31]John Calvin, *Commentary on Deuteronomy*, ed. Charles William Bingham (Grand Rapids: Baker, 1974), pp. 398-99.

[32]This is something the Nobel neuroscientist, Sir John Eccles, also assured me once at a dinner party. His approach was different from what we have explored biblically, in that he was defending the canons of science from usurping the reductionistic role of scientism. Our argument here instead expands the moral significance of memory and indeed of personhood, which calls for reform in our society.

# 17

# CHRISTIANS, SENIORS AND A
# MORE PERSONAL SOCIETY

...

Facing the demographic "tsunami" of an aging population, we will also be facing increasing disabilities in every family and every walk of life. To face these changes in ways that affirm the God-given value of all people and allow our elders to speak needed wisdom to the young, we must anticipate the need to foster a more compassionate culture, indeed, a "personal" society. Plainly we are already politically and economically unable to medicalize all of society, as the needs of national health reform measures are showing us. The escalation of medical costs, the increasing complexity of medical technology, and the need to resign how medical care addresses chronic disease are issues that must be addressed before Medicare and Medicaid systems reach their financial crisis threshold. As we have discussed, quality medical care is not enough when a person loses their capacity to live independently, social care is needed. As we have indicated, dementia is much more than a neurological disease, and its challenge is therefore more broadly personal than medical services alone can provide. Tender loving care cannot be bought and served across the counter of the pharmacist.

Just as the waning of medieval Christendom challenged the reformers to reconsider the doctrines and practice of true Christianity, we anticipate the need for another "Reformation" of the church and another "Renaissance" of society. We believe that cultural change precedes ecclesial reform. This time it will concern "the crisis of the personal," in both secular and Christian circles, since the treatment of seniors is virtually the same in both. This may seem a small issue, yet we believe it is symptomatic of much greater social issues. Churches and seminaries, not dissimilar to the institutions and professions of the secular society, are not a prophetic voice for our times. They are all constitutionally unprepared for such a revolutionary shift of perception towards the new personal resources seniors can provide for a more caring society.

**The Challenge of Cultural Transformation**

Piecemeal efforts to improve the quality of life for seniors are praiseworthy. Yet like the canary in the mine, the contemporary treatment of the old, the vulnerable and the insane alerts us to the toxicity throughout our whole culture, a culture that is still depersonalizing. By *culture* we mean the settled, established, assumed way of living together as human beings. There have been changes (assumed to be progressive) as we have moved from an agrarian to an industrial to a post-industrial, westernized urban culture. But with the care of the elderly, as with other elements, patterns within cultures tend to remain fixed long beyond the conditions which brought them about. Lesser cultures may try to effect changes—as the hippies did in the early 1970s or as the Facebook subculture is doing today—and the marginal changes they make in their own generations create a ripple effect felt long after their time. Beliefs are supported by institutions, so that they develop reciprocal reinforcement, just as popular beliefs in the advances of neuroscience are partnered by the massive support of pharmaceutical companies or religious beliefs are supported by religious denominations and their local churches. These generate patterns of power, reinforced by hierarchy, prestige, traditions, yes, and money too!

The first escape from such cultural determinism is to reject the use of such powers. A personal story from Dr. Houston illustrates just such an "escape." In 1927 the philosopher Bertand Russell gave a public lecture, "Why I Am Not a Christian," later published in 1954. Soon afterward, Professor A. Blaikock, a classics professor, invited Dr. Houston with several others to respond from their differing professions—philosopher, chemist, physicist, etc.—why they were still Christians. Dr.

Houston's response was different: he remained a Christian because he was in pursuit of being "personal," rather than just a professional; Christianity offered a much more transcending identity. The trajectory has continued ever since. He exchanged the prestige of being an Oxford don for a pioneering experiment of non-seminary advanced theological education at Regent College in Vancouver, Canada. His priority has always been "people matter more than things," institutional or otherwise.

Another example comes from economist Robert Reich, a former Secretary of Labor in Washington, D.C., who decided that family values were more important than his political career. This happened when his small son was told, "Daddy will not be home tonight to kiss you goodnight." "Well, then Daddy," the child replied on the phone, "wake me up when you come home, so that you will kiss me." So rebuked as a father, he resigned (to the complete surprise of his colleagues) and wrote a provocative book, *The Future of Success*. Indeed, a starting point for cultural change may come from the insight of "the *failure* of success." Reflection shows that "success" is intrinsically a term of reductionism; the pursuit of a limited objective is required in order to "succeed." So one can be successfully wealthy or professionally famous without social costs, such as the deprivation of time for one's family life.[1] Then in turn, the renunciation of status may require a redefinition of the primary source of identity—not in one's profession—but as a family man, a friend or in other expressions of primarily being "personal" rather than being only "professional."

In a "youth culture" focused on success, friends begin to revalue their relationships. A cartoon in the *New Yorker* pictured two boys with baseball caps and backpacks, under the caption, "Most likely to succeed," one boy is saying to the other: "I'd love to come over and hang out, but now that we're competing in a global economy I can't."[2] Freedom from this cultural expectation would suggest the opposite remark, "I can, for I am not competing!"

Even radical theory may not initiate cultural change. A theologian

---

[1]David B. Reich, *The Future of Success* (New York: Vintage Books, 2000), p. 7.
[2]Ibid., pp. 218-19.

colleague of Dr. Houston's has been instrumental in renewing the church's awareness of the doctrine of the Trinity. His wife now chuckles when recalling the time when she collapsed on the floor of his study with a heart attack. Looking up from his desk he asked: "Mary, why are you lying on the floor?" He was too remote in thought to see her plight, and yet the mysterious wonder of the reciprocity of the divine persons was his specialized theological study. Theologically he knew that "being personal" is far more radical than a mere anthropological study. But his own personality needed (like the "old" Nicodemus) to be "born again."

Ever since economic theorists began to talk about "the market" in the eighteenth century, our culture has become "market-driven." As he drove around Scotland in 1773, Samuel Johnson noticed those areas prospering under the industrial economy in contrast to those outside it. Now the spirit of commerce has so penetrated "the sale of the self" that, as Tom Peters advertises, "Your most important job is to be head marketer for the brand called You."[3] You succeed now because you believe passionately not in God but in *yourself*! How can the psyche of self-marketing moneymakers be turned toward selfless careers in old age and inevitable handicaps; how can worshipers of Mammon become worshipers of God?

A certain brand of "welfare capitalism," associated with Medicare for U.S. seniors or socialized heath in countries like Canada and Britain, challenges this solely self-focused lifestyle. (Ironically, the escalation of costs is making this type of economy impossible in many places too.) The Scandinavian countries, where taxes effectively level out the contrasts between the absurdly rich from the poor and the pensioned, have succeeded better than most in promoting a national ethic of social concern. Denmark, for example, permits seniors to have six months education at its universities to improve the educational standards of their seniors. These cultures have become more open to promoting "the greening of the economy," showing concern for the future of the planet. They value responsible stewardship for the future well-being of one's

---

[3]Ibid., p. 154.

children and grandchildren, and ownership of the global problems they will inherit. "Climate change" is certainly affecting a "culture change" as older persons become more open to a paradigm change in their thinking and actions.

Perhaps cultural change requires a specific focus, such as moving from a market-driven to a sustainable economy. In the church could we not move from valuing only the innovation of youth to affirming the wisdom of seniors? The last years of life should not be those where the frequent quest for lost golf balls on the course or the habitual pursuit of a Starbucks coffee become the most important events of the day. Rather, the elder years must be the most intensely personal years of life of inspiring, mentoring and nurturing the younger. Healing is for "the other," as Francis of Assisi's prayer expresses:

> Lord, help me not so much to be understood, but to understand;
> And to love rather than to be loved;
> For it is in the giving that we receive.

The journey is about becoming, as Henri Nouwen expressed it, "the wounded healer." The mission of seniors should be to personalize the environment around them, so that "I-Thou" is more their vocabulary and less so "I-it." This great mission changes individuals into persons, so that friendships are vital, communities are essential and "me" gives way to "you." With regard to dementia, for example, that care of the demented should become far more personalized and less dependent on medication. (Ironically, in our "greening economy" we may have more concern for the trees than for other human beings.) The challenge for Christians is to inspire a greater reverence for all human persons.

### Taking Notice of the Weak Is Revolutionary

Taking a broad view of the past three hundred years, the novel *Émile* by Jean-Jacques Rousseau (1712–1778) was explosive in a decadent, aristocratic society. It exposed what a child felt and thought, not what adults thought a child should feel and think. Yet *Émile* was severely condemned by Archbishop de Beaumont and publicly burned by order of the Genevan government. As an orphan child of eleven, Rousseau was falsely accused of breaking his foster mother's comb. Other incidents occurred unjustly to him as a child, convincing him that adults dealt unjustly with children; adults did not understand them nor realize that they were less corrupted than their adult world. With Rousseau, the world of the child was opened up to exploration, as educators like Pestalozzi and Piaget or psychoanalysts like Freud would later explore. Today, "the world of the child" is well known, but ironically "the world of the aged" is still largely relegated to geriatric medicine and the other fields associated with gerontology. Why?

Looking back, we may say we have had two major economic revolutions. The first industrial revolution was based on the massive use of energy in the basic production of materials such as textiles, iron and other metals. The second revolution has been more commercial and also more professional in its complex development of service industries. It has brought into existence the remarkable rise of the sciences and the whole network of professional life. The gist of the senior problem today is that once retired, seniors are no longer viewed or esteemed as professionals in the society or in churches. As Rousseau observed of the child, so we observe today that the aged at the end of life are now not being heard. "Professionals" have become the powerful aristocracy of our day. They are not, however, of an "elite culture" by birth, but of a "mass culture" by training. Psychotherapy as a profession is flourishing so much because it is all about listening to the other. The importance also of "the electronic revolution" is its intensification of human communication, of which youth today have taken advantage.

Yet we see new green shoots for a more sensitized outlook, such as when Jean Vanier gave new hope for the mentally retarded in his communities of L'Arche, or Mrs. Shriver persuaded Olympic sports to be opened to the handicapped. Throughout this book we have maintained that the challenge of the impending needs of the aging population will help us identify how a radical reformation of Christianity itself in the twenty-first century might occur. For whenever we concern ourselves with God we find ourselves dealing with global and indeed cosmic issues. "For God so loved the world" (Jn 3:16), we are reminded. In his sovereign governance God may therefore bring changes within culture more than we may know. Yet these are always linked with such personal and intimate issues of human life. In divine sovereignty God uses changes of culture first, in which his servants can then take advantage of bringing about ecclesial reforms too, from the redemptive issues of their own personal narratives.

One such reformer in this regard is the Swiss Paul Tournier (ironically, a citizen of Geneva like reformers Calvin and even Rousseau!). Writing about the need of a more "humane society," Tournier reminds us he, too, was an orphan. Like Rousseau, this disability became a personal asset, enabling him to express both the voice of the child, as Rousseau did, as well as the voice of a senior, as Tournier has written about in several of his books.[4] Three and four decades after Tournier's writing, the voices of seniors are growing to a critical mass. Seniors are poised to effect a transformation in society when they live prophetically, not motivated by their professional ambitions, but drawing upon a life of experience with God.

The challenge of dementia has in large part lead to silencing the voices of the aged in our society. Table 22.1 contrasts two cultures of treating senility, suggesting revolutionary practices and ways of thinking that embrace the personhood of aging members of our society.

Table 22.1

| Old Culture | New Culture |
| --- | --- |
| A physical premise. Diseases attacking the central nervous system destroy the personality and the identity of the demented patient. | A personal/spiritual presence. Dementing diseases should be seen primarily as manifest forms of disability, physical and social, so the way the loved one is treated personally is critical. |
| Ultimate authority. Brain scientists and doctors are the ultimate authority. Breakthroughs with new drugs are needed also. | The social character of a human being. A caring community of both skilled practitioners and caretakers is needed, as are medical advances. But the basic premise is that being "human" has many facets. |

[4]Paul Tournier, *A Place for You* (New York: Harper & Row, 1968); *Learn to Grow Old* (Louisville, Ky.: Westminster John Knox Press, 1972).

**Table 22.1 cont.**

| Old Culture | New Culture |
|---|---|
| Basic needs. Physical care—such as proper foods, toileting and cleanliness—is needed, as is an accurate understanding of impairments, especially of cognition. | The nature of being a "person." There are as many forms of dementia as there are persons with dementia. In addition to the physical care, caregivers need an intimate knowledge of who the person is, with abilities, values, interests, forms of spirituality, etc. Problem behaviors should be viewed primarily as attempts to communicate requiring deeper engagement, not less. |
| Diseases. All diseases are a biological phenomenon, common to both humans and animals. | Human diseases. Some diseases are peculiar to the human being and exacerbated by human stress, anxiety, depression and other psychic factors. A condition of health is personal fulfillment. So a society is also "sick" when it is impersonal. Both individual and societal sicknesses need healing. |

## Mature Persons Personalize Knowledge

We have already hinted that mature seniors are key to challenging the depersonalization of our culture. They do so by making the knowledge of God ever more personal.

The recent disenchantment with the rationalism of modernity has opened up a fresh opportunity to revive serious Christian reflection upon conventional Christian morality. The new focus in neuroscience on the complexity of the emotions should lead the Christian to explore more deeply the whole emotional context of living personally as Christians. Then we will find ourselves entering into a more personal dialogue between God's Word and our mutual responses. For the subjunctive mood given us by René Descartes, "I think, therefore I am," now needs the corrective of the indicative mood, "Thus says the Lord," to recover a deeper, living biblical faith, whether we are Protestant, Roman Catholic or Orthodox in affiliation.

Behind the basic issues of our Christian faith, we are living with the dialectic between speculative thought and human existence, between reason and faith, between the poetic and the prudent, between the personal institute and the public institution and indeed, between the temporal and the eternal. These are different spheres of our humanity, where we need to make distinctions and to establish boundaries to social thought while engaging within personal reality. The illusion of being a "thinker" is that it assumes thought and existence are united, when of course thought can merely be daydreaming about existence. Every theological student knows that such cognitive studies often drive one away from the daily practice of a devotional Christian life. Actually, the abstraction of thought indicates that one is not paying enough attention to oneself as a person in the process of merely being a thinker. That is to say, it lacks the ethical dimension of being socially related and responsible to others. For to exist in "truth" implies being both truthful to one's self and also to others, thus considerably enhancing the meaning of existence. To think and exist personally before God vastly expands both the breadth of thought and the depth of our existence.

### Spiritual Seniors Live Out the Dialectic

This life laid bare before God's truth places us squarely in the dialectic of embodying that which is eternal. The Danish word for dialectics, *gjentagelse* is more expressive than our English term, denoting a situation that is "the same" (*gjen* = already in existence) that is reinterpreted in an original way, as "the other" (*at tage* = a new reality, truly new). In his short meditation of 1843 on this term, Søren Kierkegaard speaks of dialectics as being a new creative synthesis of uniting opposites. It is the experience of being held graciously by the truth, instead of endeavoring to hold it logically by one's own way of thinking, and therefore possessively so. Life is still immanent, yet it is in process of being reunderstood and relived transcendently, as ultimately "the way of eternal life." The movements between time and eternity, flesh and spirit, the old and the new are opposites, but they are resolved into a new state of being that is more genuinely human than our natural subjectivity can ever give us.

Thus within the intrinsic issues of our Christian faith, we live dialectically all the time. This is not the Hegelian dialectic between Nature and Spirit, which is a falsely Romantic interpretation of reality. But as Christians, we live with the dialectic between thinking and being, body and soul, temporal and eternal, ordinary and extraordinary, indeed a sinner called to sanctity. We use it to reflect wisely about the different spheres of our experiences, in such a way that they are kept in balance together, in their qualitative differences. Moreover, the dialectic reminds me (Dr. Houston) of my existence as "other-relating," so that my consciousness as a redeemed sinner is very different from that which would deny this new reality. The apostle Paul cites this paradoxically when he confesses: "I no longer live, but Christ lives in me" (Gal 2:20).

Limitation, incapacity, weakness and unreality are handicaps to us in our unredeemed state. They still may haunt us as Christians. Yet if they bring us nearer to Christ, then these handicaps can become gracious assets. So the Christian dialectic is a reprise, a revival, a renewal, a rebirth, indeed a re-creation, which all come from our reconciliation with God. None of these are repetitious, implying "more of the same," like a habitual, unexamined existence. Rather it is a spirally upward motion to a new state of being, which once seemed a paradox.

# 18

# THE VITAL ROLE
# OF REPENTANCE

*If the Divine call does not make us better, it will make us very much worse.*
*Of all bad men religious bad men are the worst.*
*Of all created beings the wickedest is one who originally*
*stood in the immediate presence of God.*

C. S. LEWIS, *REFLECTIONS ON THE PSALMS*

*Wickedness, when you examine it,*
*turns out to be the pursuit of some good in the wrong way.*

C. S. LEWIS, *MERE CHRISTIANITY*

*My faithful request and admonition is that you join our company and*
*associate with us, who are real, great and hard-boiled sinners.*
*You must not by no means make Christ to seem paltry and trifling to us,*
*as though he could be our Helper only when we want to be rid of imaginary,*
*nominal, and childish sins. No! No! That would not be good for us.*
*He must rather be a Savior and Redeemer from real, great,*
*grievous and damnable transgressions and iniquities, yea,*
*and from the very greatest and most shocking sins*
*. . . Aha! You want to be a painted sinner and accordingly,*
*expect to have in Christ a painted Savior. You will have to get*
*used to the belief that Christ is a real Savior and you are a real sinner.*
*For God is neither jesting nor dealing in imaginary affairs,*

*but He was greatly and most assuredly in earnest when He sent His own
Son into the world and sacrificed Him for our sakes.*

Martin Luther

• • •

On August 21, 1544, Martin Luther wrote the letter above to George
Spalatin, one of Luther's faithful and trusted friends. Spalatin had
given some advice that he later came to regard as sinful. When he
reached this conclusion, Spalatin became immersed in grief and guilt.
He was convinced that he should have known better and that he of all
people should not have made the mistake he had made. He could not
be consoled. When Luther learned of his friend's condition, he wrote
the letter above to offer him absolution and comfort.

In a biblical example, while building the wall of the temple was a
critical symbol after the exile in Old Testament times, now that Christ
has become our temple, our recognition of him can never be adequate
enough. As a beloved follower of Jesus, even guarding him with his
sword at the betrayal and arrest of Jesus by the soldiers, Simon Peter
then wept bitterly when he denied his association with him in that very
temple area of the high priest's house (Mt 26:69-75; Mk 14:66-72; Lk
22:54-62; Jn 18:15-18, 25-27). Clearly, it is only the death and resurrection of Christ that enabled (and still enables) Jesus Christ to be more
profoundly recognized as the Son of God, our Savior and Lord. This
was the bitterness of Peter's denial, that he had denied knowledge of
the incarnate Messiah, so long anticipated by Israel, who had now appeared. Hence, at Pentecost when Peter gave his address on the fulfillment of Old Testament prophecies concerning Christ, first from Joel,
then from the Psalms, his hearers in turn, "were cut to the heart" as
Peter had been in his meeting with his risen Lord.

This is the first instance in the New Testament of a medical term
used for being pierced with a thorn (the latin *compunctio* or compunc-

tion). It is used increasingly in the early church, until it takes a place of central importance among the desert fathers. Prominence was then given in the high Middle Ages to "the seven penitential psalms" after the Lateran Council of 1215. This council decreed personal confession to a priest should occur at least once a year. The rise of the individual then gave voice to a whole series of new expressions of repentance, in living out an active Christian faith.

Today, repentance plays a minor role in Christian devotion, whereas in the later Middle Ages it dominated the Christian life of the laity. David became the great archetype of the "confessor," not as a great king, but as a great sinner who pleaded his confession openly before God. The apostle Peter was likewise viewed as the model of confession and therefore the ideal Christian. As Protestants, we tend to dismiss the need for repentance as "Catholic," and swing to the opposite extreme of far too much moral complacency and of even the loss of the sense of sin. Since seniors have seen many consequences of wrong choices and directions in their personal lives, as well as in our culture, they should become like David and Peter to the younger generations; penitence should mark our way of life.

As sinners we all need repentance as the true way of the Christian life, so those who should be most conscious of the need of repentance are seniors, who have long experienced the ravages and alienation of sin. The wisdom of the apostle Paul was to know himself as "the chief of sinners," and the wisdom of seniors should likewise be to know ever more realistically the meaning and consequences of sin before God.

Culturally, as well as personally, we have much for which to repent. For example, the birth control pill and abortion appeared attractive solutions for having small families or no children at all. Rightly so, Pope John Paul II has frequently described our culture as "death-giving, as a holocaust of innocents." All is motivated by self-convenience, so that "I" can get on with "my" professional ambitions and career. When too many have indulged in what now appears to have become a very narcissistic culture, we wake up to the reality that a top-heavy aging population will put increasing economic pressures on the next generations to sustain our social initiatives—pensions, public health or other social benefits, once considered the norm. When will the trillions of dollars of new global debts recently acquired by our government ever be paid off by future generations? Increasingly, we are discovering that, often, what one generation considers a solution is merely the agenda for further ensuing problems. The issues of human life are more mysterious and complex than flattening everything into problems and solutions.

We need then repentance from our culture of self-fulfillment and a consumer society of increasing indebtedness. We need no less than a changing identity as stewards of the planet's limited resources and stewards of the well-being of future human generations. We begin by sharing with our grandchildren how we had to earn and save money, never spending beyond our means. We teach them loyalty to personal commitments of job and community, as well as to spouses and family. We repent that often we were blind to the causes of environmental deterioration and pollution and therefore our need to be the stewards of creation.

We repent that our notions of the autonomous self have made us unaware that such is the biblical meaning of *the wicked*—not necessarily doing wicked things by our reckoning, but merely living independent of God and his Word. We repent that the American dream of the self-succeeding individual may haunt subsequent generations in nightmarish ways. We remember the appalling consequences for future generations of our divorcing culture, for family life, for wounded children, for the losses of social cohesion. How blessed are the families who can celebrate silver and golden marriages and share the benefits spiritually with their grandchildren. Yet we repent of how often our careers were given first priority over our spouses and children, so that we were not known intimately by our families. As we read about castaway children in orphanages, we must be open to how we might be sensitive to those with past histories of neglect and abuse who question spiritually whether God himself can be trusted enough. Do we then wonder why our children have not accepted the transmission of faith as we would have wanted them to enjoy and to mature spiritually?

We repent that we have not been discerning enough about the uni-

versality and power of technology to lessen and impoverish our relationships with other persons. We have already noticed this with regard
to the low social skills of youth today. We need to note that Christians
heavily involved in institutional life become unreal in their personal
relations, because politics become more important than other persons.
So too can the academy become more godlike than God, even in Christian scholarship. Indeed, whatever we need to promote can take on a
life of its own that can distort all our other relationships, the one with
God most of all. It is more likely that retirees can then look back and
see these distortions for what they are, forms of idolatry. Hence Christian seniors should see the vital importance of being a prophetic voice,
within the church, as well as within their communities. And to be prophetic is to repent and call to repentance.

In repenting, we must remain lifelong learners. Without losing sight
of how to be lovingly present, we should be open to applying new technologies. Church programs in this regard can help older members to
focus on creating e-mail and Internet distribution lists of family members and close friends. The Internet can be used to stay in touch with
our children, grandchildren and great grandchildren, and it allows
them to connect with us. We can write to them regularly using the
Internet or text message words of encouragement before a college exam.
We can add moral codicils to our will, where we can share our most
important thoughts about life, perhaps to a future prodigal when he
turns sixteen. We can repent of our isolationism by finding a ministry
in late life and by telling our story in writing or creating a video interview. Our churches can provide programs that teach us how to tell our
story of faith. Remarkable resources exist that can, for example, capture
the history of a person who served in World War II and make it a part
of the official WWII historical archives.[1] As we have noted earlier, the

---

[1]See www.wsre.org/thewar/thewar_fieldkit.pdf. This guide—a collaboration between the Library of Congress Veterans History Project, Florentine Films and WETA public television
station in Washington, D.C.—contains hands-on production tips and interview techniques
from Ken Burns and Lynn Novick, as well as information on how to send completed interviews
to the Veterans History Project. This guide was created to help individuals and groups conduct
research and preserve the stories of our nation's veterans to ensure that they become a part of
our country's collective and permanent history.

church needs to reach out to the World War II cohort, which is rapidly dying off. Important messages about faith during a sustained world war are being lost, even as America deals with its longest war in history that is leaving over 50 percent of the returning troops at risk for post traumatic stress syndrome.[2] The church could serve as a linchpin for matching returning veterans with men and women of faith from the World War II generation.

The church can help promote these initiatives community-wide. In *Dear Old Man*, Charles Wells, a geriatric psychiatrist, writes to his future, elder self.[3] He offers personal advice to himself and others who might listen about how to enter what he considers the most challenging of life's stages—old age—by keeping in touch, remaining a lifelong learner, listening more, talking less, learning to walk gently. As suggested earlier, this book and other biblical references could be used to help older people conduct a life review.

For many of us in late life, repentance is hard. Recommendations like these do not come easy, particularly if there have been long standing patterns of unkindness or self-righteousness. Some of us are too busy finding fault, like the elder son in the prodigal son's story, seeming unable to celebrate our longevity or our brother's homecoming and salvation. The Holy Spirit must do his work in each of our lives, specifically at late life because most of us are going to live far longer than we ever imagined.

In the recent movie *Gran Torino*, Clint Eastwood plays a bitter, traumatized, guilt-ridden veteran of the Korean War who sacrifices his life for an Asian family he reluctantly befriends as a lonely widower. Alienated from his own family, he mentors a young teenager threatened by a local gang, leaving a lasting legacy for his community, church and family. Our Abba Father lovely embraces prodigals of all ages and particu-

---

[2]Essential features include the development of characteristic symptoms following exposure to an extreme traumatic stressor involving direct personal experience of an event or series of events that involve actual or threatened death or serious injury to mind or body (American Psychiatric Association, *Diagnostic and Statistical Manual of Mental Disorders*, 4th ed. [Washington, D.C.: American Psychiatric Association, 1994], p. 425).
[3]Charles Wells, *Dear Old Man: Letters to Myself on Growing Old* (Nashville: Backbone Press, 1995).

larly those who might have played the role of condemning elder. May all of us be open to a fresh work of the Holy Spirit, not only in our late life calling, but also in repentance, particularly in how we relate to our family and friends.

# 19

## IN SUMMARY

### Becoming a Christian Elder in Rebuilding the Church

*In the last days, God says, I will pour out my Spirit on all people.*
*Your sons and daughters will prophesy, your young men will*
*see visions, your old men will dream dreams.*

ACTS 2:17

• • •

Though there are many theoretical arguments to be made about the positive roles seniors can be expected to play within the life of the church today, Western Protestant church life does not currently enjoy a good reputation of its treatment of seniors. In spite of the demographic trends towards an aging population in the West, the increasing medical advances to prolong longevity, the financial prosperity of some seniors that enables them to be more givers than receivers, the innumerable technical and social facilities that encourage independence in seniors and prevent them from becoming house-bound, etc., the church is failing to tap into the unique—and biblical—resource now available in its seniors. As another older gentleman observed, "I've learned that the best classroom in the world is at the feet of an elderly person." "Ask . . . your elders, and they will explain to you" (Deut 32:7).

To underscore the wealth of talent and service that is available from our seniors, the actual personal experiences and perspectives of those who are healthy, active seniors need to be examined. Dr. Houston qualifies in that category, both as an octogenarian and as a senior who maintains many personal relationships and commitments with a faith-based focus. Indeed, his primary motive for continuing to travel around the world is to encourage others in the service of Christ. After all, we have not been given a ministry of religious empire building, but of spurring individual disciples and communities on to biblical maturation. This makes Christianity credible in today's world.

Before Nehemiah initiated the work to rebuild the wall in Jerusalem, he repented when he saw the condition of his homeland. "I confess the sins we Israelites, including myself and my father's house, have committed against you" (Neh 1:6). Are we broken-hearted, like Nehemiah, about the conditions of our society today? Are our communities any better off today than those about which Nehemiah prophesied? More importantly, can we envision a revival in our churches in which older members might fuel its flames (Neh 2:19-20)? As Nehemiah did, we need to ask for God's grace and help as we welcome to serious ministry the true elders of our church.

The notion of aging successfully has garnered more and more attention as our senior population has exploded over the past few years. Research has proven that if we are to age successfully, we must avoid disease and disability and maximize our intellectual and physical fitness. Though the church has been relatively silent about how to do this, the Scriptures and science have a great deal to say about these matters. By God's grace, we must maintain an active engagement with life through Holy Spirit led ministry, and we must be lifelong learners in Christ. We must give up and overcome age-graded ways of thinking. Most of us grew up with the life plan that first, we go to school, then, we work and finally, we retire. Yet, the Scriptures have little to say about *retirement*. On the contrary, we read in the Bible of countless examples of late-life contributors to God's purpose (Moses, Joshua, John, etc.). Education, work and leisure are all lifelong concepts grounded in the Scriptures. To successfully age, we must counter the many myths of aging: old age does *not* mean we are sick and frail and the old *can* continue to learn, to be sexual, to change bad habits and to contribute in meaningful, eternal ways to God's kingdom.

In making the case that most modern Christians are not energized for a great cause, but, instead, for their own leisure, Piper offers Campbell White's countercultural perspective from an earlier century:

Most men are not satisfied with the permanent output of their lives. Nothing can wholly satisfy the life of Christ within His followers except the adoption of Christ's purpose toward the world He came to redeem. Fame, pleasure and riches are but husks and ashes in contrast with the boundless and abiding joy of working with God for the fulfillment of his eternal plans. The men who are putting everything into Christ's undertaking are getting out of life its sweetest and most prized rewards.[1]

A senior focused on work for the Lord is generally a happy, fulfilled and successful ager.

Much has been learned from research performed in the communities and churches that are providing state of the art, biblically based programs that inform older persons about how to age successfully. Some churches are partnering in imaginative ways to offer forms of assistance to their seniors where gaps in service exist: transportation of older citizens out of hurricane prone areas, caregiver support programs, fall prevention initiatives and late life legacy projects, to name only a few. These newly developed programs within the church acknowledge, affirm and incorporate the faith of our fathers and mothers in a way that no other organization on earth can do. Information about proven programs that not only help a mature person avoid disease and disability, maximize his/her intellectual and physical fitness, remain actively engaged with life and continue to grow spiritually, but also provide opportunities for ministry.

As we help our elderly become teachers again and as they are brought more into contact with younger generations, the boomer generation and younger cohorts will learn how to confront their own aging in a proactive manner. As our elders are properly mentored and loved, they, in turn, can cultivate the kind of friendships and family relations that

---

[1]J. Campbell White, "The Laymen's Missionary Movement," in *Perspectives on the World Christian Movement*, ed. Ralph D. Winter and Steven C. Hawthorne (Pasadena, Calif.: William Carey Library, 1981), p. 22.

counter our narcissistic culture. It is a biblical duty of the church to offer a counter cultural, scriptural perspective that views the aging process as the basis of hope, not of despair; caregiving as an honorable duty; successful aging practices as ways to avoid disease and disability while maximizing physical and intellectual fitness; and aging as an opportunity for meaningful ministry. Churches can uniquely facilitate intergenerational connections that will allow seniors to act as salt and light to the younger generations. Much like the relationships portrayed in the parable of the prodigal son, prodigals and elder sons and daughters need the mature, unconditional love and wisdom of Holy Spirit–inspired fathers, mothers and grandparents.

In challenging our seniors to connect with members of younger generations, other age groups or specific ministries, churches must exhort them to seek the Lord with all their hearts to find their own personal direction. Just so, all the great pioneers of faith ventured out in trust, such as Abraham, Peter, John and Paul. Not knowing what lay ahead, these focused men of faith placed their trust in their Lord and acted. So it must be with our growing senior population in the church. Sometimes this going out in obedience to God's commands results in dramatic encounters; other times there may be only a quiet exchange, but, always, it is sure to be a significant exercise in faith that intertwines the life of a senior and someone who needs an older friend.

Mother Teresa understood suffering of all kinds, but she underscored one kind that characterizes many of our elderly, as well as our younger people. "I still think that the greatest suffering is being lonely, feeling unloved, just having no one."[2] Does this not describe many of our seniors, who sit alone, day in and day out, hoping that someone they love (or even just know) will happen by? Likewise, does this not describe some of our younger generations whose parents have become so busy providing material things that they have lost the capacity to be truly present in the lives of their children? We classify generations by cohort, each seemingly sharing certain common themes and experiences that make them unique, like the boomers. As the pace of our lives has in-

---

[2]Mother Teresa, *In the Heart of the World: Thoughts, Stories and Prayers* (Novato, Calif.: New World Library, 1997), p. 14.

creased, the whole world seems to have become distraught, harried and rushed.

Therefore, it is more important than ever for one cohort to relate to another, like the World War II generation with the baby boomers. We must recognize that as one generation dies, its lessons for the next generation are lost unless they are shared relationally, with the old teaching the young. As we noted in the beginning, the prodigal son story has three primary characters, and we must be able to find ourselves in all three. As we recognize our need to return to our heavenly Father as the prodigal did in absolute confession and repentance daily, and as we must acknowledge our risk of becoming like the self-righteous elder son who was unable to rejoice over his brother's repentance, we are more able to serve like the father who symbolizes our heavenly Father. In our modern church, we need most of all "fathers" who offer mercy, grace and love to prodigals and who can challenge the self-righteous elder sons in the church. Perhaps the modern church is failing because of this one factor. Godly fathers and mothers, senior saints, are in the best position to bless those who are younger. To be blessed, two people have to have made a connection. The blessings will, undoubtedly, be reciprocal.

As we challenge seniors to "rise up and build," let us take heed to the Lord's call with a promise:

> And if you spend yourselves in behalf of the hungry
>> and satisfy the needs of the oppressed,
> then your light will rise in the darkness,
>> and your night will become like the noonday.
> The LORD will guide you always;
>> he will satisfy your needs in a sun-scorched land
>> and will strengthen your frame.
> You will be like a well-watered garden,
>> like a spring whose waters never fail. (Is 58:10-11)

PART FIVE

...

# FINISHING WELL

# 20

## FACING DEATH
## AND BEREAVEMENT

*The unremitting remembrance of death is a powerful trainer
of body and soul. . . . Vaulting over all that lies between
ourselves and death, we should always visualize it.*

ST. HESYCHIOS, "ON WATCHFULNESS AND HOLINESS"

*Enoch walked with God; then he was no more,
because God took him away.*

GENESIS 5:24

• • •

If death is what we fear above all, do we most shun the age-status of
the senior because it reminds us of our own mortality? We may not be
fully conscious of this until it is articulated to us. But when you are old,
death is meeting you everywhere, as one relative, friend or former colleague "goes" in ever greater frequency. Perhaps in our desacralized culture, we fear death most intensely because it is the only sacral territory
that remains uncontrollable and unknown. However, in the past, a
more religious society did not create such a great gulf between life and
death. Both were much more closely interrelated, where mothers gave
birth within the same homes where the old died. Moreover, religious
faith gave hope to unite this life with the afterlife. There was awareness
that just as parental love gave us birth, so too, God's love will keeps us

eternally "safe in the arms of Jesus." On both sides of death, love was
the key. A strong Christian faith has always accepted life and death in
familiar cohabitation.

## The Denial of Death in Secular Culture

Today, our secular culture denies death with a deep aversion. As one
girl replied to C. S. Lewis in a discussion: "Oh, but by the time I'm *that*
age, Science will have done something about it!"[1] (This denial has become rather like the sexual prudery of Victorian culture; for prudery
and aversion are similar in both refusing to face reality.) Otherworldly
piety may be scorned in our culture, but in former times it permitted a
comfortable accommodation to both life and death. Thus in his short
story "The Death of Justina," John Cheevers asks: "How can a people
who do not mean to understand death hope to understand love, and
who will sound the alarm?"[2] As Philippe Aries in his significant study
*Western Attitudes Toward Death* points out, death has become unnamable: "Everything henceforth goes on as if neither I nor those who are
dear to me are any longer mortal. Technically, we admit that we might
die; we take out insurance . . . to protect our families from poverty. But
really, at heart we feel we are non-mortals."[3]

Such denial come from living in a technological society where death
has become unnamable because it remains unmanageable—a scandal
for our technical mindset that there should be techniques for everything, including "terminal management."[4] New therapists for dealing
with death and dying are available to handle this "problem" too.

Today for the medical profession "saving life at all cost" has become
the norm. But after the demise of another person, the case is closed and
forgotten. Euthanasia is like that, initiating the inevitable to deceive us
that we are still in charge. And those surrounding it can sink into a void

---

[1]Quoted in Janine Goffar, *The C. S. Lewis Index* (Wheaton, Ill.: Crossway, 1998), p. 135.
[2]*The Stories of John Cheever* (New York: Ballantine Books, 1980), p. 507.
[3]Philippe Aries, *Western Attitudes Toward Death: From the Middle Ages to the Present*, trans. Pa-
tricia M. Ranum (Baltimore, Md.: Johns Hopkins Unversity Press, 1974), p. 107.
[4]Ivan Illich first used the term the "medicalisation" of death in his prophetic book *Medical Nem-
esis* in 1974. He later reviewed the trend in his article, "Death Undefeated: from medicine to
medicalisation to systematization," *British Medical Journal* 311 (1995): 1652-53.

of oblivion which keeps no memory to avoid facing their emptiness, retaining no sense of moral responsibility in being their "brother's keeper." This utilitarian mindset only accepts a naturalistic comfort, that human ashes will provide for new biological life.

*Denying death trivializes life.* Reacting strongly against to the murderous ideologies of the twentieth century, we prefer now to deny death as much as we can. But the separation of life and death becomes a banal exercise, clinically clean perhaps, but trivial also. In his poem *The Waste Land*, T. S. Eliot expresses the trivialization of our secular culture, in how many retirees spend out their time in meaningless pursuits. How then, can we live truthful lives if we live in denial of death and therefore, in denial of life as inseparable from death? The consequence can only be a great emptiness.

It is said of the filmmaker Woody Allen that at seventy-two he was terrified of the void, the "meaningless flicker" of life. The awareness of death in such films as *The Angel of Death* is disguised as "your kindly Uncle Morty," in order to change terror into banality. Allen assumes only the randomness of life, making films "not because he has a grand statement to offer, but simply to take his mind off the existential horror of being alive."[5] Yet as a filmmaker Woody Allen is aware that there is an ambiguity about the purpose of films, either to face life with realism or else to escape from life in entertainment and fantasy. As an atheist, he admits that "your perception of time changes as you get older, because you see how brief everything is . . . a meaningless little flicker."[6] Faithless, he can only be superstitious. "Every morning he cuts up his banana on his breakfast plate into seven slices . . . six slices or eight, and something bad might happen."[7]

*Denying refuses to acknowledge a transcendent relationship beyond death.* Abortion and euthanasia together, the insistence of control over both the beginning and ending of life, have been logically predictable since "the rights of the individual" and "the right-to-die movement" began their growth in the 1970s. Since that time they developed into

---

[5]Jennie Yabroff, "Take the Bananas and Run," *Newsweek*, August 18, 2008, p. 57.
[6]Ibid., p. 58.
[7]Ibid., p. 57.

an ever-narrowing culture of death.

Complex as the issues are made to appear legislatively, if human life is the gift of God as our creator, then we should not as humans throw life back in the face of the giver. As the theologian Karl Barth put it plainly, "if a man kills himself... then his action is murder."[8] Undoubtedly, medical life-support systems over the past half century have sustained dying over much longer periods of illness, and they have created new ethical issues. "Living wills," "mercy-killing," "medically assisted suicides," even "the right to be killed" are all expressive of the loss of divine transcendence in a secular society. In the Netherlands, where euthanasia has become most practiced, old people have become afraid of receiving hospital treatment in case such a stop was their final destination. As the British legal commentator John Keown has stated, "within a remarkably short time [since 1984] the Dutch have proceeded from voluntary to non-voluntary euthanasia . . . because the underlying justification for euthanasia . . . appears not to be patient self-determination, but rather acceptance of the principle that certain lives are not 'worth' living and that it is right to terminate them."[9] Far from giving patients greater autonomy, the Dutch experiment has given physicians more powers of life and death.[10]

The U.S. Supreme Court on June 26, 1997, issued its decision to uphold Washington and New York state laws against assisted suicide. Palliative care, hospice care, pain-management, psychiatric skills in the treatment of aging depression and factual disagreement among doctors in motives for mercy-killing all suggest the court's decision was wise.[11] Elderly people do need protective legislation against the cultural trend to promote suicide assistance. But the issue will inevitably come again to the fore.

One imperative element in senior care is treating depression as a

---

[8]Karl Barth, *Church Dogmatics*, ed. and trans. G. W. Bromiley and T. W. Torrance (Edinburgh: T & T Clark, 1951), 3:404.

[9]John Keown, "Euthanasia in the Netherlands: Sliding Down the Slippery Slope," *Notre Dame Journal of Law, Ethics and Public Policy* 9 (1995): 438. See also Herbert Hendin, *Seduced by Death: Doctors, Patients and the Dutch Cure* (New York: Norton, 1997).

[10]Edward J. Larson and Darrel W. Amundsen, *A Different Death: Euthanasia & the Christian Tradition* (Downers Grove, Ill.: InterVarsity Press, 1998), p. 237.

[11]Ibid., pp. 244-52.

strong factor towards the inclination of suicide. As Scott Peck wisely observed: "'true euthanasia' patients suffer not so much from a problem of death as a problem of life. . . . They have a lot to learn from being assisted to face this problem rather than being assisted to kill themselves in order to avoid it."[12] The indictment thus is against a whole society that becomes so indifferent to the loneliness and despair of deeply anguished people that it allows them to destroy themselves as the only known alternative to end their miseries! That surely is barbarism, not civilization.

### Is There a Christian Way of Dying?

Much as secularists would like to separate life from death, this remains impossible. For even the denial of death in our culture remains ineffective, since the way we may have lived in denial is highlighted by the way we shall die, as we have already seen. In contrast to Wagner's song "Im Abendrot" (at sunset) or Strauss's "Four Last Songs," both expressing the tragic embrace of death as their fate, Benjamin Britten (in the company of Yehudi Menuhin) visited the death camps of Bergen-Belsen in July 1945. The next month, Britten's response to such ghastliness was to turn to John Donne's *Holy Sonnets*, the most spiritually scouring poetry he could find, and set them to music. He finished his cycle with Donne's sonnet "Death Be Not Proud," affirming "and death shall be no more," on a rising scale, fixated for nine long beats on the word "Death," and finally over a clanging dominant tonic cadence thunders, "Thou shalt die." For this is the Christian's response to death: Death has also died in the death and resurrection of Christ. Christians actually celebrate in death's face, anticipating "the death of Death." As the apostle cries out in triumph, "Where, O death, is your victory? Where, O death, is your sting?" (1 Cor 15:55). Consequently Christians interpret the threat of dying differently, trusting in the transcendence of God as our eternal and saving hope.

Christian realism is, then, most truly grounded on being prepared for death's inevitable summons. While Christian elders are the ones

---

[12]Scott Peck, "Living Is the Mystery," *Newsweek,* March 10, 1997, p. 18.

who can most effectively challenge and remove this fantasy of "death aversion" within our society, they do so when death and love are both integrated into their own way of living, by dying many deaths to express increasing love for others. For the apostle Paul speaks of "always [carrying] around in our body the death of Jesus, so that the life of Jesus may also be revealed in our body" (2 Cor 4:10).

When my (Dr. Houston's) relative was dying from cancer in her prime of life, she called her niece to her bedside and had her open her clothes closet to try on all her favorite dresses. In spite of her niece's protests over emptying her wardrobe, the aunt commented, "There now, you look lovely in this, and that; take them all away, for I won't need them anymore." Cheerful at the prospect of meeting her best beloved, she was ready to die, ready to live eternally with her Savior. Her willingness to embrace death and to exchange this body for her eternal relationship with her Lord inspired our entire family. Recently at a college reunion, I (Dr. Houston) felt lead to pray for those present who would not again celebrate such a college reunion, knowing realistically that their mortality was limited. (It is highly unlikely that my group will all ever meet again in another twenty-five years!) In the old days such a thing was called an *amicus mortis*, someone who spoke the bitter truth while you were living, stayed with you to the end of your life and then never forgot you in loving memory until the end of their life too.

One of the deepest experiences of my life was my recent witness to the slow, painful process of cancer, the dying life of my dear colleague, Klaus Bockmuehl. I visited him every afternoon I could until the final week when Klaus bade farewell to his family and friends. Living under the shadow of death for many months only deepened our friendship as we experienced together a richness neither had ever had before. Like the God we have not seen, the undying love for such a friend has a divine quality in its endlessness. The death of a Christian friend has the capacity to make our faith stronger than it was before. Such memory never ceases, as love never ceases; and truly it is stronger than death. "The sting of death" is indeed the separation from the loved one, but just as God is deathless, so too dwelling in and sharing his love becomes deathless.

I learned from this experience that the despair of death in our culture points to a despair of love as something fickle and easily lost. Life is not meaningless when it is enveloped in meaningful, loyal and, therefore, lasting relationships. Friendship, the *amicus mortis* type, continues after death in ever deepening memory and love.

The task of a Christian elder is, then, to express through selfless service what Henry Drummond called love to be: "the greatest thing in the world." It is contrasted with the diminished capacity of the self-centered to love, which eventually can only find despair in death. If we neglect our seniors in old peoples' homes while they are still in full use of their faculties, is it any wonder that after their death they are indeed obliterated from memory? What "death of relationships" will be perpetuated detrimentally to such a society!

### Historical Vignettes of "Dying Well"

As Christians, members of the body of Christ, we have been nurtured, inspired and given direction by "the communion of saints." As our last century has changed dramatically in its embrace or denial of death, so too other cultures in the midst of change have responded differently to human mortality. A few differing vignettes enrich and deepen our ability to consider mortality: the inevitability of facing both our own death and the deaths of our loved ones.

*The funeral orations of Gregory of Nazianzus (c. 330–389).* Educated Christians mourning the loss of family or Christian leaders developed the classical panegyric (or eulogy) with a Christian perspective. Among the best-known early Christian eulogies are the fourth century orations of Gregory of Nazianzus, composed over the deaths of his brother, his sister and his father. He considered their delivery a spiritual entombment in which the reputations of his loved ones were grounded, laid to rest and protected for all posterity. In reciting the curriculum vitae of each, Gregory points out that he has more concern for their Christian godliness than their worldly successes and for their hidden life in personal devotion than what was publicly known. For in the humility of those now in the presence of the Lord, what counts is the glory of God and the fruitfulness of the life that can be imitated by those following behind. The true memorial is the one that is built into the lives of spiritual children still living.

In his eulogy about his departed father (in 374), Gregory knows his father would not wish too much said in his praise. What counts is the continuity of Christian life in its goodness, since it flows constantly from the redemptive grace of God, from father to children and to children's children. He observes that because of the Son of God's loving sacrifice on the cross, "Life and death, as they are called, apparently so different, are in a sense resolved into and successive to, each other."[13] God's love is revealed in the death of his son, and by Christ's resurrection, death is indeed conquered by the eternal reality of divine love. Every act of kindness becomes a preparation—by many little deaths of the self—for the final event of death, yet each prepares the person to dwell in the eternal kingdom of God's son. Jesus speaks of his death throughout the Gospels alongside his living acts of mercy. While the act of Christ's death and resurrection is unique, ours is made possible by that one cosmic event.

*Augustine's fear of death* (timor mortis). Advocates of the Hemlock Society have argued that first the apostle Paul[14] and then the early Christians were the first advocates for mass suicide, demonstrated by the fearless way they accepted martyrdom.[15] A contemporary rebuttal to this is fully given in the skilled researches of Darrell Amundsen.[16] But Augustine of Hippo (354–430) may have been among the first to engage the same issue due to the extremist behavior of the Donatists in North Africa (who were rather like suicide bombers today). Among Augustine's first actions as the bishop of Hippo was denying that fear and distress at dying signaled serious weakness of faith. Prudence should dictate that it is natural for us all to fear death.[17] Augustine also accepted the goodness of the body in rebuttal of the Manichees, who

---

[13]Gregory of Nazianzus, *Oration 18: "On the Death of His Father,"* in Nicene and Post-Nicene Fathers, 2nd series (New York: Christian Literature, 1894), 7:268.

[14]Arthur J. Droge, "Did Paul Commit Suicide?" *Bible Review* (December 1989): 14.

[15]Arthur J. Droge and James D. Tabor, *A Noble Death: Suicide and Martyrdom Among Christians and Jews in Antiquity* (San Francisco: Harper, 1992).

[16]Larson and Amundsen, *Different Death*, pp. 15-84.

[17]Carole Straw, *"Timor Mortis,"* in *Augustine Through the Ages*, ed. Allan D. Fitzgerald, O.S.A. (Grand Rapids: Eerdmans, 1999), pp. 838-42.

viewed the body negatively as the entombment of the soul. Later still, in his combat with the Pelagians, Augustine wrote *City of God* (412–427) and *timor mortis* took on a new focus in that debate. Pelagians argued Christians should be perfected in justice, and therefore having no fear of death became proof of their new state. But Augustine argued that even while only Christ is perfect, his death is unique and his defeat of sin and death alone have cosmic significance, the human Jesus faced his death with agony in the garden, sharing the human distress of dying. He prays: "May this cup be taken from me" (Mt 26:39). Augustine thus concludes that we face death not stoically, in heroic individualistic ideals, but by the divine help and indwelling of the spirit of Christ within us. Immanently we fear, for we are human, but transcendently we fear not, for "Christ in you" is "the hope of glory" (Col 1:27). Thus at the end of his own life, Augustine had a complete revolution in his whole thinking about death. This encourages us to share this change with him!

*Martin Luther's art of dying well.* Pastorally, Martin Luther (1483–1546) was preoccupied with death all his life. The horrors of the Black Death of 1349 generated for the rest of the Middle Ages a horrific imagination of sin, death and hell. After Luther's reformed stand of his Nine-Five Theses at Wittenberg, Luther feared the death threats of his enemies for the rest of his life.[18] But in the light of the justifying work of Christ, Luther's reformed teaching now interpreted the terrors of death as the work of the devil. False imagination must be substituted by the sacrament of Communion, where Christ is with all his people, past, present and future. As Dennis Ngien has interpreted Luther: "to be in solidarity with the dying is part of what it means to belong to the community of faith."[19]

*John Donne and preparation for dying.* After the Reformation, many classics build on these predecessors. William Perkins wrote a significant treatise, *On Dying Well*, while John Bunyan's *Pilgrim's Progress* has many moral insights, suggesting that even in the sight of the eternal

---

[18]H. Borkmann, *Luther's World of Thought*, trans. M. H. Bertram (St. Louis: Concordia, 1958), pp. 115-33.
[19]Dennis Ngien, *Luther as a Spiritual Adviser* (Bletchley, U.K.: Paternoster, 2007), p. 39.

city, across the river of death, pilgrims must sustain moral vigilance. But as the dean of St. Paul's Cathedral in London, John Donne (1572–1631) in a unique voice affirms the idea that since we all have to die, we should do so gloriously! For Christ himself, dying on the cross, "cried out loudly": "Since Christ embraced the Cross itselfe, dare I / His image, th' image of his Cross deny?"

Like Luther and Augustine, Donne affirms the unity of God's people. Just as the church bells call the whole congregation together to worship, so too, when the bell tolls at a funeral service we are reminded of our human mortal unity: "No man is an Island, intire of itselfe; every man is a peece of the Continent [of all humanity]." He reminds us further: "any Man's *death diminishes me*, because I am involved in Mankinde; and therefore never send to know for whom the *bell* tolls; it tolls for *thee*."[20] He stretches the analogy further in associating the tolling of the bell to the pulse of the blood, which one day will cease.

Like few others, Donne realized that the subject of death has no adequate genre by which to express its mysteries. But his last sermon, "Death's Duel"—perhaps anticipating his own demise—he bases on Psalm 68:20: "Unto God belong the issues of death." He firmly affirms that death lies within the context of God's sovereignty as Savior. The *exitus mortis* leads to *liberatio a morte*, our final exit by divine liberation. We still naturally fear death, but it drives us to deepen our confidence in God's grace:

> I have a sin of fear, that when I've spun
> My last thread, I shall perish on the shore;
> But swear by Thyself, that at my death Thy Son
> Shall shine as he shines now, and heretofore;
> And having done that, Thou hast done,
> I fear no more.[21]

---

[20]John Donne, *Devotions Upon Emergent Occasions* (New York: Random House, 1999), p. 101.
[21]Evelyn M. Simpson, ed., *John Donne's Sermons on the Psalms and Gospels* (Berkeley: University of California Press, 1963), p. 243.

# EPILOGUE

## Dying Elders, Living Church

*For we who are alive are always being given over to death
for Jesus' sake, so that his life may be revealed in our mortal body.
So then, death is at work in us, but life is at work in you.*

2 CORINTHIANS 4:11-12

*Now faith is being sure of what we hope for and certain of what
we do not see. This is what the ancients were commended for.*

HEBREWS 11:1-2

*I write to you, fathers, because you have known him
who is from the beginning.*

1 JOHN 2:13-14

. . .

As missionaries in Spain, living very simply in faith for our material as well as spiritual needs, my (Dr. Houston's) parents were profoundly influenced by the Spanish people with whom we lived. They helped me understand that our morals are profoundly taught from exemplary models, rather than merely by exhortation, ethical teachings or even a good education. The early church revered its martyrs, then wrote about the lives of their saints and always looked back to the patristic period (that is, the "Fathers of the church") as foundational for the later out-working of the Christian faith. With today's mass, high-tech capabilities and with educational opportunities available to everyone, Christians are poised to launch a purposed effort to publish biographies of godly exemplars or parents with inspiring faith.

A Canadian Korean lady once came to me expressing this desire: "I am now sixty-five this year. My own life has been tumultuous by divorce and much suffering. But my dear father, now in his nineties, is still a godly pastor, still serving others. Should I not collect all memories of him in a book?" "Yes!" was my answer; "indeed, inspire others by his example, as you have been inspired."

This book was begun before the full effects of the recent global financial crisis became as apparent as they now are. President Obama's reaction has been to take radical action, not only for the sake of the economy but also for the sake of medical and social well-being. Likewise, American churches should consider this economic disaster a fresh opportunity for radical reforms within their own ranks, in this case, changes toward intergenerational mutuality in church congregations. We have noted the egregious impact on the disabled and elderly of catastrophic disasters like the Katrina and the earthquake in Haiti. A final plea for establishing and strengthening the bond between younger and older generations lies in the very nature of the Christian faith, for it seeks spiritual maturity for everyone.

Yes, the Christian faith is for everyone, as N. T. Wright has written.[1] The vital communication of the early Christian faith was accomplished through letters, so that all who read could possess them; so, significantly, twenty-one of the twenty-nine books of the New Testament are letters! Indeed, Søren Kierkegaard described the Bible as "God's love letter to us!" John Donne once said, "Our letters are ourselves." Just so, a new ministry and era of letter-writing can be taken up by today's seniors that will encourage younger friends in their life of faith. When I

---

[1]See N. T. Wright, *Paul for Everyone* (Louisville: Westminster John Knox, 2004) and *John for Everyone* (Louisville: Westminster John Knox, 2004).

(Dr. Houston) was already an octogenarian, I found great pleasure in the laborious task of compiling a letter for every day of the year in the church's calendar, in celebration of the communion of saints.[2] In her restricted life today, my wife, Rita, has no greater satisfaction than encouraging others in her own constant letter-writing. Cyberspace has the potential to be filled with emails of friendship instead of pornography. As Bruce Winter notes, "the New Testament letters are addressed to the family of God, and as such are not formal but personal."[3]

The Christian life is also progressive, growing as "the garden of the Lord." As an organic metaphor, "maturity" implies ongoing growth; the Christian life never stops becoming ever more fruitful. *Retirement* is, then, not in the language of the Christian. As we have seen, the benefits of medical advances should, now, more than ever, facilitate a "no retirement" mantra for the Christian senior. As I (Dr. Houston) told my Canadian Korean friend, "Now that you are sixty-five, plan for the next forty years of your life as if you were starting life again!"

Seniors, then, should take the challenge of growing mature in Christ with utmost seriousness. The warfare against evil still continues. The race is not done until our final home-call. The harvest is still not gathered in. With such metaphors, the aging apostle Paul exhorts Timothy, "You then, my son, be strong in the grace that is in Christ Jesus. And the things you have heard me say in the presence of many witnesses entrust to reliable men who will also be qualified to teach others" (2 Tim 2:1-2; cf. also 2 Tim 2:3-9). Christian strength is not "muscular" but "spiritual" and lies, paradoxically, in one's dependence upon the grace of Christ. Young *and* old need that. Growth in spiritual maturity is, then, growing in our personal experiences with the grace of Jesus Christ.

Christian elders are to consider themselves dead to sin. Paul makes this clear in the sixth chapter of his letter to the Romans. When our old self was crucified with Christ, our new self was made alive to God in

---

[2]James M. Houston, *Letters of Faith Through the Seasons*, vols. 1-2 (Colorado Springs: Cook Communications, 2006–2007).

[3]Bruce Winter, "Why Are the New Testament Letters Not Epistles?" quoted in James M. Houston, *Letters of Faith Through the Seasons* (Colorado Springs: Cook Communications, 2007): 2:177.

Christ Jesus. So the Christian elder believes that if he has died with Christ, he will also live with Christ. For the crux of the gospel is that Christ was raised from the dead and will never die. So Christians are to deny themselves and present their bodies as instruments of God's purposes in the world. For the joy of what was beyond, Jesus endured the cross, and we are to follow him in grace, empowered by the Holy Spirit. In Revelation, John makes it clear that we overcome the hurricanes and earthquakes of this life by the blood the Lamb, the word of our testimony from a heart changed by the gospel and with a courageous love that defies death.

Within even the corpus of the New Testament documents, we can sense the inter-generational unity of faith. Mark's Gospel is written with the dash and drama of a disciple of Peter, still full of youthful energy for the challenges set forth by Jesus of Nazareth, to the old-boy religious network around the temple in Jerusalem. John the Elder writes his first epistle with the measured tread of one who is looking into eternity to see only the rule of divine love becoming all-in-all. "This is the message you heard from the beginning: We should love one another" (1 Jn 3:11). However much we appreciate the freedom in Christ about which Paul writes to the Galatians and which Luther, as a much older man nearing the end of his life, also extolled, Paul's letter to the Romans is no longer like the new wine offered to the Galatians, but vintage port indeed! What can exceed Paul's maturity than communicating the gospel of which he is now no longer ashamed? Perhaps our dear seniors have lived too long ashamed to let their Christian faith be known, remaining silent about their faith. But no Christian maturity will come until we are unafraid of what others may think of us for sharing our faith!

Reflect, then, on the apostle Paul's epistle to the Romans, as he shares his mature understanding of the gospel with his friends in Rome. He concludes, ". . . that I might have a harvest among you" (Rom 1:13). This "harvest" Paul has described earlier to the Galatians as the receiving of "love, joy, peace, patience, kindness, goodness, faithfulness, gentleness and self-control" (Gal 5:22-23). Now, in Romans 5:1–8:39, Paul wants his fellow Christians to pursue the fruits of godliness, just as in classical humanism, the pursuit of arête, or excellence, remained a life-long task. For the Christian, this involves reconciliation and peace with God, living in the constant tension of "living" and "dying," and which focuses on having one's identity "in Christ" and walking in "the Spirit." Christians are called not only to receive the gospel, but to become mature persons in the gospel. Only mature persons in Christ can communicate this gift to others. As one mature missionary put it, "It takes many of us years to learn what preaching the gospel means."[4]

In the final season of life, we are in a position to have the greatest influence, if we don't grow weary. If we live as spiritual orphans, afraid of change, slothful and isolated from the world, we may fill up the crevices of our remaining time in idle (and idol) pursuits. When the will of the flesh does not yield to the will of God, "there must follow the painful breaking up of hopes and expectations."[5] May our last years be what one missionary called her "soldiership years!"[6] We have been saved to serve and this could involve the care of a loved one suffering from Alzheimer's disease, or we might need to take the rear in the cue of leadership and during our final days learn to be the recipients of care, remembering that all should be done with Christ in mind. At the core of our late life ministry, whatever our physical state, should be private prayer, waiting in silence for God alone. In facing all of the challenges associated with late life, whatever they might be, the church should be in the position of reminding Christians that "Jesus Christ is the same yesterday and today and forever" (Heb 13:8).

Amy Carmichael, the tireless nineteenth-century missionary to the very poorest in India said: "Dear, you are coming to a battlefield. You cannot spend too much time with Him alone. The keys of the powers of the world to come are not turned by careless fingers. So few are willing to pay the price of the knowledge of God. They play through life, even Christian life, even missionary life."[7] But, as sons and daughters of

---

[4]Elisabeth Elliot, *A Chance to Die : The Life and Legacy of Amy Carmichael* (Grand Rapids: Fleming H. Revell, 1987), p. 308.
[5]Amy Carmichael, *Though the Mountains Shake,* quoted in Elisabeth Elliot, *A Chance to Die* (Grand Rapids: Fleming H. Revell, 1987), p. 334.
[6]Ibid.
[7]Elliot, *Chance to Die,* p. 304.

the living God, we can do all things if we are empowered by the Holy Spirit. It is the spiritual responsibility of Christian seniors to settle, alone with God, the immensely important matter of their late life calling. Will they be a part of "rebuilding the wall," as in the days of Nehemiah? Will they "rise up and build together" without concerns for their reputation (Neh 1–2)? Will they be willing to commit to the exigencies of laborious, self-sacrificing work? Will they trust "the Rock" and not the "sands of self-confidence" to meet all their needs?[8] If yes, then those seniors will leave an eternal legacy, even if they are a "burden" for a season. For every person's work shall be tried by fire (1 Cor 3:12-14). The purer the aim, the more vehement the opposition will be. While seniors must plan, perhaps for a period of dependency, they must not forget that in matters pertaining to his calling: "Our fight is not against any physical enemy, but it is against organizations and powers that are spiritual. We are up against the unseen power that controls this dark world and spiritual agents from the very headquarters of evil" (Eph 6:12 Phillips). With daily, persistent focus on the One who has overcome all evil, today's seniors can lead lives of assured, eternal victory and in so doing, light the path for those behind them.

We offer no modern psychological screening for selection on this late life version of the crucified life. Nor do we offer a life filled with guaranteed prosperity and health; our poster simply reads: "Wanted! Seniors with a love that loves in deed unto death!" As Ugo Bassi reflected: "Measure thy life by loss and not by gain; not by the wine drunk, but by the wine poured forth, for love's strength standeth in love's sacrifice, and he that suffereth most hath most to give."[9] And who were the heroes of our faith, the men and women of old? By faith, Abel, Enoch, Noah, Abraham, Sarah, Isaac, Jacob, Joseph, Moses, Rahab, Gideon, Barak, Samson, David, Samuel . . . "conquered kingdoms, administered justice, and gained what was promised; . . . quenched the fury of the flames, and escaped the edge of the sword; whose weakness was turned to strength;

---

[8]Ibid., p. 258.
[9]Elisabeth Elliot and Lisa Barry, "The Grace to Forgive," BacktotheBible.org, <www.back tothebible.org/index.php/Gateway-to-Joy/The-Grace-to-Forgive.html> (accessed July 11, 2011).

and who became powerful in battle. . . . They were stoned; they were sawed in two" (Heb 11:33-34, 37; see the entire chapter). So "let us run with perseverance the race marked out for us. Let us fix our eyes on Jesus, the author and perfecter of our faith, who for the joy set before him endured the cross, scorning its shame, and sat down at the right hand of the throne of God" (Heb 12:1-2).

If you live long enough, life has a way of bringing its unexpected scars. For the Parker family, this would include a spinal cord injury to one their children, and for the Houstons, it would involve another caregiving trajectory with a loved one suffering from increasing dementia. What a responsibility it is, then, to be a Christian elder—someone who is willing to serve in any or all of the "missions" outlined throughout this book, in planting the seeds of eternity and in rebuilding the walls, as in the days of Nehemiah, together—sometimes giving and sometimes receiving, but always united in Christ and by the scars affixed from a lifetime of service!

> Hast thou no scar?
> No hidden scar on foot, or side, or hand?
> I hear thee sung as mighty in the land,
> I hear them hail thy bright, ascendant star,
> Hast Thou no scar?

> Hast thou no wound?
> Yet I was wounded by the archers, spent,
> Leaned Me against a tree to die; and rent
> By ravening beasts that compassed Me. I swooned:
> Hast *Thou* no wound?

> No wound? No scar?
> Yet, as the Master shall the servant be,
> And pierced are the feet that follow Me;
> But thine are whole: can he have followed far
> Who has no wound nor scar?[10]

---

[10]Carmichael, quoted in Elliot, *Chance to Die*, p. 264.

# Appendix A

## "The Life Review" Preparation Tips and Questions

### Everyone Has a Story to Tell

What are the main steps in recording an oral history?

Get permission from church leaders. Plan a group, educational format. Plan for the respective interviews and get permission (sign release form) from the participants.

Give list of questions that will evoke memories, ahead of time.

Be prepared. Check equipment.

Be on time. Begin with easy questions. Try not to ask questions that can be answered with yes or no.

Be a good listener and be encouraging. Moments of silence can be helpful.

Never go over two hours.

Keep subject on track and on schedule.

ID every tape, with date, time, subject.

Transcribe the tape. Give copy to subject of oral history.

*Sample questions to ask when recording a person's history or for general discussion in a group format:*

### Spiritual History

• What is your spiritual story?

• What is your faith tradition?

- Describe how you arrived at your faith or lack thereof.

- Regarding your profession or professions, did you feel "called" to that profession(s)?

- If your answer to question 3 was that you experienced a "call," how has the nature of that "call" changed for you over the years you have practiced your profession?

- In what ways how has your spirituality and/or your religious beliefs/practices influenced your daily work? Your family? Your health?

- Was your faith helpful during troubled times? Please share how it was helpful.

- Please describe how your private religious practices have helped you cope with tough times.

- How has your involvement with organized religion, like a congregation, been helpful? Please share stories.

- Have you lived a crucified life? Have you done humble things joyfully for Christ's sake?

- Does the thought of hardness draw you to a project or repel you?

- Apart from the Bible, can you name three or four books that have been of vital help to you?

- What refreshes you most when tired?

- Have you ever had opportunity to prove our Lord's promises (i.e., to supply temporal as well as spiritual needs)?

- Can you mention any experience you have passed through in your Christian life which brought you into a new discovery of your union with the crucified, risen and enthroned Lord?

- How has your congregational membership been difficult?

- How has your faith helped you to mature?

- How has your faith helped you with personal illness or disability?

- How has your faith changed your life for good? For bad?

- How has your faith affected your marriage? For good? For bad?

## Family and Friends

- What is your greatest hope for your children? Grandchildren?
- What is the most important message you want to give your children? Grandchildren?
- Do you have one important message to share with your family or one person in your family?
- What would you want to say to your best friend?
- What is your full name? Why did your parents select this name for you? Did you have a nickname?
- When and where were you born?
- How did your family come to live there?
- Were there other family members in the area? Who?

## Personal History—Childhood

- What was the house (apartment, farm, etc.) you grew up in like? How many rooms? Bathrooms? Did it have electricity? Indoor plumbing? Telephones?
- Were there any special items in the house that you remember?
- What is your earliest childhood memory?
- Describe the personalities of your family members.
- What kind of games did you play growing up?
- What was your favorite toy and why?
- What was your favorite thing to do for fun (movies, beach, etc.)?
- Did you have family chores? What were they? Which was your least favorite?
- Did you receive an allowance? How much? Did you save your money or spend it?
- What was school like for you as a child? What were your best and worst subjects? Where did you attend grade school? High school? College?

- What school activities and sports did you participate in?
- Do you remember any fads from your youth? Popular hairstyles? Clothes?
- Who were your childhood heroes?
- What were your favorite songs and music?
- Did you have any pets? If so, what kind and what were their names?
- What was your religion growing up? What church, if any, did you attend?
- Were you ever mentioned in a newspaper?
- Who were your friends when you were growing up?
- What world events had the most impact on you while you were growing up? Did any of them personally affect your family?
- Describe a typical family dinner. Did you all eat together as a family? Who did the cooking? What were your favorite foods?
- How were holidays (birthdays, Christmas, etc.) celebrated in your family? Did your family have special traditions?
- How is the world today different from what it was like when you were a child?
- Who was the oldest relative you remember as a child? What do you remember about them?

### Family History—General

- What do you know about your family surname?
- Is there a naming tradition in your family, such as always giving the firstborn son the name of his paternal grandfather?
- What stories have come down to you about your parents? Grandparents? More distant ancestors?
- Are there any stories about famous or infamous relatives in your family?

- Have any recipes been passed down to you from family members?
- Are there any physical characteristics that run in your family?
- Are there any special heirlooms, photos, Bibles or other memorabilia that have been passed down in your family?
- What was the full name of your spouse? Siblings? Parents?
- When and how did you meet your spouse? What did you do on dates?
- What was it like when you proposed (or were proposed to)? Where and when did it happen? How did you feel?
- Where and when did you get married?
- What memory stands out the most from your wedding day?
- How would you describe your spouse? What do (did) you admire most about them?
- What do you believe is the key to a successful marriage?
- How did you find out you were going to be a parent for the first time?
- Why did you choose your children's names?
- What was your proudest moment as a parent?
- What did your family enjoy doing together?
- What was your profession and how did you choose it?
- If you could have had any other profession what would it have been? Why wasn't it your first choice?
- Of all the things you learned from your parents, which do you feel was the most valuable?
- What accomplishments are you the most proud of?
- What is the one thing you most want people to remember about you?

## Unique Internet Sites on Life Review

www.wsre.org/thewar/thewar_fieldkit.pdf

This guide—a collaboration between the Library of Congress Veterans History Project, Florentine Films and WETA public television station in Washington, D.C.—contains hands-on production tips and interview techniques from Ken Burns and Lynn Novick, as well as information on how to send completed interviews to the Veterans History Project. This guide was created to help individuals and groups conduct research and preserve the stories of our nation's veterans to ensure that they become a part of our country's collective and permanent history.

www.lastchapters.org

Last Chapters offers a collection of inspiring stories and video interviews of people who are facing death or chronic illness. These stories shed light on a range of issues about quality of life, including: spirituality, talking about dying, managing pain, caregiving, coming to terms with grief and more. The Last Chapters Forum is a discussion board where site visitors can comment on featured stories and share their own experiences, concerns and encouragement.

www.growthhouse.org/lifereview.html

In hospice care and in many nursing homes, the process of thinking back on one's life and communicating about one's life to another person is called life review. Life review is an important part of bringing one's life to a close. As life ends, we want to know that we have truly been seen by someone in this world and that our life has had value and meaning.

www.uwsuper.edu/cee/lll/reminiscence/index.cfm

The International Institute for Reminiscence and Life Review (IIRLR) brings together participants to further define reminiscence and life review as an interdisciplinary field of study in the areas of practice, research, education, volunteer and individual application. Similar to a membership organization, the IIRLR enrolls individuals throughout the year to utilize and participate in networking, collaboration and research. They also provided a newsletter that discusses key issues in the field.

www.guidedautobiography.com/aboutus/index.html

A group of colleagues and professionals interested in promoting Guided Autobiography teamed up with Jim Birren more than six years ago. They meet on a regular basis and develop new venues for Guided Autobiography, create new products and research the effects of the Guided Autobiography process. They call themselves, The GAB Workgroup.

www.personalhistorians.org/

The APH is an international organization of skilled professionals passionate about preserving life stories.

www.usc.edu/dept/gero/

USC life course center

www.storiesunfolding.com/

Stories Unfolding offers multiple services to engage in Life Review. Each service affords you opportunities to develop contentment with who you are and a sense of mutual caring and connectedness with others. Your active participation in Guided Autobiography Groups and Spiritual Legacy Groups will allow you to pass a written legacy on to others.

www.your-life-your-story.com/

Personal History Featured Resources—Your Life Is Your Story provides you with many wonderful family and personal history resources.

www.memoirsinc.com/

Memoirs, Inc., interviews, writes and publishes hardcover books for elders and their families that can serve as a source of intergenerational connectedness and blessing.

# Appendix B

## Church Survey Questions

Our Senior Ministry Association is an ecumenical organization with four primary goals: (1) to challenge elders in our congregations to God-inspired ministry, service, volunteerism and leadership; (2) to help our seniors age successfully by avoiding disease and disability, maximizing their physical and intellectual fitness; (3) to support and encourage pastors and lay leaders in "ministry" to older persons; and (4) to foster faith-based partnerships for new, needed programs that target seniors and their caregivers. In this regard, we are organizing a Senior Resource Directory for our community to be used by the Senior Ministry Association and local churches and agencies that work with older persons. Please take a few minutes to complete the following survey about your congregation. This information will be used to help older persons and their caregivers better understand the range of programs and services offered by your congregations and to address gaps in our larger, faith-based community.

**Community Survey**

*Congregation*
Name of your Congregation
Denomination
Street Address
City                    State                    Zip
Phone Number
Fax Number
E-mail Address

How many members belong to your church? _____
What percent of your membership fall into the following categories?
65 and older _____ %
85 and older _____ %

1. What are the major issues facing your seniors?

2. Does your church offer a program or set of activities for seniors in your church or community?

3. Do you have any requirements for participating in your senior programs? If yes, please list your requirements (e.g., age, mobility, church membership, fees)

4. Are you willing to partner with other churches to establish new programs for seniors?

5. Have you developed a unique program or activity to meet the needs of your seniors? If yes, please describe briefly.

6. Do you offer special exercise programs that target older persons (e.g., balance-related exercises, Tai Chi)?

7. Does your church maintain an up-to-date bank or information service on older adult services in the local community? If yes, do you refer members of your congregation to other programs?

8. Does your church assist seniors and their caregivers in finding additional services they might need that are not offered by your church?

9. Does your church currently offer regular support services and resources to elder caregivers in your congregation?

10. Does your church currently offer classes or programs to seniors in your congregation on how to age successfully?

11. Does your church operate a systematic home-visitation program for elderly shut-ins?

12. Does your church offer help for elderly members of your congregation who do not live nearby?

13. Does your church have a preplanned evacuation service to elderly

members for disasters and catastrophic events (e.g., tornadoes) or hazards (e.g., power outages)?

14. Does your church make an effort to integrate the elderly into Sunday school classes with different age groups represented?

15. Do most of the elderly in your church belong to age-graded Sunday school classes?

16. Does your church offer regular transportation to the elderly members of your congregation? If yes, what is the transportation used for: religious services, medical appointments, business, shopping, other?

17. Does your church provide special services to disabled members of your congregation (e.g., parking, hearing assistance, wheelchair access to worship and Sunday school programs)?

18. Does your church have access to experts in the field of aging who speak regularly about aspects of successful aging (e.g., cognitive health, driving assessment, falls prevention, opportunities for ministry and community leadership, aging in place initiatives) with your seniors (Sunday school classes, Wednesday night programs, special events)?

19. Does your church provide decisive encouragement for ministry and volunteerism targeted at seniors?

20. Does your church partner with other churches and denominations in meeting the needs of seniors throughout the community (e.g., developing a hospice program, designing an aging in place community, designing caregiver support programs)?

21. Does your church participate in national ministries (denominational or ecumenical) that focus on ministry to seniors and their caregivers?

22. Does your church promote small groups (home Bible studies) that target all age groups and provide regular sources of fellowship and opportunities for the old to teach the young?

23. Have you developed a list of services (such as those mentioned above) for which you would like some assistance in developing programs for seniors or elder caregivers in your congregation?

24. Does your church offer a program that might encourage seniors to share and capture their life stories with their families and with younger people in the congregation?

25. Does your church offer meal programs for older members? If yes, please list the meal program(s) offered: congregate meals, home-delivered meals, food pantry, grocery shopping, emergency food, other.

    Are these meal programs available to anyone in the community?

    Are these meal programs offered for free?

26. Does your church offer an information and referral program for church members?

27. Does your church have a Parish Nursing program?

28. Does your church offer health promotion programs?

29. Does your church provide emergency financial assistance to older persons in the congregation? If yes, please list the service: debt management, energy assistance, income-tax help, other.

30. Does your church offer legal assistance for older persons?

31. Please list and describe any other services provided uniquely by your church to its older members.

# APPENDIX C

## Parent Care Readiness Program

As the baby boom generation enters retirement, pastors and adult children of all ages are increasingly concerned about fulfilling the fifth commandment of honoring parents. Though eldercare is a predictable developmental experience for most people at midlife, our interdisciplinary research has confirmed that most adult children are not prepared to care for their aging parents. Despite the growing technological literacy of most American churchgoers, a holistic, viable, interdisciplinary program to effectively address the needs of caregivers and older loved ones has not been available. *We have provided a list of common parent care tasks and challenges on the book's webpage at ivpress.com.* You'll find four domains of tasks: medical, legal-financial, familial and spiritual-emotional. A review of each domain and each task that makes up the domain is provided, along with some websites that can serve as sources of information in each area.

This information is part of a web-based program currently under development, but the benefits of the content have been demonstrated in research conducted with the U.S. military and faith-based organizations. Much of the content at the site is taken from the Parent Care Readiness Program, or PCRP, which attempts to fill this informational void for families, congregations, organizations and caring professionals. The content was originally developed for military personnel and their families, and is based on the premise of a soldier's "family care plan" that is constructed before he ships out. The content at ivpress. com was adapted for congregational use and created to offer a high-quality system of evaluation and tailored interventions to help educate, motivate and support caregivers to become more proactive (*ready*) and less reactive (*unprepared*) in the development of a comprehensive program for their aging parents.

Over the past twenty years, Dr. Parker, supported by an interdisciplinary team of geriatric professionals, conducted a series of longitudinal, cross-sectional, prospective feasibility and clinical trial studies to develop an empirically based, comprehensive assessment and intervention program for eldercare. The first series of studies was aimed at military caregivers and their parents, and the studies were later expanded to academic, health care and faith-based groups. The research was funded in part by the Department of Defense, the John A. Hartford Foundation, the Gerontological Society of America, the National Institute on Aging, the Center for Mental Health and Aging at the University of Alabama, the Research Advisory Committee at the University of Alabama, the Significant Living Network, and the U.S. Air Force's Chaplains' Institute.

The authors have also worked extensively with national experts in businesses or services related to the PCRP, including scientists and practitioners like Richard Allman, M.D., the director of the University of Alabama in Birmingham Center for Aging and director of the VA Geriatric Research, Education and Clinical Center; Michael Hardin, Ph.D., the senior associate dean and the associate dean of research of the University of Alabama's Culverhouse College of Commerce and Business Administration; Linda Harootyan, M.S.W., the deputy director of the Gerontological Society of America; Daniel Winstead, M.D., the chair of the Department of Psychiatry at Tulane University; Harold Koenig, M.D., professor of geriatric psychiatry at Duke University; James Martin, Ph.D., previous director of the Army's Research and Development Command, consultant to the Department of Defense's Chaplain's Institute, and professor at Bryn Mawr College; Richard Powers, M.D., professor of pathology and psychiatry at the University of Alabama in Birmingham and primary spokesperson to the U.S. Congress for Alzheimer's' Foundation; the National Center on Caregiving; Thomas Cassidy, M.S., an economist, professor and former senior investigator with the New York Attorney General's Medicaid Fraud Control Unit; Andrew Achenbaum, Ph.D., a leading gerontologist, former dean and director of the Institute of Gerontology at the University of Michigan; and Barbara Berkman, Ph.D., the director of the Hartford Foundation's Geriatric Scholars Program at Columbia University.

If you would like access to the PCRP website, which is still under development, please contact Dr. Parker at mwparker@sw.ua.edu.

# APPENDIX D

## Sample Senior Ministry Association Correspondence

October 30, 2001
Dear Pastor:

The Tuscaloosa Senior Ministry Association is a new ecumenical organization with three primary goals: to challenge seniors to God-inspired ministry and leadership; to support and encourage the individual church "ministers" to the elderly in our area churches; and to foster church-medical partnerships that help seniors age successfully God's way. This is the same organization that was responsible for the "Successful Aging Conference" held at the Bryant Center in June, 2000.

To encourage Christian seniors to Spirit-led ministry, we hope to organize an annual conference aimed at challenging seniors to spiritual growth and leadership. The success of our last conference has led to national recognition within and across denominational lines. Other communities are emulating our model, and national and international interests in our faith-based approach have been expressed repeatedly in professional publications and forums.

To lend support to the individual adult ministers, a monthly newsletter is being created that will include state-of-the-art medical and practically helpful information about opportunities available to all Tuscaloosa senior adults and will highlight the "doings" of the elderly in individual churches. Points of contact will be provided that will enable a senior adult minister or lay leader to connect with any event that appeals to him/her for the seniors in his/her church. Another major goal of this ministry is to draw out our senior adults to enriching programs that are surrounded with lots of FUN! Nothing is more rejuvenating than a SMILE and a LAUGH!

One goal of the Tuscaloosa Senior Ministry Association is to partner religious and medical aspects of aging that will provide tangible ways for our Christian senior adults to more successfully age. Church-sponsored partnerships for the development of on-going programs with leading Christian medical professionals are planned to help seniors avoid disease and disability, maximize their cognitive and physical fitness, and remain actively engaged with life (e.g., hypertension, falls prevention, memory enhancement).

We hope that you will be involved in this ministry. You and/or your church can subscribe to the newsletter for $25 a year. This charge is to cover the costs of mailing and publication. We meet the fourth Thursday of each month, from 1200–1:00 at the Focus Building 1920 6th Street, Tuscaloosa. If you provide us with a church or personal email address, we can provide a copy of the newsletter free. Because we use color, and photographs, you will need a large memory (RAM 256 minimum) to print the newsletter. You can use what you like, or reproduce it for your seniors. We're all in this ever-growing senior population together, and, with God's guidance and blessing, we can support and encourage each other in our individual efforts. Hoping to meet you soon!

Serving Christ together,

*Michael W. Parker Sr., DSW, LTCR, BCD, LCSW*
Acting Chairman, Tuscaloosa Senior Ministry Association
John A. Hartford Foundation Geriatric Scholar
Associate Professor in the School of Social Work at the University of Alabama
Associate professor of Medicine, Division of Gerontology and Geriatric Medicine at the University of Alabama at Birmingham (UAB)

# Appendix E

## State Agencies on Aging

Alabama Department of Senior Services
Phone: 1-800-AGE-LINE
Website: www.adss.alabama.gov

Alaska Commission on Aging
Phone: 907-465-4879
Website: www.alaskaaging.org

Arizona Aging and Adult Administration
Phone: 602-542-4446
Website: www.azdes.gov

Arkansas Division of Adult and Aging Services
Phone: 1-866-801-3435
Website: www.daas.ar.gov

California Department of Aging
Phone: 1-800-510-2020
Website: www.aging.ca.gov

Colorado Division of Adult and Aging Services
Phone: 303-866-5700
Website: www.colorado.gov/cs/Satellite/CDHS-SelfSuff/CB
ON/1251579250975

Connecticut Department of Social Services, Elderly Services Division
Phone: 860-424-5274
Website: www.ct.gov/agingservices/site/default.asp

Delaware Division of Services for Aging and Adults with Physical
Disabilities
Phone: 1-800-223-9074
Website: http://dhss.delaware.gov/dsaapd

District of Columbia Office on Aging
Phone: 202-724-5622
Website: http://dcoa.dc.gov/DC/DCOA

Florida Department of Aging Affairs
Phone: 850-414-2000
Website: http://elderaffairs.state.fl.us/index.php

Georgia Division of Aging Services
Phone: 1-866-55AGING
Website: http://aging.dhr.georgia.gov/portal/site

Hawaii Executive Office on Aging
Phone: 808-586-0100
Website: http://hawaii.gov/health/eoa/index.html

Idaho Commission on Aging
Phone: 208-334-3833
Website: www.idahoaging.com/IdahoCommissiononAging/tabid/36/
Default.aspx

Illinois Department on Aging
Phone: 1-800-252-8966
Website: www.state.il.us/aging

Indiana Bureau of Aging and In-Home Services
Phone: 1-800-457-8283
Website: www.in.gov/fssa/ddrs/2872.htm

Iowa Department on Aging
Phone: 1-800-532-3213
Website: www.aging.iowa.gov

Kansas Department on Aging
Phone: 785-296-4986
Website: www.agingkansas.org/index.htm

Kentucky Office of Aging Services
Phone: 1-800-372-2973
Website: http://chfs.ky.gov/Services/Seniors.htm

Louisiana Governor's Office of Elderly Affairs
Phone: 225-342-7100
Website: http://goea.louisiana.gov

Maine Bureau of Elder and Adult Services
Phone: 1-800-262-2232
Website: www.maine.gov/dhhs/oes

Maryland Department of Aging
Phone: 1-800-243-3425
Website: www.mdoa.state.md.us/index.html

Massachusetts Executive Office of Elder Affairs
Phone: 1-800-AGE-INFO
Website: www.mass.gov/?pageID=eldershomepage&L=1&L0=Home
&sid=Eelders

Michigan Office of Services to the Aging
Phone: 517-373-8230
Website: www.michigan.gov/miseniors

Minnesota Board on Aging
Phone: 1-800-333-2433
Website: www.mnaging.org

Mississippi Division of Aging and Adult Services
Phone: 601-359-4929
Website: www.mdhs.state.ms.us/aas.html

Missouri Department of Health and Senior Services
Phone: 573-751-6400
Website: http://health.mo.gov/index.php

Montana Department of Public Health and Human Services
Phone: 1-800-332-2272
Website: www.dphhs.mt.gov/index.shtml

Nebraska Department of Health and Human Services State Unit on Aging
Phone: 1-800-942-7830
Website: www.hhs.state.ne.us/ags/agsindex.htm

Nevada Aging and Disability Services Division
Phone: 775-687-4210
Website: http://aging.state.nv.us/index.htm

New Hampshire Division of Elderly and Adult Services
Phone: 603-271-4680
Website: www.dhhs.state.nh.us/dcbcs/beas/index.htm

State of New Jersey Department of Health and Senior Services Division of Aging and Community Services
Phone: 1-800-367-6543
Website: www.state.nj.us./health/senior/index.shtml

New Mexico Aging and Long-Term Services Department
Phone: 1-800-432-2080
Website: www.nmaging.state.nm.us/default.asp

New York State Office for the Aging
Phone: 1-800-342-9871
Website: www.aging.ny.gov/

North Carolina Division of Aging and Adult Services
Phone: 919-733-3983
Website: www.dhhs.state.nc.us/aging/

North Dakota Department of Human Services
Phone: 701-328-4601
Website: www.nd.gov/dhs/services/adultsaging/

Ohio Department of Aging
Phone: 1-800-266-4346
Website: http://aging.ohio.gov/home/

Oklahoma Department of Human Services Aging Services Division
Phone: 1-800-211-2116
Website: www.okdhs.org/divisionsoffices/visd/asd/

Oregon Senior and Disabled Services Division
Phone: 503-945-5921
Website: http://egov.oregon.gov/DHS/spwpd/index.shtml

Pennsylvania Department of Aging
Phone: 717-783-6207
Website: www.aging.state.pa.us/portal/server.pt/community/ deparment_
of_aging_home/18206

State of Rhode Island Department of Elderly Affairs
Phone: 401-462-3000
Website: www.dea.state.ri.us/

South Carolina Lieutenant Governor's Office on Aging
Phone: 1-800-868-9095
Website: http://aging.sc.gov/seniors/Pages/index.aspx

South Dakota Department of Social Services Division of Adult Services and Aging
Phone: 605-773-3656
Website: http://dss.sd.gov/elderlyservices/index.asp

Tennessee Commission on Aging and Disability
Phone: 615-741-2056
Website: www.state.tn.us/comaging

Texas Department of Aging and Disability Services
Phone: 1-800-458-9858
Website: www.dads.state.tx.us

Utah Department of Human Services Division of Aging
and Adult Services
Phone: 1-877- 424-4640
Website: www.hsdaas.utah.gov

Vermont Department of Disabilities, Aging & Independent Living
Phone: 802-241-1228
Website: www.ddas.vermont.gov

Virginia Department for the Aging
Phone: 1-800-552-3402
Website: www.vda.virginia.gov

Washington Aging and Disability Services Administration
Phone: 1-800-422-3263
Website: www.aasa.dshs.wa.gov

West Virginia Bureau of Senior Services
Phone: 304-558-3317
Website: www.wvseniorservices.gov

Wisconsin Department of Health Services for the Elderly
Phone: 608-266-1865
Website: www.dhs.wisconsin.gov/aging

Wyoming Division on Aging
Phone: 1-800-442-2766
Website: http://wdh.state.wy.us/aging/index.html

# ABOUT THE AUTHORS

**James M. Houston**, M.A., D.Phil., is founding principal, former chancellor and emeritus professor of spiritual theology at Regent College in Vancouver, British Columbia. He is the author of some forty books, including *Joyful Exiles, Believe in the Creator, The Transforming Friendship, In Search of Happiness, The Heart's Desire* and *The Mentored Life*. Dr. Houston is a highly acclaimed scholar and pioneer in the field of evangelical spirituality. He moved from England in 1968 to help found and lead Regent College in Vancouver, Canada, an international graduate school of Christian studies. He received a B.Sc., M.A. and D.Phil. from Oxford University, as well as an M.A. from the University of Edinburgh. He is currently a Board of Governors Professor of Spiritual Theology at Regent College and serves as senior fellow of the C. S. Lewis Institute, Washington, D.C.

**Michael W. Parker Sr.**, Ph.D./DSW, LCSW, PIP, serves on the executive board of the Center for Mental Health and Aging and is an associate professor with the School of Social Work at the University of Alabama. He holds an adjunct associate professor appointment with the University of Alabama at Birmingham (UAB) in the Division of Gerontology, Geriatrics and Palliative Care, where he has active collaborations with interdisciplinary teams of faculty affiliated with UAB. He serves as coinvestigator on the National-Institute-of-Aging-funded UAB Study of Aging. Dr. Parker completed a two-year NIA postdoctoral fellowship at the University of Michigan, and he is a retired Lieutenant Colonel from the US Army (AMEDD), where his record of military service was noted in the Congressional Record. He was selected as one of ten national geriatric scholars by the Hartford Foundation and Gerontological Society of America (GSA) in 2003, and he helped to establish a Hartford Scholar Program within the Department of Veterans Affairs. He serves as a mentor to Hartford Scholars, as well as on the selection committee for the Hartford Geriatric Scholars Program. He serves on the Governing Council of the American Society of Aging Forum on Religion, Spirituality and Aging, and he remains active in the special interest group on spirituality and aging within the GSA. He and his Ph.D. students have received local and national awards for their community-based research with older persons and the church. He has over 100 peer-reviewed articles, chapters and presentations, and he has worked with the U.S. Air and Army War Colleges and the U.S. Army's Chaplain's Institute on aging-parent issues for military families.

# Index